THE MECHANICAL SONG

Edison talking doll, ca. 1890. Courtesy of the U.S. Department of the Interior, National Park Service, Edison National Historical Site.

THE
MECHANICAL SONG

Women, Voice, and the
Artificial in Nineteenth-Century
French Narrative

FELICIA MILLER FRANK

Stanford University Press, Stanford, California
1995

Stanford University Press
Stanford, California
© 1995 by the Board of Trustees
of the Leland Stanford Junior University
Printed in the United States of America

CIP data are at the end of the book

Stanford University Press publications
are distributed exclusively by Stanford University Press
in the United States, Canada, Mexico, and
Central America; they are distributed exclusively by
Cambridge University Press throughout the rest
of the world

For Russ

Acknowledgments

Thanks first to my parents, as always, for their unfailing love and support.

During the early stages of this project, the following grants made needed time and research opportunities available to me: the Georges Lurcy Fellowship for French Studies Abroad, the University of California Chancellor's Dissertation Year Fellowship, and the Chancellor's Patent Fund Grant. Generous and helpful guidance from Bertrand Augst created the lucky conditions under which I wrote the first version of this book. Instead of crediting him in the first note, I will suggest that this study could be read as a footnote to the challenge and stimulation offered by our conversations.

Robert Alter and Ann Banfield gave me suggestions early on in the project; Leslie Bary, Joanna O'Connell, Mary McGarry, Nancy Ciccone, and Ellen Greene gave me invaluable feedback and support at the same time.

Thanks to Frances Ferguson for her kindness in reading the manuscript and for her useful comments. Finally, I would like to thank Helen Tartar of Stanford University Press for her help and encouragement in bringing this book to press.

Contents

THE MECHANICAL SONG

Introduction

What is the source of the special relationship of women and the voice? Women have traditionally been accorded a privileged relation to the voice, in the antique figures of sibyls and sirens of ancient narratives, in the fantastic successes of such singers as Maria Malibran and Jenny Lind in the nineteenth century, and in contemporary texts that reflect a fascination with the figure of the diva: Jean-Jacques Beinix's film *Diva*, Federico Fellini's *Et la nave va*, and Marlene Dietrich's smoky *Blue Angel*. During the seventies, the feminine voice became the focus of theoretical discussions among French and American feminists in response to writings by Luce Irigaray, Hélène Cixous, and Julia Kristeva. Their work, and the psychoanalytic theory that influenced it, gave rise to a polemic about the significance of the maternal voice they seek to valorize, and about the feminine voice taken in a broader sense, that is, of the position from which women may speak, and of the nature of representations of the feminine.

One suggestion I will make here is that though these recent critical discussions arise out of a cultural tradition that represents women as associated closely with the voice and its expressive power, the woman's voice as it emerges in representation functions as a construct within a discursive system that is structured in terms that elide feminine subjectivity: the song of the siren, like Echo's, mirrors Narcissus's desire. The problematic efforts of the French feminists to valorize the feminine voice may be seen as a response to this representational tradition, as an effort to hear Echo's lost words. In differing ways, Irigaray and Jean-Joseph Goux argue that Western metaphysics is predicated on an underlying, and double, association of the feminine with the maternal, and denial of both.

It is out of this critical context that my own project emerged. I was struck by a curious recurrence in a number of modern French narrative texts of an association between women, the voice, and some version of the notion of the artificial or the technological: the texts that I first considered were Marcel L'Herbier's 1924 film *L'Inhumaine*, Jules Verne's *Le Château des Carpathes*, and Villiers de l'Isle-Adam's *L'Eve future*. Working to untie this thematic knot, I followed the threads further back in the nineteenth century, to a reading of Honoré de Balzac's *Sarrasine* and works by George Sand, as well as of such non-French texts as the stories by E. T. A. Hoffman about Olympia, the singing mechanical doll, and Antonia, whose voice is assimilated to her father's violin, and the tale of George du Maurier's created diva, Trilby. The course of my readings also led me to a consideration of the parallel significance of the maternal voice for Jean-Jacques Rousseau and Marcel Proust, bookends, as it were, of French romanticism, and of Gérard de Nerval's fascination in "Sylvie" with a remote, angelic female voice, placed in a complex relation to that of an actress and a country girl.

My study draws in a second set of questions about the way women have been identified with artifice and artificiality in romantic and postromantic French literature. Though I began with something like the theme of the woman, the machine, and sexuality that has been discussed elsewhere by Carolyn Lake, Michel Carrouges, and others, what emerged as germane to the texts and the problematic I broach in my study has to do with how literary figures of women, represented as sexless or artificial angels, are figured in a progressive way through the nineteenth century as emblematic of an experience of the sublime on the one hand and of artistic modernity on the other, or put differently, the angelic and the artificial.

The argument I make for the imbrication of the three terms of women, the voice, and the artificial in the narratives I discuss is indebted to the polemic over the maternal voice. In its turn, this critical matrix derives from the contributions of psychoanalytic thought to literary study. Thus, I place my discussion of the emotional appeal of the feminine voice in the context of certain psychoanalytic writings about the voice: in particular, those of Denis Vasse and Didier Anzieu, who argue for the importance of the voice in the development of the psyche. Their work seems generally supportive of the ideas of Kristeva on the maternal voice and the *chora*. I am especially interested in the way these ideas about the maternal voice, in particular what Anzieu calls the "sonic mirror," are congruent with Philippe Lacoue-Labarthe's analysis of the weakness of our received theory of the subject in "L'Echo du sujet." Here he combines psychoanalytic and philosophical approaches to show the lack of foundation for the visual metaphor as it is used in the psychoanalytic model of the constitution of subjectivity. His deconstruction of the primacy of its role in favor of the modes of the auditory and of rhythm is congenial to Kristeva's account and provides a philosophical support for the arguments I present for the voice as foundational ground for the psyche, and for the importance of the maternal voice in this process. At a much later point in the study, in a seemingly different context, readers may be reminded of this pulse of rhythm when they come to Jean-Luc Nancy's description of the rhythmic "pulsation" (*battement*) at the structural heart of the sublime moment.

The feminine voice emerges as a signifier that is erotically charged with nostalgia for the maternal but circulates in a system based on the devaluation of the feminine. The woman's voice functions as a double term that refers to a certain affective plenitude, but whose signification is yet structured by a representational system the defining terms and resulting perspectives of which elide the representation of feminine subjectivity. The result is an effacement of a genuine feminine subjectivity as "voice," reflected in representation by its structural position as echo.

The psychological dimension of explanation offered by psychoanalysis forms an underlying support for the historical argument I develop about the role of the female voice in romantic and postromantic narratives. One implication of this nostalgia for the maternal voice forms the subject of my first chapter, in which I show how in writing by both Proust and Rousseau, the act of writing, the creation of a self through a text autobiographical in nature, is tied to a deep sense of loss of the mother's voice, "heard" in a sense as a disembodied absence. The odd result is an association with the voice as feminine that is yet profoundly bound to an assumption of a (male) writer's writerly self.

Another implication has to do with the fetishization of the voice in these texts. Drawing on Michel Poizat's thesis in *L'Opéra ou le cri de l'ange* about the privileged position given to the feminine voice in nineteenth-century opera, in which it is identified as a sexless, angelic object of aesthetic pleasure, I show how a number of literary works by Sand, Hoffman, Balzac, Théophile Gautier, and du Maurier represent such sexless, inhuman, constructed voices. In the course of designing the chapter in which I suggest the association of female singing voices with angels, bells, violins, and struck crystal, I also found a curious ambiguity or doubleness in the sense of the gender of these singers. They were female, or feminized, but engaged in travesty, were considered as containing "other" voices in themselves, and so on. This gender ambiguity no doubt owes a great deal to romantic opera's inheritance from Italian castrati voices, long considered the greatest, purest, and most angelic. There may yet be something further: a kind of inherent doubleness or instability in gender structure of the kind Kristeva points out.

In a subsequent chapter, I place my discussion in the contexts of literary and art criticism, turning to Jacqueline Lichtenstein's discussion of the treatment of women and artifice and to Mario Praz and Frank Kermode's writings on romantic images of women. Through my analysis of Charles Baudelaire's association of the artificial woman with modernity as a positive value, which is supported by Kermode's arguments about the impassive dancer as a figure for the romantic image, I suggest a progressive identification of the woman with the inhuman in French letters and art.

I say French letters, because though one finds narratives in other literatures about opera singers during this time (in Spanish, for example, there is Leopoldo Alas Claría's *Su unico hijo* and Fernan Caballero's *La Gaviota*), the particular association of the female voice with artificiality has to do with Baudelaire's watershed contribution to the theory of art in modernity, his association of art with artifice. It may also have something to do with a particularly French rejection of the castrato elsewhere more successful: Poizat speaks of the transformation, the assumption of center stage by the soprano voice in romantic opera, but in looking at these French texts, one may as easily speak of the transformation through appropriation of the Italianate castrato into a woman. The artifice of the castrato voice transfers to artifice, *tout court*.

A few years after Baudelaire, Villiers de l'Isle-Adam crystallizes this dual image of the woman as artifice. The Android in *L'Eve future* is a sexless angel whose singing is sublime, an artificial woman fabricated by a fictionalized Thomas Edison. Like the phonograph on which the Android is patterned, she is essentially a device for recording and reproducing the human voice. Jacques Perriault's book on the early history of the phonograph and cinema, *Mémoires de l'ombre et du son*, suggests how the yearning for a way to preserve the voice against loss and death led to the invention of the phonograph. Villiers's phonograph-woman, the artificially incarnated bearer of a disembodied voice, recapitulates the romantic themes of the work of art as artifice and that of the sexless angelic singer and unites them in a female figure at once totalizing Wagnerian artwork and uneasy metafiguration of the coming age of the work of art as mechanical reproduction.

The closing years of the nineteenth century were the era of posters of ladies on bicycles; the "fairy of electricity" exhibited at the Exposition Universelle, which Edison took home with him to New Jersey; Edison's line of talking dolls, perhaps reminiscent of Pierre Jaquet-Droz's clockwork automata—with a difference: it was a time when technological innovation was projected upon the figure of the woman, no longer a sign of nature, since Baudelaire, but rather the screen for the modern, a technological echo, like Villiers's phonograph-woman. The Android figures this "neo-technic" revolution of which Lewis Mumford spoke and does so in an oddly modern way, for the doubt about whether she is or is not sentient, is or is not a machine, anticipates curiously the terms of A. M. Turing's Imitation Game, an early formulation of the question of artificial intelligence: if you can't tell, does it make a difference? The woman and the machine thus become strangely interchangeable on the modern scene, a fantasy played out again and again, no longer in French nineteenth-century texts, but in science fiction films and novels like

Bladerunner and Stanislaw Lem's *Solaris*. One finds yet another parallel configuration of the woman and the technological in the contemporary Verne text that creates another artificial woman singer, anticipating cinema in its use of lantern-slide *trucage* to make a dead woman's disembodied voice and body appear from nowhere.

In closing, I find in Jean-François Lyotard's discussion in *L'Inhumain* the terms to suggest that the voice functions as a vehicle of the sublime in the nineteenth-century texts I discuss. Positing a continuation of the aesthetic of the sublime through romantic art to the avant-garde movements of the twentieth century, Lyotard argues for a link between the inhuman or the indeterminate and the sublime, and for the sublime as the mode of aesthetic experience that characterizes modernity in art. In this way, the inhuman, artificial voice of the woman singer may be seen not only as representing the persistence of the aesthetic of the sublime in the texts I discuss but as figuring the idea of modernity.

That the feminine voice should come in the nineteenth century to denote art and artifice is a curious and perhaps surprising notion: generally, one thinks of the feminine as bearing a traditional association with nature. This shift may be understood in the terms in Goux's *Iconoclastes*. As I stated above, Goux traces the ancient but historically continued dichotomy between masculine and feminine reproductive roles in idealist philosophy that associates the masculine with the spirit, the unrepresentable, the feminine with matter, materiality. According to this system, the *physis/techne* dichotomy (used by Martin Heidegger in his essay "The Question Concerning Technology") corresponds to a correlation in western thinking of the male with spirit or idea and female with matter, which may be worked. The implications of this epistemological alignment of the female with the material is interesting when seen in the context of the argument I make for the voice as vehicle of the sublime, for the woman's voice as identified with the artificial, the inhuman, not nature, as one may expect.

I suggest that the representation of the woman's voice as inhuman continues the tradition of objectification of the woman as material and other, making of her voice a simulacrum, an echo, of itself and simultaneously signals the advent of a period in which the transformations effected in the world by technological innovations threaten to denature matter itself, piercing an aperture in the world as nature that admits the element of the inhuman, denoted in art as sublime. Within the familiar thesis of the romantic valuation of nature emerges a secondary counterthread of a preoccupation with artifice and the artificial, of an emerging anxiety about the implications of an inhuman modernity: Echo's voice is heard as a mechanical song.

Nostalgia for the Maternal Voice

The motif of the maternal voice and its nostalgic rediscovery is a familiar one: not only does it occur in the first-person narratives, whether fictional or autobiographical, of such writers as Rousseau and Proust, but as an aspect of the broader question of the feminine voice it also emerges as a problematic term in recent critical and theoretical discussions of language, subjectivity, and gender. Under the rubric of the maternal voice we find a complex cluster of elements that includes the erotic, the suppressed feminine, the foundational divisions in the psyche, and the role of the mode of the acoustic in all of these. The questions it raises inevitably bring up the feminist debates over how to theorize feminine subjectivity. While the theme of the maternal voice seemed to present opportunities for a "rescue-reading" to certain proponents of women's writing (*écriture féminine*), such a line of thinking, despite its initial attractiveness as a validating feminist term, has since been criticized as utopic or essentialist by American feminist critics. For example, in her article on the voice in film, Mary Ann Doane has written:

The notion of a political erotics of the voice is particularly problematic from a feminist perspective. Over and against the theorization of the look as phallic, as the support of voyeurism and fetishism (a drive and a defense which, in Freud, are linked explicitly with the male), the voice appears to lend itself readily as an alternative to the image, as a potentially viable means whereby the woman can "make herself heard." Luce Irigaray, for instance, claims that patriarchal culture has a heavier investment in seeing than in hearing. . . .

Nevertheless, it must be remembered that, while psychoanalysis delineates a pre-oedipal scenario in which the voice of the mother dominates, the voice, in psychoanalysis, is also the instrument of interdiction, of the patriarchal order. And to mark the voice as an isolated haven within patriarchy, or as having an essential relation to the woman, is to invoke the specter of feminine specificity, always recuperable as another form of "otherness."[1]

For Doane, the problem is that of the classic bind for feminists, for grounding a politics in a conceptualization of the body—and the voice retains a link to the body—reinforces it as guarantee of lack and difference, but the body as "site" of oppression is also contested ground, the possible site of redefinition.

In discussing the nostalgia for the maternal voice and its relation to the role of the voice in the fabrication of subjectivity, in seeing the memory of the maternal voice as imbricated in a broader way in the appeal of the female voice, I do not make an appeal to nature or to any biological foundationalism, but rather conduct my inquiry in terms of the historical and cultural determinants that construct and motivate these relations. The suggestion that the feminine has been bound to the maternal in the discursive framework we have inherited and that cultural systems of values work to negate or efface both is no longer a new argument. Of numerous variants of this idea, the homologous arguments of Goux and Irigaray can serve here as exemplary and provide a backdrop to my own proposition that the feminine voice in its literary representations repeats within the modality of the acoustic the specular structure of the psyche, like Echo, Narcissus's other mirror. While I will not gesture repeatedly toward the myth of Echo as an organizing figure, it may be seen to govern the discursive situation I outline and may be traced *en filigrane* throughout the literary instances discussed in the book.

It is not possible to invoke the Echo-Narcissus myth, the story that casts in human figures the logic dictating the feminine position reflecting male subjectivity in discourse, without pointing to Irigaray's work. Her argument in *Spéculum de l'autre femme*, for example, has become well known. She shows there how the specular logic of the "same" positions the subject as always male and the feminine as a mirror of the phallic, a structure she presents as that underpinning Western discourse, philosophical, social, and psychoanalytic, through her discussions of Freud, Plato, and Descartes. Writing of the subject in *Ethique de la différence sexuelle* she calls for a different look at these relations:

Everything about the relations of subject and discourse, the subject and the world, the individual and the cosmic, the micro and macrocosm is being re-interpreted. Everything, and first off, that the subject writes itself in the masculine, even if "he" wills himself to be universal or neuter: *man*. Never mind that man (at least in French) is not neuter but sexed. Man has been the subject of discourse: theological, moral, political. And the gender of God, guarantor of every subject and of all discourse, is always masculine-paternal in the West.[2]

Within the phallocentric system thus set in place, the feminine position is that of the mute ground that makes discourse possible, but which is by definition out of the picture:

If the woman traditionally, and as mother, represents *place* for man, the limit signifies that she becomes a *thing*, with some possible mutations from one epoch to another. She finds herself hemmed off as a thing. Now the maternal-feminine serves also as an envelope, with which man limits his things. The relation between *envelope and things* constitutes one of the aporias, or the aporia, of Aristotelianism and the philosophical systems that derive from it.[3]

The philosopher Goux articulates a parallel argument about sexual difference in his book *Les Iconoclastes* (selections of which are translated in *Symbolic Economies: After Marx and Freud*). He discusses the ways in which an idealizing injunction against figuration structures the process of symbolization in the Western philosophical tradition. In his argument tracing the history of the symbolic economy with its equivalence between the phallus and gold (i.e., value), Goux insists on the repression in this system of the maternal, equated with the feminine. His last chapter, "Sexual Difference and History," presents a "sexual archaeology of idealism" derived from the metaphors used by Plato and Aristotle on the model of sexual difference found in ancient procreation myths. These metaphors underpin the elaboration of idealism, and of history in a more general sense. Goux argues against the transparency of philosophical concepts to affirm the historical roots of idealism in a repression of *mater*, hence matter. It is grafted onto an underlying structure he calls "paterialism," which identifies man with form and thought, woman with matter and death:

What does idealism say? It says that the conscious power of thought is of an entirely different order from that of nature. It bars mother and matter from generative power. Matter is dead; it is *mater* and not *genetrix*. It desires an order. It requires a meaning it does not have, which must come from without. Thought is not the product of matter, the offspring (however sublime) of organized living nature: it is wholly other.[4]

To reduce Goux's argument somewhat, the symbolic system inaugurated by idealism works through a process of unconscious systematization of the opposing terms provided by sexual difference. Thus, biological difference becomes the "prop and pretext" for symbolic divisions at another level, so that they pass from a position of external reflection to an internal one, becoming thereby naturalized. In pointing to the homology between the Freudian symbolic system and that of the dominant order out of which it arises, Goux argues, like Irigaray, that it reduplicates its phallus-centered logic.

This perhaps now-familiar position, that phallocentric logic structures all symbolic thinking, has been criticized by Monique Plaza, who seeks to cut the knot of phallomorphic "bouclage," looping or closure, in a well-known article directed at attempts to use Freudian theory for feminist ends.[5] Such a formulation remains controversial, particularly for American feminists, since it seems to close off the possibilities for an articulation of a theory of female subjectivity. In her introductory essay to a recent issue of *Hypatia* devoted to critiques of French feminist philosophy, Nancy Fraser raises the issue of the dangers posed to feminist thinking by views that posit phallocentric thinking as monolithic and univocal rather than contested and plurivocal. Arguing that Irigaray's critique of phallocentrism unwittingly extends it, she suggests that it should "be possible to replace the view that phallocentrism is coextensive with all extant Western culture with a more complicated story about how the *cultural hegemony* of phallocentric thinking has been, so to speak, erected."[6]

When qualified by such caveats as this, the analyses by Goux and Irigaray remain useful to describe the unconscious emplacement of sexual difference within the structures of history and discourse, an emplacement that carries a heavy ideological freight. In elaborating his argument for how reproductive models provide the generative formulae for the symbolic order, Goux traces out how, from Plato to Hegel, the feminine gets tied to the maternal, the maternal to matter and nature and thus devalued. This logic "glorifies" the phallic, identifying the male and the paternal with idea and form. In this process that objectifies imaginary constructs, "history" is itself conceived in imaginary terms, predicated on the terms of biological difference: "If the phylogenetic odyssey of libidinal positions of knowledge, through which social access to reality is gained, comprises a multiphased shift from inclusion in nature as mother, through a separation, and finally to an inclusive reciprocity with the *other* nature, human history through the present has been limited to the history of *man*: history is masculine. It has never been conceived otherwise." In fact, Goux suggests that history itself must be seen as a masculinist construct, based on the negation of the mother: "History is the history of man." Goux offers the corrective of a materialist dialectic that considers "material organizational potency as including the production of concepts, [and that] to make mind the offspring of organized matter, is to explode the *paterialist barrier* between concept and materiality."[7] This would be an "other" matter, the work of another feminine not the mother, yet to be conceptualized. This "other woman" of whom Goux speaks bears some traits in common with the "other woman" whose concave mirror Irigaray theorizes.

To show how Echo gives voice to Narcissus's concerns, as I seek to do in this study, may not work to restore Echo's body and voice, her absent outline, but perhaps holds up a mirror in which her absence may be seen.

Several texts by Proust and Rousseau can serve as examples of works written in an autobiographical mode that tie the voice to the maternal and to the paired association with origin and with death invoked by the writer's self-constitution in writing. Behind the voice of the writer's "I" attempting to realize itself one hears the echo of the voice of his earliest cognizance of life, the echo of the subject's own intrinsic division.

The second volume of Proust's *A la recherche du temps perdu* contains a passage that vividly invokes the motifs both of a disembodied female voice and of nostalgia for the maternal. The voice is that of Marcel's grandmother, with whom he has a conversation over the telephone, a still unfamiliar device at the time the narrative is placed. The passage falls early in *Le Coté de Guermantes*, which opens with a meditation on the evocative power of names. The resonant sounds of certain names (those of Guermantes, Berma, the names of officers at the garrison town Marcel visits) evoke places, artists, distinguished people still beyond Marcel's experience; he fills the neutral frames of the words with qualities projected from his own imaginings. Proust's work here is, of course, a progressive emptying and refilling of these names with new associations and qualities, ironic and surprising in their differences from Marcel's naive expectations.

Marcel's conversation with his grandmother takes place within this thematic matrix of familiar names paired with unfamiliar realities, potent incantations that call up emptiness—in short, the jarring or gratifying mismapping of language to the world it aims to represent. The shock of the grandmother's voice heard over the telephone line operates a transformation of these same thematic materials in another sphere: the seeming fullness of presence implied in the warmth of her voice inverts itself into a sharpened awareness of her absence and approaching death. A second framework sets up the conversation as well, that of the Proustian motif of absences, minor and major, temporary and permanent, that recurs throughout the novel: Marcel's separation from his grandmother is occasioned by his trip to Doncières where Saint-Loup is stationed, and the bass note of his resulting anxiety is preceded and comically paralleled by the goings-on surrounding Saint-Loup's separation from his mistress.

Proust couches his description of the unfamiliarity of the telephone in a hyperbolic and ironic vocabulary of fairy tale and myth that allows him to render a variation on his recurrent theme of the anesthetizing force of habit: the magic of the unfamiliar telephone quickly yields to banality, and we wait irritably during the slow connection, wondering whether to lodge a complaint. Proust humorously invokes the "sacred forces" at work in the establishment of telephone communication, comparing a person speaking to a loved one on the phone to the hero of a fairy tale aided by a sorceress to defeat distance, and the characterization of the faceless female operators as "Vigilant Virgins" and invisible, jealous "Guardian Angels" in fact introduces the real enchantment of his grandmother's transformed voice. From his ironically cadenced mythologizing of the operators as the "All Powerful by whose intervention the absent rise up at our side," "the Danaids of the unseen who incessantly empty and fill and transmit to one another the urns of sound," "the ever-irritable hand-maidens of the Mystery, the umbrageous priestesses of the Invisible, the Young Ladies of the Telephone," he moves to the actual shock of hearing the loved voice. It only requires a call to them, he writes, and distance is abolished: "And as soon as our call has rung out, in the darkness filled with apparitions to which our ears alone are unsealed, a tiny sound, an abstract sound—the sound of distance overcome— and the voice of the dear one speaks to us."[8]

Proust develops the material in the telephone conversation over several pages, moving through the logic of the emotions implicit in it. The telephone, which seems at first to abolish distance and sepa-ration, ends in reinforcing it. Thus, Marcel's joy at hearing the be-loved voice gives way to a pang of Proustian anxiety over separation, when the sense of proximity of the beloved voice on the telephone provokes a paradoxical realization of the actual gulf that intervenes between them:

It is she, it is her voice that is speaking, that is there. But how far away it is! How often have I been unable to listen without anguish, as though, con-fronted by the impossibility of seeing, except after long hours of journeying, her whose voice was so close to my ear, I felt most clearly the illusoriness in the appearance of the most tender proximity, and at what a distance we may be from the persons we love at the moment when it seems that we have only to stretch out our hands to seize and hold them. A real presence, perhaps, that voice that seemed so near—in actual separation! (Proust, 135)

Instead of deriving comfort from the sound of his grandmother's voice heard over the telephone, Marcel experiences a wrenching sense of loss. Because of the way her voice is isolated, he hears it in a new way, as if for the first time. The very familiarity of her voice thus resolves into a poignant newness: he hears in it an unaccustomed sweetness and aged fragility that moves him painfully. The present

separation brought home to him by this isolation of her voice gives
him an intimation of her mortality, of the permanent separation to
come. The mythological register on which Proust plays earlier in the
passage remains to provide another, more serious reference, at first
only implicit:

Many were the times, as I listened thus without seeing her who spoke to me
from so far away, when it seemed to me that the voice was crying to me from
the depths out of which one does not rise again, and I felt the anxiety that
was one day to wring my heart when a voice would thus return (alone and
attached no longer to a body which I was never to see again), to murmur in
my ear words I longed to kiss as they issued from lips forever turned to dust.
(Proust, 135)

Like the disembodied voice of Villiers de l'Isle-Adam's Android,
heard in a tomblike chamber, like the memory of Eurydice that
haunts Orpheus, after her death the grandmother's voice will haunt
Marcel from the depths.

The allusion to Orpheus and death becomes explicit at the end of
the passage, after the description of the interruption of Marcel's connection to his grandmother. Their tender conversation gives Marcel
"an anxious, an insensate desire" to return home and provokes in
him a response of grief, as though she were already dead:

"Granny!" I cried to her, "Granny!" and I longed to kiss her, but I had beside
me only the voice, a phantom as impalpable as the one that would perhaps
come back to visit me when my grandmother was dead. "Speak to me!" but
then, suddenly I ceased to hear the voice, and was left more alone. . . . It
seemed to me as though it was already a beloved ghost that I had allowed to
lose herself in the ghostly world, and, standing alone before the instrument,
I went on vainly repeating: "Granny! Granny!" as Orpheus, left alone, repeats the name of his dead wife. (Proust, 137)

The grandmother's voice, at first seemingly the vehicle of their inti-
macy, bears another meaning as well: isolated by the telephone, it
carries an awareness of loss and death. Marcel's initial dismay when
he realizes that her voice has been broken off turns to anguish, an
emotion fed by the return of an early memory of being suddenly separated from her in a crowd and being overwhelmed by a feeling of
grief and loss. The child Marcel called her name then as hopelessly

as he does in the telephone passage. This incident in turn clearly echoes the Freudian motif of the primordial "lost object," the mother's breast, whose loss, attended by intense grief, becomes a drama repeatedly reenacted in later life. The isolated thread of the maternal voice pulls the two moments of separated time together, imbricating them in an affective matrix of memory, nostalgia, grief, and foreboding sense of mortality in this passage, a small fractal of the structure of Proust's narrative itself.

For Rousseau, as well, the thread of feminine voice binds together a childhood memory of maternal sweetness, a sense of mortality, and a narrative project that stages the self in the fusing of a dual temporal frame. Two separate studies that appeared within several years of each other center on the fascination of the feminine voice for Rousseau. Louis Marin's takes as its point of departure a passage from the *Confessions* and focuses on Rousseau's association of the feminine voice with the maternal in connection with the writer's self-constitutive act. The other, by Alain Grosrichard, moves from a similar perception of the importance of the maternal voice for Rousseau to develop the implications of the erotic character of the voice. In these analyses, the feminine voice—a voice often notably detached by memory or by a purely physical barrier from its human origins—reveals itself not only as the source of a profoundly erotic appeal, one deriving from an association with Rousseau's memory of maternal tenderness, but also as a kind of flash point that illuminates the problem of the writer's identity.

Marin's piece, "Un Filet de voix fort douce," starts from the passage in the *Confessions* where Rousseau, immediately after identifying the circumstances of his birth (the place, the date, the death of his mother in childbirth), tells how his aunt's attentions saved his life, and how he grew up by her side:

I was always with my aunt, sitting or standing by her side, watching her at her embroidery or listening to her singing; and I was content. . . . I am convinced that it is to her that I owe the taste, or rather the passion, for music, which only became fully developed in me a long time afterwards. She knew a prodigious number of tunes and songs which she used to sing in a very thin, gentle voice. This excellent woman's cheerfulness of soul banished dreaminess and melancholy from herself and all around her. The attraction which her singing possessed for me was so great, that not only have several of her songs always remained in my memory, but even now, when I have lost her, and as I grow older, many of them, totally forgotten since the days of my childhood, return to my mind with an inexpressible charm. Would anyone believe that I, an old dotard, eaten up by cares and troubles, sometimes find myself weeping like a child, when I mumble one of those little airs in a voice already broken and trembling?[9]

His Aunt Suson's singing is what Rousseau remembers her by most vividly, and this memory of the voice of the woman who was mother to Rousseau organizes and suffuses his other memories of early childhood like a light or a scent.

One of his aunt's songs in particular haunts the memory of the aged Rousseau as he begins his *Confessions*. Marin relates Rousseau's efforts to recall the melody sung by his aunt with his project in writing the *Confessions* and suggests that writing his life history means recovering his origins, means writing the succession of selves that make up the voice that says "I":

What machinations, what ruses must one need in order to write: "I was born," "I died," "I write my own self, this self peculiar to me," "I write the truth?" Machinations, ruses of which the operator will always be a mask, placed in the place of the inappropriable, will always act out on another stage, the stage of fiction or of dream, origin and end at the same moment, the beginning where everything is still possible and the perfection where the singular essence closes itself on its immobile truth. What image? What face? The one that makes visible and legible the originary voice, forever inaudible except as its echo, a voice that will always be nothing but an echo.[10]

The scene of his writing evokes another scene, which intrudes itself on his memory at the very outset of his writing. Finding the voice to write of himself, finding the source of his voice, means for Rousseau recovering the echo of the originary voice of his Aunt Suson.

Rousseau speaks of being moved by one melody she sang in particular, yet he cannot remember it in its entirety: the whole of the text curiously eludes him. Marin cites part of the passage and what Rousseau includes of the song:

One of them, especially, has come back to me completely, as far as the tune is concerned; the second half of the words, however, has obstinately resisted all my efforts to recall it, although I have an indistinct recollection of the rhymes. Here is the beginning, and all that I can remember of the rest:

> Tircis, je n'ose
> Ecouter ton chalumeau
> Sous l'ormeau;
> Car on en cause
> Déjà dans notre hameau
> . . . un berger
> . . . s'engager
> . . . sans danger;
> Et toujours l'épine est sous la rose.

[Tircis, I dare not listen to your pipe under the elm; people are beginning to talk about it in the village. A shepherd . . . To engage oneself . . . without danger; there is no rose without its thorn]. (Rousseau, 7)

Rousseau mentions thinking of writing away to Paris to find out if anyone knows the song, but he is sure much of his pleasure in remembering it would dissolve if he had proof that anyone else sang it: he wishes to keep his memory intact. As Marin and Grosrichard both show in their discussions, he misremembers the song tellingly. The actual text of the ending reveals itself to be: "Un coeur s'expose / A trop s'engager / Avec un berger / Et toujours l'épine est sous la rose" ["It is dangerous for a heart to have too much to do with a shepherd; there is no rose without its thorn"]. Marin points out the reversal that Rousseau operates as:

In Rousseau's memory	*In reality*
un berger [a shepherd]	s'expose [runs a risk]
s'engager [to engage oneself]	s'engager
sans danger [no danger]	un berger [shepherd] (Marin, 16)

Rousseau's telling lapse traces a miniature portrait of desire and conflict, with the voice as mediating term: the song itself thematizes the voice as a vehicle for eros and its risks. Marin suggests the song as meaning a shepherdess to say: I dare not listen to your song (your pipe), although I desire to; I dare not listen to your voice because of the talk, the voices of the others who whisper and spy. The rose and the thorn hint at virginal innocence and the piercing danger of erotic *jouissance*.

In his reading of the song, Grosrichard makes a similar point: "Tircis: the one to whom the song is addressed, as response to a request signified by his pipe. Tircis, as a result, whose place the child occupies while he listens to the song, all eyes and ears, to the maternal voice sending him that confession of love held back by modesty, is the same shepherd as in Virgil's VIIth Eclogue."[11] Whether Rousseau remembers or not, the theme of memory appears itself in the eclogue, where Tircis, competing with Corydon in a vocal duel, singing of the beauty of Lycidas, prays to his god Priapus and promises to cover his statue with gold if he wins. Grosrichard cites it: "*'Haec memini*, here is what I remember' concluded Melibea, arbiter of the contest, *'et frustra victum contendere Thyrsum*, and Thyrsis protested in vain, he was beaten'" (Grosrichard, 134). Risk and danger are doubly implied in the love song, first in the Virgilian reference, and then in Rousseau's transposition of "sans danger" for "s'expose . . . un berger." Risking love means exposing oneself to the danger of death, of castration, to spell out a Freudian reading. For Marin, it also implies the danger of exposing oneself to the eyes and judgment of others ("they are talking already") through the world of language, of exchanged signs, hence the risk Rousseau assumes in writing his history:

To listen to the music, the melodic thread of the pipe, is already to make oneself visible, to be seen and spoken about, to get caught by signs. This warning, it is your *entire* story, your destiny, your truth, caught by the slender thread of the sweet voice of aunt Suson, by Tircis' piping song, the voice of Eros. And this warning, you must forget it, for the song that haunts you gives you an inexpressible and recurring pleasure taken at the price of the mortal danger of words, signs and looks. (Marin, 16)

For Marin, the voice of the song is double, even multiple, and undecidable, floating between that of the shepherdess of the lyrics, that of Rousseau's unknown lost mother, that of Aunt Suson, and that of the old man "eaten up by cares and troubles," approaching his end, and attempting to recover his past to write of himself. Grosrichard elaborates further the risk implied in the song as part of his larger discussion of the erotic significance of the voice for Rousseau. His reading becomes intelligible only when the rest of Rousseau's remarks about the effect of the song are completed: "I ask, where is the affecting charm which my heart finds in this song? It is a whim, which I am quite unable to understand; but be that as it may, it is absolutely impossible for me to sing it through without my being interrupted by my tears" (Rousseau, 7). As Grosrichard shows, Rousseau was unable to complete another love song, was stopped by convulsive weeping on other occasions, as well. He appears to have always found a thorn beneath the rose there to discourage him when he reached out to possess the object of his desire.

Grosrichard anchors his discussion of Rousseau's conflictual investment of the female voice with the erotic in his experience of reawakening to music during 1743, the year he spent as a diplomatic attaché in Venice working as a cryptographer. Grosrichard operates his own work of cryptography to decipher the affective key to the consistent theme of the voice that runs through Rousseau's writings, from his theoretical pieces on opera that appear in the *Dictionnaire de musique* through *La Nouvelle Héloïse* to the *Confessions*. Framing this discussion are Grosrichard's analyses of two key episodes that reveal Rousseau's erotic identification of the voice with a forbidden maternal object: Rousseau's account of his experiences with Mme de Warens and the nostalgia for Aunt Suson's song.

Grosrichard invokes the enigma of the passage from the *Confessions* in which Rousseau speaks of his awakening to the enchantment of Italian music at an opera: having fallen asleep during a performance at the theater of Saint Chrysostom (he has not been much of an admirer of Italian music), he awakes in ecstasy during the singing of one aria which he remembers as "Conservami la bella / Che si m'accende il cor." Rousseau's double awakening in the theater reads as a conversion experience that leads him to seek a theoretical ground for his new passion through his subsequent writings on music. Grosrichard notes Rousseau's interest in the representative powers of music, its synaesthetic capacity to "place the eye in the ear," and his belief in the voice as source of music: "It is then, in the last analysis, from the pathetic and accented voice out of which it is born that music holds its double power, making one see and feel while giving something to hear, that 'paints objects to the imagination and brings feeling to the heart.' And it is this originary and essential music that Rousseau discovers suddenly on arriving in Venice" (Grosrichard, 115). In part Rousseau's fascination for hearing and the voice can be placed in the context of the general eighteenth-century interest in the nature of the senses and their mutual substitutability: Denis Diderot's *Lettre sur les aveugles* describes the extreme tactile sensitivity of a blind woman, Mélanie de Salignac, as "a sensitive mirror" and mentions her attribution of colors to voices.

Grosrichard notes that Rousseau also shows himself to be highly sensitive to qualities of the voice in the *Confessions*, in particular, that of his "mamma," Mme de Warens. Her "silvery" and "youthful" voice had had such an effect on Rousseau that he writes he can never hear the pretty voice of a young girl without being moved. Grosrichard reads Rousseau's relationship to his beloved "mamma" specifically in terms of the voice. In the *ménage à trois* at Chambéry, Mme de Warens shared her apothecary passions with her lover Anet, but with her "little one," she engaged in the innocent pleasures of song. Gifted with a pleasant voice ("she had a good voice"), able to play the harpsichord, she taught the young Rousseau to sing; music created a special bond between them through which he was able to beat out his rival on a spiritual field:

What at that time made this study particularly a pleasure, was that I could pursue it together with mamma. With very different tastes in other respects, we found in music a bond of union, which I gladly made use of. She made no objection; I was at that time almost as advanced as she was; after two or three attempts we could decipher an air. Sometimes, when I saw her busy around a furnace, I used to say: "Mamma, here is a charming duet, which seems to me just the thing to make your drugs smell of *empyreuma*." "On my honor," she would reply, "if you make me burn them, I will make you eat them." While the dispute was going on, I pulled her to the piano, where we soon forgot everything else; the extract of juniper or absinthe was reduced to powder; she smeared my face with it—and how delightful it all was! (Rousseau, 164–65)

Grosrichard draws from Rousseau's piece on the duet in the *Dictionnaire de musique* to point out the importance for the quality of emotion in the duet—most affecting between two lovers—of the equality of voice of the singers. He speculates that by age 17, Rousseau's voice would have lost the childish purity that made him her matched partner. Despite his expressed wishes, "mamma" heard the voice of a maturing young man and decided that she should undertake his sexual initiation. The day arrived, to his dismay:

My heart sealed all my vows, without desiring their reward. However I obtained it. For the first time I found myself in the arms of a woman, a woman whom I adored. Was I happy? No; I tasted pleasure. A certain unconquerable feeling of melancholy poisoned its charm; I felt as if I had been guilty of incest. Two or three times while pressing her in ecstasy in my arms, I wetted her bosom with my tears. (Rousseau, 179)

Rousseau's oedipal guilt is compounded by the illness and death of his older rival, the description of which immediately follows this account. Henceforth, his role as "petit" is over with, and Rousseau finds himself able neither to revive the safe joys of the duet nor to assume the role of lover to his "mamma." Elsewhere in the *Confessions* he maintains that for him sexual love remains in some way impossible: "Enjoyment [Jouir]? Does this ever fall to the lot of man? If I had ever, a single time in my life, tasted all the delights of love in their fulness, I do not believe that my frail existence could have endured it; I should have died on the spot" (Rousseau, 200).[12] Rousseau could not participate in the compounding of the drugs in which "mamma" engaged with his older rival Anet; sexuality would always appear to him in the light of a poison. Grosrichard asserts that having broken the "miroir sonore" of the duet in the sexual act, Rousseau's idyll with Mme de Warens is shattered: "In attempting to take hold of the object the voice suggests to those 'eyes' found only in the ears, not only does he fail to find what he expected, but in fact loses what he does possess, the true object of his pleasure: mamma's very voice itself" (Grosrichard, 120). Full of desire "without an object," Rousseau's reaction is twofold. He throws himself into mathematical studies, and he develops an overwhelming and disabling tinnitus: a ringing in his ears that renders him hard of hearing and so forces him to abandon music.

It is only in Venice that Rousseau rediscovers the pleasure of song, specifically in Italian singing, with its pleasing continuum between the spoken and musical voice. Grosrichard gives the lie to Rousseau's claim that he avoided sex while in Venice, dividing his time between his ciphers and the opera, asserting that "in fact . . . Rousseau never

stopped moving toward sex, even and above all when he was listening to singing voices" (Grosrichard, 123). He is especially captivated
by the pure singing of the charity students at the school of Saint Chrysostom. The exquisite voices that emerge from behind closed grills,
detached from their sources, suggest that the students are exquisitely
beautiful; their ugliness when he actually sees them is crushing.
Sand's description in *Consuelo* of the meeting at the school of the
Mendicanti between the singing student Consuelo and her wealthy
admirer follows the same curve of expectation and disappointment
that characterizes this episode and was evidently modeled on it:

I cannot imagine anything so voluptuous, so touching as this music. The
abundant art, the exquisite taste of the singing, the beauty of the voices, the
correctness of the execution—everything in these delightful concerts con-
tributes to produce an impression which is certainly not "good style," but
against which I doubt whether any man's heart is proof. . . . What drove me
to despair was the confounded gratings, which only allowed the sounds to
pass through, and hid from sight the angels of beauty, of whom they were
worthy. I could talk of nothing else. . . . When we entered the saloon which
confined these longed-for beauties I felt an amorous trembling which I had
never before experienced. M. le Blond presented to me one after the other
these famous singers whose names and voices were all that I knew about
them. Come, Sophie . . . she was a horrible fright. Come, Cattina . . . she
had only one eye. Come, Bettina . . . she was disfigured by small-pox. Hardly
one of them was without some noticeable defect. (Rousseau, 288)

Rousseau says in continuing to attend their concerts, he ended in
finding them almost beautiful anyway, despite the evidence of his
eyes.

  Grosrichard suggests a parallel here with the denial of the
fetishist:

I know very well (that they all have some marked defect), but nevertheless. . . . This reality that these voices have made me, alas, desire to see, these
same voices, in bringing the eye back into the ear, in retouching the images,
are also the most convincing denial, the privileged instrument of his *Verleugnung*. *Verleugnung*: it is the term which Freud uses in his article on fetishism. Rousseau, fetishist of the voice? Perhaps. (Grosrichard, 124)

Grosrichard finds a common thread of the denial of sexual difference,
implicit in fetishism, in his analysis of Rousseau's sallies into sexual

adventure in Venice, in which the theme of the "horrible flaw" recurs repeatedly: the lush courtesan *la Padouana* sings voluptuously, but the sexual act with her repels him: he runs to a doctor, convinced he has been poisoned by *la vérole*; Zulietta, who speaks only Italian ("her accent alone would have been enough to turn my head"), at first arouses him, but she turns out to be a "monster." As the seduction, or transaction, approaches its final stages, Rousseau struggles against a mounting anxiety. At the critical moment, she reveals a terrible "flaw," and Rousseau finds a locus for his uneasiness: she has a "blind nipple." A mortal chill replaces his ardor, and he dissolves in tears. She advises him to leave women alone and study math (*lascia le donne, e studia la matematica*), as he has indeed done before. In his final adventure, a proposed threesome with a friend and a twelve-year-old, Anzoletta, he finds himself unwilling to proceed. Instead, he pays for the girl's singing lessons and becomes attached to her in a paternal way: the pattern of Chambéry is restored, peacefully reversed.

Rousseau renounces sexual pleasure with its poisonous threat, the concealed defect of its forbidden object, to return to the theater of Saint Chrysostome, where he falls asleep during a concert, then awakens, thinking himself in Paradise. Grosrichard writes: "This Paradise was only 'the gods' [*un paradis*: an opera gallery]. For it is not upon the banal reality of things that the sleeper suddenly opens his eyes and ears. He awakens *in a dream*, in a fantastic world which the most extreme artifice cleverly orchestrated to create illusion" (Grosrichard, 129). Rousseau's pleasure is inextricably bound up with his effort to *conservar la bella che mi accende il cor*: for him an object of desire must remain untouched. The fetishistic pleasure taken in the female voice is one that will crop up repeatedly in the texts I discuss: it emerges in *Sarrasine* and, more obliquely, in other texts that figure an ambiguity in the singer's gender; it is visible in *L'Eve future* and in Leopold von Sacher-Masoch's *Venus in Furs*.

The crisis posed by sexual difference that underlies the logic of fetishism serves as a key to Grosrichard's reading of *La Nouvelle Héloïse*. He finds its trace in Saint-Preux's horror of the beauty he hears in the singing of a castrato, regretting that it was not Julie's voice that so moved him, and in his injunctions to her to be more like a man and to study Italian singing.

Grosrichard's analysis concludes with the passage on Aunt Suson discussed above: he notes that for Rousseau the object of desire, heard in a long series of echoes throughout his work, remains forever untouchable: a thorn always lies hidden beneath the rose. His reading of the imbrication of Rousseau's erotic conflict with his love of the feminine voice provides a gloss on Marin's insights about the relation between Rousseau's autobiographical project in the *Confessions* and the melody that haunts him: a voice from the past reverberates within the present voice of the author writing of himself. Marin writes: "The maternal voice of Eros is the song of innocence, of birth, and no sooner articulated, then also of danger and of death by signs and looks: birth and death, origin and end, beginning and ending at the same moment and in the same place, insurmountable contradiction" (Marin, 16).

In the writings of both Proust and Rousseau discussed in these pages, self-narration becomes implicated with memory, with echoes of the lost mother, with grief, and with the mortal risk implied in the gesture of entry into the world of signs, the world of others. In both texts, the act of writing, of assuming a voice, calls up the shadow of a lost maternal voice. Not only nostalgia and the anxiety about death are at work in the implication of the maternal voice in the creation of a narrative self in these texts; rather, the conditions for the emergence of the very sense of self are imbricated with the maternal voice.

That these two writers bracket the edges of the nineteenth century is not irrelevant here, nor that voice is linked to the maternal. As numerous writers have shown, the nineteenth century was a time in any number of European societies in which women became firmly emplaced in the domestic sphere. The Rousseau material anticipates the post-Napoleonic scene in which the law itself would treat women as primarily wives and mothers, restricting inheritance rights for women and their abilities to control property and to maintain the guardianship of children, enforcing their dependence on men, and restricting the spheres of activity open to them, as the historian Edward Berenson has described in *The Trial of Madame Caillaux*.[13] Likewise, Mary Poovey's well-known work describes the division in England in these years between a public male sphere and a private feminized one.[14] Finally, the production of a fantasy of the maternal voice as ground for the literary production of German romanticism is a central argument in Friedrich Kittler's study of the shift from romanticism to modernism in *Discourse Networks: 1800/1900*.[15] If the feminine is identified with the maternal in the founding symbolism of the culture, an insistent construction of women as mothers is a historically demonstrable feature of this period.

Marin's and Grosrichard's readings of narrative voice in terms of reminiscence of the maternal voice owe much to the interest generated in France a few years ago by certain psychoanalytic studies of the voice. Studies by analysts like Denis Vasse and Didier Anzieu, who conceive of the voice as a key component of psychic structure, emerged during the same period that feminists such as Irigaray, Cixous, and Kristeva made feminine voice the object of a theoretical discourse that sought to employ it as an empowering model for gender studies and for feminist writing.

Denis Vasse's book *La Voix et l'ombilique* comes out of his work with children as a practicing psychoanalyst and derives from the writings of Jacques Lacan and the clinical work of Françoise Dolto. His discussion intercuts theoretical chapters with case studies of particular children. He focuses especially on their drawings, which he asserts are as individual and revelatory as a person's penmanship and can be read as a kind of writing. Citing years of clinical work by Dolto that reveals repeated patterns of representations of the umbilicus in children's drawings and speech, he shows how the voice replaces the umbilical cord and serves, like the belly button, as the mark of severance.

Vasse grounds his account in the Lacanian hypothesis of the psychic alienation produced by an unconscious hidden object of fixation—the "object (a)"—that confuses subject and object and freezes the psyche, tying the subject to an objectifying and inexpressible alienation. Vasse refers to Lacan's thesis that this object has to do with a series of reifications: the impossible materiality of the penis, of the expression or retention of excrement, of color and form, of the voice, and of nothingness. The goal of psychotherapy is to recover this object without referent, which is inaccessible to symbolization or specularization, through the discourse of the patient. Through the

disappearance of the object (a), the subject is returned to his own desire, and to the Other, who is the place of his speech. The voice, as
support of the subject's speech, addressed to the Other and is subject
to the desire of the Other, is the point at which the symbolic knot is
made, can make itself heard at the moment when the object (a) shatters: "It is the symbolic place par excellence, because it is indefinable
other than through the link, the gap, the articulation between the
subject and object, the object and the Other, the subject and the
Other."[16] When the voice can be heard, it reestablishes the relation
of alterity that founds the unconscious and the speech of the subject,
breaking the materiality of the object (a) and restoring the subject to
the symbolic dimension. Vasse's conception of the function of the
voice thus stresses its enabling role within the symbolic order.

In his account of the function of the voice, Vasse associates it with
the umbilical cord. As the physical bond that links the fetus to its
mother, the umbilical cord is the first object of adult care: cut and
tied off at birth, it is the primordial locus of the infant's anchoring in
its mother. The scar of the belly button remains as the mark of desire
at the center of the child's body, the desire of the parents that conceived it, and the child's own desire to live. The moment when the
umbilical cord is tied off is simultaneously the moment when care is
taken to cleanse the infant's mouth to prepare it for its first cry and
its first breath: "The voice moves into the place of the umbilical severance" (Vasse, 16). The baby's first cry signals its entry into the
world and makes up, with the tying off of the cord, a single act of
individuation that is completed by its naming. Thus, the umbilicus
represents the closure that marks the newborn's definitive rupture
with the body of the mother and the beginning of its new life, one
that will be mediated by the voice, its own as well as that of the parents. The child calls to its mother by crying; she responds with needed
attentions and her own speech. Through the voice, the child becomes
subject to the laws of exchange that determine its place as a human
subject, laws ruling a structure of alliance whose terms dictate its
participation in a social web of desires within the matrix created by
language.

If the umbilicus marks closure, the voice is its subversion, for it
traverses closure without breaking it. At the same time the voice sig-

nifies the body's limits, it dislodges the child from simple localization in its body, ushering it into a realm of relations governed by speech: "So, in the same act, the voice attests to and frees one from this limit. It cannot be heard or proffered except as an effect of resonance within a particular volume whose limit, while it can be sealed off at all points, nevertheless authorizes a reasoning/resonating effect [*raison-nance*] that situates the subject outside itself, in speech, which utters him to the Other" (Vasse, 20). The voice is thus situated in the space between the organic and the social, so that neither the body nor the social body can be conceived without it: the social order is constituted by the relations of the voice and thus language: "The order which it establishes between subjects . . . comes to substitute for the bond of umbilical blood, and it is through [the voice] that the speaking subject is constantly linked, on the one hand, to the particularity of his body and blood, to his personal history and, on the other hand, to the universality of language and to others, to humanity" (Vasse, 21). The voice marks the symbolic point of limit that implies separation and relation, out of which are constituted the relations of language that imply and make possible the individual's self-recognition and recognition by others.

It is by the quality and tone of one's voice that one is known to others: the voice reveals a person's affective state, something of his character. Arising from the body, separate from it, contiguous with it, the voice serves as a token of presence. Any number of expressions relate the voice to presence and to recognition: to be "heard," to "have a voice in something"; in French, electoral votes are counted as "voix." To speak, however, means also to be heard, implies the act of reception by another. In speaking, one is simultaneously localized and taken up from one's place in the exchange of speech. Within the notion of the voice are implicated those of place and discourse:

The voice belongs neither to the order of representation (knowledge) nor to the order of self-presence (place). It cannot be conceived other than as the crossing that *establishes the limit that it crosses*: as the founding passage of the limit, the voice specifies the limit that separates and counter-distinguishes body and discourse, place and knowledge. . . . Outside of the concept of which the voice is the agent, there is neither presence nor knowledge. *The voice is the in-betweenness originary of knowledge and place.* (Vasse, 185)

For Vasse, it is not possible to separate the voice from the body and from presence, or from discourse, knowledge, or representation. There is no inside or outside to the voice. Rather than as a simple support for difference, Vasse suggests thinking of the voice as an objectified difference, appealing to the limits of both its origin and destination and serving as the ground of the formal coherence of representation: "Let us say that in the voice become articulated the phoneme and the seme, *resonance* and *reasoning*, and that through it, presence becomes discourse *for* someone" (Vasse, 186). Out of this analysis Vasse elaborates a theory of psychosis as lost voice, of confounded limits between the body and discourse, that results in the loss of the defining matrix of human reality of knowledge and naming, place, and mortality. For Vasse, the voice poses itself as the enigma of human reality: arising from silence and inconceivable either as the place of presence or as the knowledge of representation, irreducible to either, it is the relation between them that articulates them in their difference. Absent from representation, it yet organizes knowledge. It is an "establishing rupture" of self and other, an "enigmatic passage" that simultaneously lays down the grid that makes human reality coherent and retains in itself the traces of the subject's origin.

Vasse's conception of the voice as the psychic umbilical cord that simultaneously marks the subject's act of individuation and organizes his integration into the social order provides one way of reading the preoccupation with the maternal voice that emerges out of the passage from Proust and Marin's and Grosrichard's interpretations of Rousseau's writings: the privileging of the maternal voice as constitutive of the individual's identity leads to its direct thematization in these autobiographically based narrative works, in which what is originary becomes directly implicated in the very act of writing itself.

Following a somewhat different line of thinking, one that departs from a Lacanian grid, the analyst Didier Anzieu arrives at a not dissimilar emphasis on the role of the maternal voice in the foundation of psychic structure in his book *Le Moi-Peau*. Anzieu postulates a double organization of the psyche, grounded in both the biological body and in the social body, and proposes the notion of a "skin ego" (*moi-peau*) that functions as an intermediary structure. Among the earliest and most important components of the human psychic envelope is what he calls "the sound envelope," the sea of sounds and voices in which the infant bathes and which first engages him in the development of his sense of self.

Anzieu prepares for the introduction of his "vast metaphor" of the *moi-peau* by reviewing a series of epistemological issues that led him to his theory. He observes that from Freud's time to ours there has been a shift in the kinds of psychological disorders commonly seen, from hysteria and obsessional and phobic neuroses, produced in a society in which sexuality and discussion of sexuality were repressed, to currently more common neuroses involving problems with the sense of limits: narcissistic and boundary disorders. Contemporary society is one in which the issue of limits is endemic, in which unmeasured ambitions are promoted and the individual is taken in charge by a succession of institutions. Noting the erosion of the sense of boundaries in the contemporary world, with its easy access to the artificial ecstasies of drugs and its progressive isolation of children in an overheated nuclear family life, Anzieu suggests that the cultural atmosphere in general promotes immaturity and generates disorders of psychic limits. He develops his theme of the envelope in tracing the predominance of the epistemological theme of the shell and core: since the Renaissance, to know means to break through the shell to expose the kernel of truth of a matter. One result of this line of thinking has been the explosion of the atom bomb. Anzieu notes a paradox in this dichotomy emerging from physiology: the cerebral cortex lies out at the edge of the brain; the true center of thinking is at the periphery. His own hypothesis extends this observation to propose that thinking is as much a matter of the skin as of the brain and that the self has the structure of an envelope.

Anzieu breaks down the simple dichotomy of shell and kernel by reviewing findings from embryology, anatomy, and cell biology that support a more complex concept of internal and external, in which subtle structures of interface emerge. Notable among these is the embryological concept of "invagination" in the development and structuring of human physiology: many structures that are at one point external become folded in to form the body's orifices (lips, nose, eyelids, and so on). Recent research in cell structure reveals a complex double membrane that serves both to contain and to communicate. Borrowing perhaps as well from Jacques Derrida's use of the term, Anzieu elaborates from these recently evolved biological models and calls for psychoanalytic theory to extend its analytical model to present a view of psychic content that includes an appreciation of the themes of containment and communication.

He explores the semantic richness of the English and French words referring to touch and feeling to argue for the role of the skin as an organ of central importance in mental and social life (the entry under "touch" is the longest in the *Oxford English Dictionary*; in *Robert*, those for skin, hand, and touch [*peau, main, toucher*] are among the largest; myriad idioms attest to the metaphoric significance of words having to do with touch and skin, as for example "to rub someone the wrong way," "to enter into contact with someone"). He passes under review the complexity of the biological function of the skin, of the number of professions that occupy themselves with the skin and hair, and points out the many paradoxes that govern the skin: it is permeable and impermeable, superficial and deep, betrays the truth and conceals it, is the cause of pleasure and pain, ages and renews itself continually. Its position is one of transitionality, in-betweenness, its role, that of intermediary. One implication of his estimation of the skin's significance in psychic life is his call for a redefinition of the oral stage in infancy that would move emphasis from the breast to the child's contact with the mother's skin in general. It is in this context of the importance of the skin as primordial source of contact with the mother that Anzieu presents his notion of the *moi-peau*.

The establishment of the skin ego in the infant arises from its need to create a narcissistic envelope that ensures the development in the psychic apparatus of a ground of certainty and well-being. Psychic activity in the child is anchored in the skin's function simultaneously to contain, to mark a limit, and to serve as means of communication with the world. In both normal and abnormal cases, the sense of self is modeled on the physical experiences of the body's surface, and its figuration remains mingled with them:

By Skin Ego, I mean a mental image of which the Ego of the child makes use during the early phases of its development to represent itself as an Ego containing psychical contents, the basis of its experience of the surface of the body. This corresponds to the moment at which the psychical Ego differentiates itself from the bodily Ego at the operative level while remaining confused with it at the figurative level.[17]

The creation of this envelope allows for the individuation of the child to take place. Much of Anzieu's book explores the psychological implications of various failures and distortions of this sense of the self as bounded by a permeable envelope.

Anzieu analyzes the dyad formed by the mother and child as a double feedback system characterized by a process of mutual vocal solicitation: it is as much through her voice as through her actual handling of the child that the mother brings appeasement and care, an idea that restates in different terms Vasse's notion of the role of the voice. Anzieu signals, among other elements of the feedback system, the early identification of the "familiar melody of the maternal voice." The skin ego is an intermediary structure that defines boundaries, but equally important, it gives contact with the world beyond. Through this Janus-faced formation the integrity of the self's unity is ensured: the developing child needs as much to have its separateness acknowledged by the mother's speaking to it of itself, as it needs to be reassured by her proximity. This communication takes place not only through physical contact but also through the voice.

Among several sensory envelopes that Anzieu adumbrates (the thermal, olfactory, muscular), the one primary is what he calls "the sound envelope" (*l'enveloppe sonore du moi*). He describes it as developing in parallel with the establishment of two-dimensional boundaries and limits that are anchored in tactile sensations. Through the introjection of the world of sound, the child begins to prepare a sense of individuality and unity. Crying, she is engaged in a three-dimensional world, which will begin to orient her in space and time. Reviewing the Lacanian notion of the *mirror stage* and Winnicott's idea of an early mirroring effect in the mother's face, Anzieu argues for an anterior stage, for a sound mirror: "I would like to demonstrate the existence at an even earlier stage of a sound mirror or of an audio-phonic skin, and the role this plays in the acquisition by the psychical apparatus of the capacity to produce meaning, and then to symbolize" (Anzieu, 158). The sonic bath that surrounds the child, made up of alternation of his own cries and the voices of those around him, prefigures the "moi-peau," with its Janus-faced structure looking simultaneously inward and outward, and provides him with a first "image" of himself as an individual body/self:

Before the look and smile of the mother who feeds and cares for him reflect back to the child an image of himself which is visually perceptible to him, and which he interiorizes to reinforce his Self and develop the rudiments of his Ego, the bath of melody (the mother's voice, her singing, the music she causes him to hear) have made a first sound mirror available to him. He makes use of it first in his crying (to which the mother's voice responds with soothing), then in his babbling, and lastly in his early games of phonemic articulation. (Anzieu, 169–70)

Anzieu's notion of a sound mirror that antedates the famous mirror phase is a theoretical idea of great force: one of the most heavily used and overused concepts that literary criticism has borrowed from psychoanalysis, the mirror stage carries with it a freight that has gone generally unexamined. With the notion of a primordial visual mirror as constitutive of the subjectivity of the individual, one is led to privilege vision and the visual image in speaking of subjectivity. In doing so, Lacan evidently was following the lead of Freud, in interpretations of whose work there is relatively little emphasis on the auditive in the early development of the self (beyond the role of "things heard in the night" in the imagination of the primal scene).

If one posits an auditory mirror that precedes the visual, it anchors the voice and the auditory sense at a deeper or earlier level in the inauguration of subjectivity, with interesting implications. Anzieu's evocation of a "melodic bath," his use of the notion of harmony to describe the child's listening to "familiar melody of the maternal voice" ("and what term but a musical one would do?") recalls the melody that haunted Rousseau; it resonates with the analysis by Philippe Lacoue-Labarthe in his essay "L'Echo du sujet" of a profound relation between "the haunting melody" and subjectivity, between the mode of the auditory and the adumbration of subjectivity, which I discuss in the following chapter. The mode of the auditory, with the metaphors that it offers, presents itself as a rich and relatively underexplored source of understanding of subjectivity. One may think of Henri Meschonnic's use of the notion of rhythm, for instance, to recast the relations of language and discourse, a point to which my discussion will return below. Film scholars have in recent years taken a renewed interest in the study of the voice and sound in general in cinema.[18] One of the most influential of these critics, Michel Chion, has written a book on the voice in cinema that takes off from Vasse's theories.[19]

Anzieu turns to the myth of Echo and Narcissus to explore some implications of his notion of the auditory mirror: within its elements he finds expressed the imbrication of the visual and acoustic mirrors in the constitution of primary narcissism in the psyche. The youth Narcissus, while exciting passion in the nymphs and girls he meets, remains insensible to them. Echo also falls in love with him, and disappointed in her turn, retires into solitude, where she wastes away. Soon, nothing remains of her but her voice that repeats the last syllables she hears. The nymphs obtain their revenge from Nemesis: returning thirsty from a hunt, Narcissus leans over a clear pool where he falls in love with his own image. In symmetry with Echo, he perishes in the contemplation of his own features. Even during his descent to Hades, he seeks his reflection on the surface of the river Styx. Anzieu comments: "The legend well indicates the precedence the sound mirror has over the visual mirror, as well as the primarily feminine character of the voice and the connection between the emission of sound and the demand for love" (Anzieu, 169).

Several points emerge from Anzieu's observations here. In finding a structural parallel between Narcissus and Echo, he shows the common element of reflection that binds them. In the disembodiment of Echo, caused by Narcissus's self-absorption but preceding his own dissolution, Anzieu sees a confirmation of his theory of the primal nature of the auditory mirror. The accompanying implication of the association between the voice and a demand for love corresponds with the emphasis both Anzieu and Vasse place on the mediation of the mother-child relation by the voice and points to this dyad as the source for the power of the voice in its avatars as vehicle of the erotic and the lyrical.

Anzieu's intimation of a primary relation between the voice and the feminine is suggestive to me but also problematic. Though I argue that such an association can be found and seems to be very old (sirens, oracles, "dread goddesses endowed with speech"), and though I borrow from his notion of an acoustic mirror, I would not wish to argue that the voice is inherently or predominantly a feminine mode. To do so suggests the maternal to be the feminine destiny. I would prefer to emphasize the functional, culturally typified nature of the association of the voice with the feminine, and thus of its role in the formation of the psyche. It is not necessarily a woman who cares for the pre-oedipal infant, though it generally was and often still is in our culture. On the basis of her analysis of how gender roles in child rearing reproduce themselves through the differential passage of boys and girls through the oedipal drama, Nancy Chodorow suggests an egalitarian sharing of infant childcare as a way to restructure gender and, in the process, mitigate male hostility to women.[20] In some other societies, women have not been the only primary child-tenders. In an issue of the linguistic journal *Langue française* devoted to the "mother tongue," an article by A. Khomsi underscores the cultural determinations behind this notion. Evoking the ambiguities surrounding the term, Khomsi notes that the linguistic development of the child must be seen in the context of the socializing forces. It is not always the mother who cares for the infant, even in our society, not only a female care-giver who occupies this function. Among some groups, the arrangements may be quite different:

In two recent translations, *Mother-Child* (D. Stern, 1978) and *Maternal Behavior* (R. Schaffer, 1981), the titles, which appeal to the reader's unconscious, are corrected at the very first page, since for R. Schaffer, the mother, necessarily designated by a feminine pronoun [in French], becomes "every person who takes care of small children." The mother can, then, *not* be the mother, and we will be obliged to come back to this question when discussing the innatist argument of D. Slobin (1981) according to which little Samoans learn to speak "despite the fact that parent-child conversations are very limited"; it is necessary, in fact, to take into account this other fact presented by Slobin himself: in Samoan families, it is the older children who take care of the little ones.[21]

Samoans, then, might not grasp what Khomsi calls the "appeal to the unconscious" of the notion of the "mother tongue": it may not carry the same resonance for them as for Europeans.

In appropriating Anzieu's figure of the sound mirror, I trace out where some of this cultural baggage ends up. In fact, the female figures in the texts I analyze in the second part of this study, while they are persistently defined in terms of their voices, turn out to be just as persistently defined as ambiguously gendered, asexual, or in some way constructed. The bodiless and feminine Echo is emblematic of the deployment of the female figures in these texts and may be seen in the broadest sense as a vivid image of the structural position of the woman's voice in representation, serving in the myth, as in the texts, as an acoustic reflection of male desire.

Echo's Haunting Song

The Voice in
Feminist Psychoanalytic Theory

During the 1970's and 1980's, the theoretical and fictional work of women writers such as Luce Irigaray, Michèle Montreley, Marguerite Duras, and Hélène Cixous, with her conception of the "primarily feminine character of the voice," brought before feminist readers a particular conception of the voice as a privileged term. The strategic decision to take theoretical advantage of sexual difference, to insist on the value of "feminine" traits in order to use them as a point of departure for a mode of female writing, characterizes in a general way the movement of "women's writing" (*écriture féminine*). Whether or not one finds this a congenial way of thinking, one should certainly see it as a response to the discursive and cultural denegation of the feminine, and of the feminine as maternal, for which Goux and Irigaray argue in the accounts sketched out above. Thus, a key move made by these feminist analyses was to accord a new value to feminine writing through a valorization of the mother and the maternal voice.

Such an approach has elicited a strong response, in particular from American feminists and gender theorists, who see this line as dangerously close to ghettoizing essentialist or normative conceptions of the discursive and social positions available to women. In part to situate my own material in context, since my interest in female voice was stimulated by the currency the debates of French writers gave it, I will rehearse some of these critical responses through readings of relevant articles by Domna Stanton, Claire Kahane, and others, as well as Kaja Silverman's *The Acoustic Mirror*,[1] to examine in what ways the notion of the mother's voice has seemed to fall short and in what ways it may still be useful. I am interested in retaining aspects of the argument about the female voice for what a reconsideration of the acoustic mode can give to ideas about the construction of subjectivity.

The critical gain I hope to derive is not a "rescue reading" of maternity per se nor a model of feminine subjectivity in particular, but rather the perhaps elusive gains that acknowledging the primacy of the acoustic dimension may bring. One such result is the questioning of the hegemony of the Lacanian model (insofar as it is based on the mirror stage) produced by the reworking of subject theory, which Lacoue-Labarthe effects in "L'Echo du sujet" and which bears some comparison with Kristeva's ideas as well as with those of Meschonnic. It is a useful dividend for a study that focuses primarily on representations of singers to find that an archaeology of acoustic sense seems repeatedly to bring up the rhythmic as basic to the foundations of the structuration of the self in language. Rhythmic pulsation is, in turn, a notion that Nancy uses to describe the structure of sublime experience, an idea to which I will return at the close of my study, where I argue that representations of female song owe much of their shape and force to the aesthetic of sublimity and to an underlying conception of what is inhuman. I propose then, that the perception of the role played by the maternal voice in the constitution of the subject remains useful for descriptive and contestatory purposes and thus offers, when taken as itself a historical construct and carefully framed, a useful tool for a study of the voice within a feminist perspective.

The problematic nature of the project to valorize the voice and its inherent limitations has been cogently presented by Domna Stanton in "Difference on Trial: A Critique of the Maternal Metaphor in Cixous, Irigaray and Kristeva" and by Claire Kahane in her recent article "Questioning the Maternal." Noting that a truly complete analysis of the maternal metaphor in contemporary French women's

writing would have to take into account the work of writers like
Chantal Chawaf, Duras, Sarah Kofman, Marcelle Marini, Michèle
Montreley, and Eugénie Lemoine-Luccioni, Stanton holds up the
three writers she studies as emblematic of a widespread movement
that sought to subvert phallocentric discourse through an exploration of feminine difference. Stanton states that female difference as a
metaphor for difference is a theme that has formed part of the theories of modernity of Lacan, Lyotard, Gilles Deleuze, and Jacques
Derrida, referring to Alice Jardine's point in *Gynesis* that the modernist masters in France have "consistently coded as feminine that
which exceeds the grasp of the Cartesian subject—be it called non-
knowledge or nontruth, undecidability or supplementarity, even
writing or the unconscious."[2] Stanton suggests that the female authors of texts that rely on the notion of female difference have been
deeply influenced by these ideas and questions to the extent that the
metaphor of the maternal actually opens up a viable alternative tex-
tual strategy to represent the unrepresentable. Within these texts that
valorize the maternal, the mother's voice is frequently represented
as the marker of a specifically feminine space that predates and
eludes inscription in the oppressions of a phallocentric discursive
system.

Stanton asserts that for these writers the feminine is associated
with the maternal "metaphor." For Irigaray, difference is "the
maternal-feminine"; for Cixous, the essence of femininity lies in the
womb, and women are "the maternal sex." While Irigaray writes that
"when we are women, we are always mothers," Kristeva discusses the
feminine function as the maternal, and unrepresented feminine sexuality as maternal *jouissance* (pleasure) (cited in Stanton, 159–60).
Later in my discussion I will take a closer look at certain of the problems posed by Kristeva, for this seems to be a somewhat simplistic
take on her positions. Stanton notes the break these writers make
with the stance of Simone de Beauvoir, who emphasized the oppressions of motherhood and oriented her analysis through the historic
and political dimensions, holding to her sense of the primacy of wom-
en's task of liberation. Instead, Stanton says that Cixous and Kristeva
affirm maternity as a locus of feminine specificity and seek to redefine
the field of possibilities for women in terms of its symbolic force. For

Kristeva "only a full elaboration of maternity and its relation to creation" will allow "a true feminine innovation," while Irigaray claims for this a new cultural syntax, arguing for the idea of the murder of the mother as foundational in Western culture. Thinking of the mother in every woman is a forbidden act that will undermine the patriarchal edifice and bring about a revolutionary ethic of sexual difference. The pre-oedipal has served as the ground for the maternal metaphor in these writers who claim it as a gynocentric space. For Cixous, it is an "originary point for the future feminine" and represents an archaic past before the advent of the symbolic that has been abducted and buried alive, like Persephone (cited in Stanton, 164–65). Stanton's discussion of the valorization of the pre-oedipal in Kristeva and Cixous points up the privileged role they accord to the maternal voice.

In Cixous's writings, the theme of the maternal breast and voice is central to her focus on the mother-daughter relation as metaphor for "femininity in writing." Stanton evokes numerous instances of this privileging of the voice as figure for female writing. The voice is the "song before the law, before . . . the symbolic," able to "make the text gasp or fill it with suspense or silences, anaphorize it or tear it apart with cries." She contrasts masculine "writing by the written" to feminine "writing by the voice," identifying the voice with the maternal woman's essential connection to the uterus: in *Illa*, she writes that "the voice is the uterus"; in *La Jeune née*, she identifies the maternal voice with the breast: "Voice. Inexhaustible milk. Is rediscovered. The lost mother. Eternity: voice mixed with milk" (cited in Stanton, 167–68). Stanton finds most typical of Cixous her use of milk as the predominant metaphorical vehicle for writing in the feminine, exemplified in her notion of *le langelait*, of the mother who writes with the white ink of her good milk. Like Irigaray, Cixous plays with the traditional associations of femininity with water and its attributes of rhythm, movement, fusion, and diffusion to posit the notion of an alternative feminine space that escapes identification and provides a model for the overcoming of binary phallocentrism.

Stanton rightly finds a danger in attempts to define feminist writing in terms of such metaphoric feminine attributes, since despite their underlying project of a revalorization of the feminine, they end in reinforcing the binary logic of opposition that produced them: the structure does not change, and the female writing becomes ghettoized, as it were, in a traditional essentialism. She argues that Kristeva, Cixous, and Irigaray countervalue the traditional antithesis that associates man with culture, woman with nature, and thus reproduce and even reinforce the dichotomy between male rationality and female materiality traced by Irigaray (and Goux, as I show) to Greek metaphysics.

Stanton deconstructs this use of the maternal, arguing that while these writers consciously use the maternal as metaphor, thematizing the metaphoric in their discussions, they ignore what she calls the essentializing, metaphysical, even theological implications of metaphor: its equations plug it into a metaphysical frame that reinscribes its terms into the "structures of phallagopresence," what Irigaray has called the logic of the same in *Speculum de l'autre femme*. Thus, to Stanton's way of thinking, the unrepresented and unrepresentable female difference, defined as absence, made present in texts through the maternal metaphor, becomes recuperated into the very system it seeks to subvert. Parallel criticisms may be heard from both Kahane and, more recently, Nancy Fraser in her introduction to *Hypatia*'s special issue on French feminist philosophy.[3]

Kahane shows substantial agreement with Stanton in her discussion of the maternal in both these French writers and American women writers like Nancy Chodorow, who uses object-relations theory that emphasizes the maternal, and Alicia Ostriker, whose work *Stealing the Language* surveys contemporary American women poets' use of the female body. Like Stanton, she characterizes this approach as a strategic dead end. In her view, such a project romanticizes the maternal in a way that is ultimately damaging for feminist analysis and must be renounced as utopian, although she affirms a certain value for feminists in its affirmative vision of the feminine. She parts ways with Stanton, however, in finding value in Kristeva's opposition of the semiotic and the symbolic.

Kahane locates her discussion in the polemical context of Jane Gallop's talk at the 1985 MLA panel on "Psychoanalysis: Its Place and Potential," where she critiqued *The (M)Other Tongue*, a collection of feminist psychoanalytic essays edited by Kahane. In her talk,

Gallop argued that the dominance of object-relations theory, which focuses on the maternal, in the collection of articles, notably in Chodorow's work, resulted in an idealization of the mother as heroine of a pre-oedipal narrative that resisted the otherness implied in the title. This mother didn't "want" separation, argued Gallop, who characterized the imagining of a mother tongue that would be outside language as a dream-wish, since language is based on difference, and urged an approach that "explored the radical alterity within the mother."[4] While conceding that accepting the premise that patriarchal discourse narrates even the pre-oedipal implies a renunciation of the notion of a "prelapsarian period" before language promising an "unmediated access to maternal fullness," Kahane maintains the value of a "public articulation of [such] a dream." It is in terms of a feminist construction of empowering representations of the mother, a "rescue fantasy," that Kahane describes this idealizing project in which the daughter gives birth to the mother she has always wanted, an event that inscribes her as a figuration of discourse itself.

Kahane turns to the Kleinian theory of infant phantasms of the breast to criticize the idealized image of a primordial fusional relation to the mother. In Melanie Klein's work, introjected *imagos* of the breast incorporate aggressive and destructive fantasies as well as reassuring ones and result in a split between representations of the good and the persecuting mothers in an effort to rescue the good one. As Kahane puts it, "It is the movement from the paranoid-schizoid position of persecution and splitting to the depressive position, marked by loss and separation, that allows the recognition of both the mother as a separate and whole object containing the splits and the self as a separate subjectivity" (Kahane, 85).

The Kleinian view of the infant's relation to the breast implies an earlier experience of individuation than that emerging from the work of the proponents of women's writing. Kahane points out that by denying ambivalence, these writers who affirm maternal plenitude promote the repression of the mother's other side and thus "deny her a human form." She recalls André Green's remark that the good breast is not always good when it is present, not always bad when it is absent. The good may be good precisely because it leaves an empty space needed for individuation. Kahane parts ways with Stanton, however, when she evaluates the implications of Kristeva's version of the function of the pre-oedipal stage. Stanton includes Kristeva with Cixous in her critique of the French women writers' idealization of the mother, while Kahane finds room in her theory for a feminist appropriation of the notion of difference, indeed for a differential conception of the movement of the female child into language.

Stanton writes that the pre-oedipal stage is especially important for Kristeva's theory of poetic language and of a subversive production. The semiotic logically and temporally precedes the symbolic order, which is identified with the paternal law of the father. A "revival of archaic pre-oedipal modes of operation," the semiotic is described by Kristeva in *Révolution du langage poétique* as the preverbal period during which the child is bound to and depends on the mother's body and rhythms. This relation to the mother's body is repressed when the child acquires language, but the heterogeneity and richness of the semiotic remain inherent in the symbolic and may erupt into it and threaten its position in certain types of subversive discourse, notably poetic language, defined as the semiotization of the symbolic.

According to Stanton, Kristeva's theory is weakened by its reliance on certain traditional images, in particular, that of the child at the breast: "The superego and its linear language . . . are combatted by a return of the oral glottic pleasure" of suction and expulsion, fusion and rejection (cited in Stanton, 166). The maternal voice is associated with the primordial rhythms that characterize the semiotic: "with a material support like the voice, this semiotic network gives 'music' to literature," and "melody, harmony, rhythm, 'gentle' and 'pleasing' sounds" (cited in Stanton, 166). The poetic text derives its radicality from a return of the repressed and from a kind of metaphorical incestuous act of appropriating this forbidden maternal territory. Stanton challenges the acceptance implied in this account of the phallocentric Freudian script and claims that Kristeva's characterization of the artist is usually made as male, the only articulate mother in her work being the Stabat Mater of *Histoires d'amour*: "Although the maternal/semiotic is crucial to the Kristevan theory of art as the exemplary subversive practice, the mother remains, as the phallotext defines her, a passive instinctual force that does not speak, but is spoken: 'the artist speaks from a place where she is not, where she knows not. He delineates what in her is a body rejoicing' (*un corps jouissant*)" (Stanton, 167). For Stanton, Kristeva's ideas about maternity imply a reinscription into the patriarchal metaphysics of the Freudian "script," resulting in a kind of theoretical failure to clear the gravitational force of phallocentric discourse, or put another way, in the ambivalence toward feminism more than one critic has detected in Kristeva.

It may be worth pointing out, however, that other discussions of this aspect of Kristeva's work give a somewhat different picture, for they draw from remarks she makes in other texts like "Women's Time," "L'Héréthique," and "Polylogue." In *The Daughter's Seduction*, Gallop engages in a careful triage of Kristeva's notions of motherhood, pointing out the problems posed by her heterosexual bias and the uneasy linkage of the maternal with the semiotic. Yet Gallop also shows how Kristeva conceives of the maternal state as not governed by fantasies of unity but, on the contrary, as characterized by a state of double division, "a space both double and foreign." Gallop emphasizes Kristeva's efforts toward subversion, not only of the phallus, but of the phallic mother. Kristeva "dreams" dangerously, says Gallop, of the socially and politically critical position available to a woman, precisely because of her already alienated state: In "Polylogue," Kristeva suggests that the doubly alienated position of the mother might prepare her to call many things into question. Gallop likewise draws her reader's attention to Kristeva's positing in "L'Autre du sexe" of such a state of negative capability assumable by a woman who is simultaneously mother and artist. Gallop dismisses as fantasy Kristeva's suggestion that such a person would be able to stand outside of the symbolic order and "enjoy" its collapse, but one can see that Kristeva works, at least, to theorize a nonutopic, nonregressive relation to maternity precisely through the figure of an articulate, artistically creative mother.

In arguing that Kristeva's semiotic is not assimilable to Lacan's imaginary, that the former is disruptive, the latter basically conservative, Gallop makes a useful distinction, one elided by Stanton in her critique. She does so, however, by way of pointing to the problem posed in Kristeva's use of the semiotic:

The danger in Kristeva's theory is that "the semiotic" fall into "the imaginary"—in other words, that the potential disruption of the maternal becomes the alibi for what actually functions as a comforting representation. The incompatibility of Lacanian and Kristevan theories, the difficulty in thinking a relation between the "imaginary" and the "semiotic," ought to be attended to as a locus of conflict between two maternals—one conservative, the other dissident—as a way of keeping the position of the mother "both foreign and double," of guarding against a complacent assimilation of the mother to one side or the other, against a smug attribution of superior dissidence to one sex or the other.[5]

Gallop closes her discussion through an analysis of the efforts Kristeva makes to think through a relation that is "heterosexual not homological" between the sexes in "Polylogue." She shows in this text Kristeva's ambivalence toward both maternity and homosexuality, but she also shows the richness of its dialectic, its double duplicity that gestures toward a different type of discourse, one not reducible to phallocentric terms.

In her chapter on Kristeva in *Sexual/Textual Politics*, Toril Moi arrives at her discussion of the semiotic by way of stressing that Kristeva's antiessentialism leads her to refuse definitions of "woman," as well as belief in any fixed form of identity. Moi also makes it clear that Kristeva is not a subscriber in any way to *écriture féminine*, a point that does not emerge from Stanton's discussion, which tends to lump together differing French women writers in one group. As a corollary to her claim that Kristeva does not biologize, Moi suggests that critics are mistaken who claim that Kristeva identifies the semiotic solely with the feminine. She observes that while the semiotic is linked with the pre-oedipal mother, this phantasmatic phallic mother encompasses both masculine and feminine traits. Moi opens up a gap within the structure of gender by arguing that this figure

cannot . . . be reduced to an example of "femininity," for the simple reason that the opposition between feminine and masculine does not exist in pre-Oedipality. And Kristeva knows this as well as anybody. Any strengthening of the semiotic, which knows no sexual difference, must therefore lead to a weakening of traditional gender differences, and not at all to a reinforcement of traditional notions of "femininity." This is why Kristeva insists so strongly on the necessary refusal of any theory or politics based on the belief in any absolute form of identity.[6]

Moi thus emphasizes Kristeva's focus on the role of positionality, rather than inherent identities, with the fluidity this may suggest.

Kahane also turns to Kristeva's conception of the pre-oedipal process in her discussion of the maternal voice, finding she articulates it not as idealized fusion but as the term that opens up difference, serving as the ground for the symbolic. Like Gallop, Kahane takes note of Kristeva's use of maternal voice to provide a theoretical vocabulary for the double alienation of the female subject in language. She evokes the prevalent use of hysteria in recent studies as a "trope for the truth of the body, the hysteria speaking through her body the truth which language does not allow" (Kahane, 85). Unable to use language to address the father, the hysteric lodges a protest against paternal discourse by using her body to subvert the limits that define it. Hysteria is bound up in its very nature with the voice: "[it] problematizes the voice both as object (that which is heard out there) and as subject (speaking an interiority)." Noting the now familiar point that the beginnings of psychoanalysis were associated with Freud's research on hysteria, she cites, following Kristeva, an early paper in which he acknowledges the connection between hysteria and the voice:

The point that escaped me in the solution of hysteria lies in the discovery of a new source from which a new element of unconscious production arises. What I have in mind are hysterical phantasies, which regularly, as it seems to me, *go back to things heard* by children of an early age and only understood later. The age at which they take in information of this kind is very remarkable—from the age of six to seven months onwards. (Cited in Kahane, 88)

These acoustic memory traces of the primal scene imply an assumption by the subject of a mobile position, a multifaceted act of identification. The understanding of the "things heard" marks the passage from the semiotic to the symbolic, with the initial mobility of the child's perceptual position becoming anchored in the symbolic structure of difference. The child grasps sexual difference in his secondary revised symbolic participation in the scene: the relative positions of power and vulnerability become assigned later to the father and mother, respectively. Thus, in Kristevan terms, the reinterpretation of "things heard" marks the transition in which the mobility of the semiotic subject is fixed in the structure of sexual difference.

In contrast to Stanton, who interprets Kristeva's theory of the process by which the semiotic is subsumed by the symbolic as an unintentional capitulation to a phallocentric definition of the subject, Kahane argues for its usefulness. In her reading of Kristeva's writing on the voice, she underscores its differences with the Cixousian voice as plenitude. Kahane emphasizes that although Kristeva celebrates the pre-oedipal mother, she grounds the symbolic as "the inescapable determinant of her signification," while positing the lived experience of a differently constructed space of meaning: "Kristeva theorizes a presence beyond/before the symbolic that is linked to the real elsewhere and, moreover, to a biological real that materially supports representation. In the unconscious is the lost trace of an archaic experience of the body before language, an experience of a sensuous continuum to which mothers and artists have privileged access" (Kahane, 86). While Stanton subsumes the Kristevan semiotic in the register of the imaginary and metaphoric whose use she criticizes in the proponents of the maternal, Kahane points to the experiential ground for this theory, and by stressing the crucial role of the semiotic process to the formation of the symbolic discounts its metaphorization through antinomy.

Kahane further argues (like Gallop) that Kristeva's account of the maternal voice—unlike that of Cixous—defines it as the "site of a primary splitting." She points to the idea in Kristeva's writing of the infant's identification of the voice as a signifier of otherness even before its apprehension of the mother as object. She quotes Kristeva's statements in "Freud and Love" that "there is an immediacy of the child's identification" with a "maternal desire for the other." This experience is associated with sound and the voice: "[It is] not visual, but a representation activating various . . . perceptions, especially the sonorous ones; this because of the precocious appearance in the domain of neuropsychological maturation, but also because of their dominant function in speech. [The voice is an] ideal signifier, a sound on the fringe of my being, which transfers me to the place of the Other, astray, beyond meaning, out of sight" (Kahane, 86). Thus read, the maternal voice in Kristeva is to be seen not as utopic fusion but, from the very outset of the child's experience, as a vehicle for individuation and even splitting through the processes of identification. This identification with the other is equally the source of the discovery of otherness; the *chora* contains the seeds of abjection and pain.[7] Like Anzieu's acoustic mirror, this view of the voice as an acoustic bridge does not point away to an imaginary other realm but functions from the start to prepare the infant for participation in the symbolic and is a prerequisite to the structures of identification that make individuation possible.

While Kahane observes with Stanton that for Kristeva the subject of enunciation is gendered as male, she stresses Kristeva's progressive use of such a definition. In the French psychoanalytic model, the subject enters language by identifying with a paternal figure. Without the third term provided by the paternal signifier, the "law of the father," the mother-child pair would be locked in psychotic fusion. The mother who turns away to address an other opens a space for separation. As Kahane puts it, "the triangulating instance allows the move to object loss; the mother who turns to the world creates a space for the subject-in-language, for the signifying 'I'" (Kahane, 87). In accepting this characterization of how the subject is inserted in language, Kahane follows feminist psychoanalytic critics who view such a description of the *status quo* not so much as an inevitable reinforcement of it but rather as an opportunity for discussion: the description of such a process is not necessarily a capitulation to it; naming it may instead provide a way to get a handle on its effects. Kristeva's choice as a psychoanalyst and linguist to begin from where she sees things to be, rather than from where she would like them to be, would seem, in fact, to remove her from the rolls of the utopian feminists Stanton criticizes.

While Kristeva is interested in the insights potentially available to the woman who goes through the double alienation of maternity, she does not extol it as a desirable state. Her writings question the ideological and psychological workings of "the material basis for women's oppression: motherhood."[8] In "Polylogue" Kristeva in fact argues the necessity to go beyond the mother in a passage that supports Kahane's reading:

No language can sing unless it confronts the Phallic Mother. For all that it must not leave her untouched, outside, opposite, against the law, the absolute esoteric code. Rather, it must swallow her, eat her, dissolve her, set her up like a boundary of the process where "I" with "she"—"the other," "the mother"—becomes lost. . . . Within the experiencing of the phallic, maternal mirage, within this consummated incest, sexuality no longer has the gratifying appeal of a return to the promised land. Know the mother, first take her place, thoroughly investigate her *jouissance* and without releasing her, go beyond her. The language that serves as a witness to this course is iridescent with a sexuality of which it does not "speak"; it turns it into rhythm—it is rhythm. What we take for a mother, and all the sexuality that the maternal image commands, is nothing but the place where rhythm stops and identity is constituted. Who knows? Who says so? Only rhythm, the designating and dissolving gesture, scans it.[9]

The Kristevan notion of a phase prior to the classic mirror stage which is a kind of boundary intrinsic to the beginnings of the symbolic bears some affinities with Anzieu's notion of a sound mirror. His *miroir sonore*, the adumbration of the *enveloppe sonore du moi* (discussed above), also creates the beginnings of a sense of the boundary between self and other and inaugurates in the logic of his system as well the founding of the capacity for language.

In the vocabulary of Anzieu's work, as well as in Kristeva's, the maternal voice provides the term that makes difference possible, and it retains some significance as a constituting element in the founding of subjectivity. Kristeva's conclusions are thus consonant with the vocabulary of the envelope and the sound mirror that emerge in Anzieu's physiologically and behaviorally oriented rethinking of psychoanalysis, as well as with Vasse's work on child psychology, which describes the voice as the term that founds the symbolic. It is less a fusional space than a traversal, a crossing-through of both mother and child by the structuring order of language that binds both to the social realm. Their findings do not deny the primal role of the maternal voice or relegate it to an imaginary never-never land outside the foundation of the subject in language. Rather the reverse: in its capacity as sound mirror and vehicle of the social, as agent not simply of a reassuring sense of fusion but of a necessary sense of boundary, the maternal voice becomes in fact a primary and enabling agent of the individual's assumption of subjectivity. The maternal voice, then, does not stand simply for an undifferentiated milky nurturance, but, emerging itself out of division, offers a simultaneous gift of connection and separation, drawing the child into social affiliation and opening to him or her the foundational experience of difference, inscribing in its echo the double nature of the subject. Thus, I would place Kristeva in different company than does Stanton: her ideas about the voice are congruent with those of Vasse and Anzieu.

For the purposes, too, of certain connections I hope to make in this discussion, Kristeva's ideas are also worth consideration (however qualified they should be, given the advances in feminist theory in the years since her material first appeared): in its evocation of rhythm in association with the maternal voice in the subject's early history, Kristeva's *chora* resonates, so to speak, with the philosophical study of Lacoue-Labarthe that revises the visual model of subjectivity to stress the role of the auditory in the foundations of subjectivity. Both Kristeva and Lacoue-Labarthe trace the auditory, along with the pulse of rhythm, to the threshold of what can be theorized about the formation of subjectivity. Later, I will put forward some other arguments that show how the singing voice is characterized in certain literary texts in terms of the vocabulary of the sublime aesthetic. In this quite different context, rhythmic pulsation (Nancy's "syncopation") will again be in question, but here as a sort of vanishing movement at the edge of the imagination's faculty of presentation. In these antipodal thresholds, in the formation of subjectivity as in a perceived form of sublimity, one finds the instance of voice and pulse, a certain relation between the auditory and the rhythmic.

A number of critics have found Kristeva problematic for what seems to be a heavy-handed bias against homosexuality, for her focus on male artists to the exclusion of women, and for a kind of turning away from a firm political stand.[10] Kaja Silverman takes up some of these criticisms in her discussion of Kristeva in *The Acoustic Mirror: The Female Voice in Psychoanalysis and Cinema*. This book combines a study of the female voice in cinema (a topic stimulated by the writing of recent French theorists of the voice in cinema like Chion, of whose work this book is in part a critique) with a theoretical examination of the voice in (French) psychoanalytic thought. While Silverman appropriates the term "acoustic mirror" used by Anzieu and

Guy Rosolato as a basis for her discussion, she is yet careful to criticize what she calls the "maternal fantasy" in the conception of the maternal voice she finds in their work, in Mary Ann Doane's article on voice in the cinema, and, especially, in Kristeva's work.

Silverman works to create a nuanced position in what is an awkward and tricky subject for feminists, since a celebration of traditional maternity is not at all where one wishes to wind up. Thus, she affirms the neglected importance of the mother's actual social function as language teacher to the infant, while opposing an idealizing, retrograde conception of the mother's role. It seems to me, however, that in her rigor she makes certain sweeping, perhaps overstated, criticisms of these writers. Doane, for example, does not seem to me to harbor any nostalgic dreams about the maternal voice—in fact, as the passage I have quoted shows, she warns specifically against such dangers. Likewise, Silverman finds Anzieu's notion of the *enveloppe sonore* to be a dream of undifferentiated, blissful fusion between mother and child. Anzieu, however, as I hope I have shown, thinks of the *enveloppe sonore* as one of several psychic "skins" that function complexly as structures of separation and containment as well as of contact. The auditory/vocal mirror, as he describes it, is precisely what makes psychic boundaries, psychic differentiation, possible.

Silverman shares with Gallop and others, such as Judith Butler,[11] some serious reservations about the usefulness of Kristeva's theories because of the bias against female homosexuality in her work. Silverman counters by opening up a discussion of the female child's psychic development that explores the implications of the little girl's continued attachment to her mother through the vicissitudes of her oedipal trajectory. Much of Silverman's discussion of Kristeva, then, includes a focus on the *chora*. One of the criticisms that emerges has to do with Kristeva's marginalization of the mother/daughter relationship. Silverman's discussion of the maternal voice here moves away from the voice itself and becomes reoriented toward Silverman's interest in providing an account of the female oedipal trajectory and of the difficulties in conceptualizing the daughter engaged in a "negative Oedipus."

Silverman is engaging here in a very appealing and intriguing project, which she conducts through a multipronged critique of Kristeva that aims to show not only that she grounds maternity in biologistic, regressive terms and conceives of the maternal condition in nostalgic, fusional terms, but also that she is defensive and fearful toward it all at the same time, and thus ends in silencing the mother. While her analysis of some of Kristeva's texts ("Freud and Love," for example) is persuasive, her reading, at a closer glance, may not seem entirely fair. Silverman seems to conflate the remarks Kristeva makes about pregnancy, for example, with those she makes about the *chora*; she takes up an early theory of Freud from *The Ego and the Id* positing several possible oedipal trajectories (disregarding his later position in, say, "Femininity") in order to bring out her theory of the negative oedipal but denies Kristeva the same luxury. Silverman focuses on Kristeva's remarks in her "Freud and Love" as a disturbing new paradigm that abandons the mother and the semiotic (for which Silverman has criticized her for identifying with the mother) in favor of the father. Silverman herself calls her reading "unorthodox," for it depends on a psychoanalyzing of Kristeva's unconscious dispositions, read as meanings opposite to the expressed statements, as in the following passage:

If we penetrate the Kristevian fantasy at a third point of entry, we eventually stumble upon the same homosexual-maternal scene. . . . That point of entry is indicated by the sentence that reads: "[Is it not true] that in order to have access to the symbolic-thetic level, which requires castration and object, [the mother] must tear herself from the daughter-mother symbiosis, renounce the undifferentiated community of women, and recognize the father at the same time as the symbolic? . . . No answer follows, but as with all rhetorical questions, one is implied.[12]

Silverman plays off the ambiguity inherent in a rhetorical question to suggest that Kristeva is only paying "lip service" to the reality of castration, that in fact her unconscious desire is to negate "the desire to negate," to deny "the desire to repudiate the force of the symbolic imperative." Thus, she finds Kristeva guilty of *Verneinung*, of saying the opposite of what she means: "This is precisely what happens in the text under discussion, which simultaneously states and conceals that desire which is at the center of the Kristevian fantasy—the desire to fuse the daughter with the mother, and the mother with her own mother. 'Is it not true' corrects and covers the parapraxis which is on the tip of Kristeva's tongue . . . which would have read: 'It is not true'" (Silverman, 110).

One may not wish to endorse Kristeva's peculiar notion of the "undifferentiated community of women," yet Silverman's reading of the meaning of this passage as the opposite of what it states may not seem convincing to all readers. In accusing Kristeva of "reducing [the mother] to silence" as Silverman does (112), of identifying the artist as only male (a judgment she is not alone in making—it is a point that has disturbed numerous critics), she ignores the texts in which Kristeva discusses the tensions and possibilities available to the woman artist, even, and in particular, the artist who may also be a mother. Elsewhere, Silverman points out with dismay Kristeva's statement "I long for the Law" in "Stabat Mater." One might note that this remark comes in the part of the text where she seems to be recording her emotions after giving birth; while one might not want to read such "confessional" material, it doesn't seem fair to take it as programmatic. Moi and Gallop have, in differing ways, read the same passages, and if they note Kristeva's limitations and ambivalences, they also offer somewhat more generous readings of her gestures.

If I have spent so much time here defending Kristeva against her critics, it is not because I find her theory of the semiotic entirely progressive or her relationship to both feminism and the paternalist order free of ambiguities: these are problems. It is also time for someone to write about the collective French *intello* shrug of renunciation of the possibilities of politics after the seventies. Despite her shortcomings, Kristeva did make an important, even pioneering, effort to articulate a theory of maternity within its ideological frame in a way that sought to be neither utopian nor essentialist. At the same time, she took the risk of speaking quite personally about an ungrateful subject, one almost taboo, certainly, in French circles at the time. For my purposes here I propose not to toss out Kristeva with the bathwater, since I find that in her association of the maternal voice, the early experiences that form the basis of language, the formation of the subject, and the notion of rhythm, she isolates a suggestive nexus of material. Her questioning of the relations of rhythm, the acoustic, and the constituting division of the individual psyche brings her into the company of others primarily concerned not with feminist issues but with other possible critiques of the theory of the subject. Philippe Lacoue-Labarthe and Henri Meschonnic, coming from very different perspectives as they do, have also underscored the imbrication of rhythm in language and subjectivity.[13]

Echo and the Division of the Subject

The concept of an acoustic echo provides the organizing question in Lacoue-Labarthe's "L'Echo du sujet" in which he interrogates a thematic link between a haunting melody and the autobiographical impulse similar to the one Marin makes in his study. Noting the occurrence in the modern history of philosophy of several instances in which an intense "haunting by music or musical obsession" is linked to an autobiographical compulsion, specifically in Nietzsche and Rousseau, Lacoue-Labarthe points in passing to its appearance in the works of numerous other writers such as Diderot and Proust, certain German romantics (Hoffman in particular), Michel Leiris, Roger Laporte, and the modern German novelists Hermann Hesse and Thomas Mann. Identifying the problem of the subject that lies at the heart of the possibility of autobiography, a mode that has colored modern philosophic discourse, he suggests that since Kant the concept of the subject has been open to question, and since Heidegger, to a process of deconstruction. He traces to Nietzsche's destruction of the figure a questioning of the philosophic discourse that is based on an uncritical acceptance of the autobiographical subject. Lacoue-Labarthe argues that the question of what links the autobiographical urge to musical preoccupations allows one to examine the infraphilosophical distinction between the visible and the audible to arrive at a theoretical threshold behind the theory of the subject, putting into question its "privileged apparatus," which he calls both a specular instrument and an instrument of speculation. Proposing to "go back from Narcissus to Echo," he investigates in this essay the philosophical implications for the theory of the subject of the question: what is a reverberation or a resonance; what is a "catacoustic phenomenon"?

Lacoue-Labarthe grounds his discussion in the problems posed by Theodore Reik's 25-year fascination with the inner echoing of a melody that came to him on hearing of the death of his mentor Karl Abraham and that provided the focus of his dual theoretical and autobiographical project, ultimately published in two works: *Fragment of a Great Confession: A Psychoanalytic Autobiography* and *The Haunting Melody*. Referring to Reik's account of experiencing an emotion of disquieting familiarity in hearing Max Bruch's Opus 47, based on the *Kol Nidre*, he introduces the Freudian motif of the *Unheimlichkeit* (whose significance reappears later in his discussion of the affective aspects of music) and underscores the relation between Reik's interest in the auditory aspects of analysis (his notion of "hearing with the third ear," borrowed from Nietzsche) and his personal experience of an internally "heard," recurring melody. The problem preoccupied Reik in his writings for many years, and he ultimately renounced hope of finding its key: Lacoue-Labarthe argues that Reik's theoretical difficulties in finding the terms with which to address his problem take place at the interstices of the Freudian theory of the subject, at the point where the verbal model is problematically juxtaposed (as it describes the operations of the unconscious) with the figural (as it is made to account for the dream scene and the phantasmatic).

It is not possible here to retrace each step of Lacoue-Labarthe's densely reasoned reading of the narrative of Reik's haunting by the theme from Mahler's Second Symphony, based on the Klopstock poem "Resurrection"; of how grief and oedipal rivalry inform the quartet configuration of Reik/Abraham/Mahler/von Bulow in which musical and analytic filiations are doubled and mirrored; or of Reik's lapsus in associating Abraham with Hamburg, the city where Mahler found inspiration for his symphony at the funeral of von Bulow. The term on which it hinges—Abraham's accent—poses for Lacoue-Labarthe the term of style, the point at which the tonal aspect of voice offers something extra, something associated with character, not reducible to the content of speech:

What is heard and begins to make sense (to "signify," not in the mode of signification but, if one may rely on a convenient distinction, in that of *significance* [in Benveniste's sense]) is not, strictly speaking, of the order of language. Rather, it affects a language, and affects in the use of a language (although this cannot be understood in relation to the Saussurian *parole* [speech], or in relation to linguistic "performance") its *musical* part, prosodic or melodic.[14]

Lacoue-Labarthe writes that what interested Reik was the voice (grain, tone, color). These qualities that lend themselves to musical or stylistic analysis are what is precisely least amenable to theorization "because, more fundamentally, they escape the metaphysical (theoretical) distinctions that always underlie them (sensible/intelligible, matter/form, body/spirit, thing/idea, and so on). A phenomenon of this sort is, finally untheorizable" (Lacoue-Labarthe, 160). He evokes Reik's analytical interest in the voice as indirectly revelatory of the unconscious, noting that Reik's notion of the analyst as listening with a "third ear," which privileges hearing as a metaphor of analytic understanding, derives from Nietzsche's "third ear": sensitivity to style, the artist's ear. Thus, Reik's use of hearing is paradigmatic for perception in general, of language as mimetic: hearing and seeing become conceptually fused. He demonstrates from this fusion the conceptual knot in which Reik tangled himself through his vocabulary borrowed from the visual register to describe the audible that uses the Goethean motif of "repeated reflections."

Lacoue-Labarthe thus reads Reik's "failure" as a failure of theory, of a specular reduction that is also a theoretic reduction, tracing this problematic and curious linguistic circuit back to the "old secret heritage of Platonism: the voice, diction, the audible in general (and music) are attainable only by speculation" (Lacoue-Labarthe, 163). The unexamined passage from the optic analogy to the acoustic, from reflection to echo, then, opens up the problematic of specularity in the theory of the subject.

Lacoue-Labarthe departs from his observation of the doubly specular configuration of identification in Reik's autobiographical "novel" to enter into a discussion of Lacan's refiguration of the oedipal triangle as quaternary. Noting that the concept of identification (primary identification in particular) is the "nodal point" of Freudian theory, he shows the production of an effect of alienation in the subject by this quaternary system. Just as the gap between the real father and his symbolic function creates his double to fulfill this function, the subject itself is created as double:

> This splitting, or, as Lacan also said—an inevitable word here—"alienation" of the subject "with respect to itself," makes it oscillate vis-à-vis its double between distancing (where the substitute bears every "mortal menace") and a "reintegration" of the role (where desire is inhibited). A well-known situation in the "romantic" or "fantastic" novelesque forms (that of Hoffman, for example). In short, Lacan sketched out, though within psychoanalysis and while retaining the Oedipus complex, a "mimetology" fairly comparable to the one that Girard, with quite different intentions, will elaborate later. (Lacoue-Labarthe, 170)

This quaternary system determines at once the impasses of neurosis and also the possibility of the assumption of one's position as subject by the self. This doubled structure of alienation is the frame for Lacan's mirror stage, the foundational experience of the subject's narcissistic relation to himself in alienation as an image. Out of the Freudian imago and the mirror stage, argues Lacoue-Labarthe, emerges a theory of the *figure* and of *fiction*, of death as figure, of the double and double death as *Gestalt*. Through the mediation of the imaginary death which the subject undergoes as part of the process of the constitution of his self comes the possibility of meaning. This imaginary death described by Lacan is, for Lacoue-Labarthe, the struggle to the death for prestige described in Hegel's *Phenomenology of Mind*: an imaginary, hence specular, death. He locates Lacan's text on the mirror stage with its implication of a doubly specular structure within the scene of figural ontology or fictional ontology. Operative in Reik's dual project of autobiographical and autoanalytical study, this "fiction" dramatizes him as subject of the theory of the subject, framing the theoretical enterprise in the order of the novel, which proceeds by figures or types. Lacoue-Labarthe finds problematic here not only Reik's position but the theory of the subject itself based on a dissymmetry found in the doubly specular relation of the quaternary structure. At the heart of Reik's text, as in the specular relation itself, Lacoue-Labarthe argues for a fundamental instability in the nature of the subject:

And thus, because it takes into account this discord that no speculation can dialectize because it is inscribed in the specular relation itself, it is very likely that we are dealing here with a *loss of the subject*, undermining in advance any constitution, any functional assumption, and any possibility of appropriation or reappropriation. This loss of the subject is imperceptible, however, and not because it is equivalent to a secret failing or hidden lack, but because it is strictly indissociable from, and doubles, the process of constitution or appropriation. (Lacoue-Labarthe, 174)

The subject in the mirror is then, for Lacoue-Labarthe, a subject *"en désistement,"* able to appropriate his status only within the limits of a mortal inadequacy that spells his inability to assume it; undermined by the very work of the imaginary that creates the dimension of his being, he attains self-assumption at the price of self-loss. This paradoxical instability of the subject implies a destabilizing division in the figure:

The "theoretical consequence" (though at the limit of the theorizable): the figure is never *one*. Not only is it the Other, but there is no unity or stability of the figural; the imago has no fixity or proper being. There is no "proper image" with which to identify totally, no essence of the imaginary. What Reik invites us to think, in other words, is that the subject "desists" because it must always confront *at least* two figures (or one figure that is *at least* double), and that its only chance of "grasping itself" lies in introducing itself and oscillating *between* figure and figure. (Lacoue-Labarthe, 175)

Within the space opened by this conception of the destabilizing partition of the figural, Lacoue-Labarthe sees the operation of the association of the "musical obsession" and the autobiographical compulsion, allowing as it does for an examination of the "prehistory" of the subject beyond the frame created by the model of narcissistic recognition. Like Anzieu, Lacoue-Labarthe turns to the register of the acoustic to account for what predates the mirror stage, and like Kristeva, he attributes a fundamental significance to rhythm as a structuring principle.

Lacoue-Labarthe returns to Reik's effort to relate the *"hantise musical"* to affectivity, and he describes his first gesture to locate music in the Freudian conception of music as deriving its impact from repressed material, as the representation of an unconscious *Stimmung*. He then turns to the Nietzschean reading Reik gives of musical catharsis as arising from feelings nonverbal in nature, hence inexpressible in words. In *The Birth of Tragedy*, Nietzsche argues for a nonverbal preliminary to poetic creation. For Lacoue-Labarthe, this Nietzschean reading, which gives anteriority to the dionysian, or musical, over the apollonian, or figural, also attempts to articulate the inarticulable passage from chaos to the figure, from the pain of "originary Unity" to the phenomenal. Lacoue-Labarthe evokes Nietzsche's assessment of the undoing of the self in the dionysian process, of the illusory status of the poet's "I" to underscore his own argument about the nearly untheorizable "abîme" from which the subject emerges: "The 'I' of the lyrist therefore sounds from the depth of his being: its 'subjectivity,' in the sense of the modern aestheticians, is a fiction" (quoted in Lacoue-Labarthe, 187).

In these terms, music would be seen as catharsis through a kind of mimetic reduplication of original pain, bringing consolation for the sense of mortality, for the grief it evokes. Lacoue-Labarthe notes that this pleasure, partaking of the theatrical and the tragic, is specifically a "masochistic" one. He argues that by stopping with the notion of musical catharsis, Reik renounces making the step that would allow him to complete his thought, reproducing the suspension or caesura created by the masochistic *jouissance* itself. Reik finally renounced his project, admitting to theoretical failure. For Lacoue-Labarthe, Reik's inability to make the jump between the phenomenon of unconscious repetition and the determination of the subject as ethos or character left him in a theoretical impasse. The critical term that would have allowed him to make this transition is the notion of rhythm as anterior to the visible figure, of whose appearance it is the condition.

Lacoue-Labarthe reads a passage from Reik that describes an experience of the unheimlich in terms of a scene that seems like a senseless dance. It concludes with the sense that what is missing is rhythm, the key to all the movements that otherwise appear bizarre. One may think here of the wild dance of Hoffman's mechanical doll Olympia as she spins out of control, her uncontrolled movements spelling out the truth of her uncanny nature. For Lacoue-Labarthe, rhythm is the specifically musical or acoustic element that orders the movements and repetitions of dance. It is anterior to the schema or visible figure and is the precondition for the possibility of its apprehension. As repetition, it creates the possibility of the event (or dance); missing, it creates the emotion of disquieting unfamiliarity, the "nothing" of the unheimlich:

> *Nothing* occurs: in effect, the *Unheimliche*, the most uncanny and most unsettling prodigy. For in its undecidability, the *Unheimliche* has to do not only with castration (this *also* can be read in Freud), the return of the repressed or infantile anxiety; it is also that which causes the most basic narcissistic assurance (the obsessional "I am not dead" or "I will survive") to vacillate, in that the differentiation between the imaginary and the real, the fictive and the non-fictive, comes to be effaced (and mimesis, consequently, "surfaces"). Without the beneficial doubling (or because, according to Freud, of the change in "algebraic sign" the double undergoes in the development of the Ego), the immediate certitude of "primary narcissism," its confused, blind, ante-specular recognition, is shaken.
>
> In which case, rhythm would also be the condition of possibility for the subject. (Lacoue-Labarthe, 195)

Rhythm thus appears as the *sine qua non* of the subject, as the underlying condition of subjectivity. Definable only through repetition ("the repeated difference from itself of the Same"), inaccessible to conceptualization insofar as it pertains to the prespecular and the prefigural, rhythm becomes in Lacoue-Labarthe's argument the term that creates the fissure between the visible and the audible, the temporal and the spatial, retrievable not in these terms but in terms of a Derridean *archi-écriture*.

Lacoue-Labarthe arrives at the final step of his argument by associating rhythm, type, and character (in both the ethical and stylistic or lexical senses of the words) through a reading of the rhetorical tradition that identifies *rhusmos* with *skema*. He cites Emile Benveniste in *Problems in General Linguistics* and Werner Jaeger in *Paideïa*, who show an early identification of *rhuthmos* or *rhusmos* with *skema*, form or figure. In the "materialist" tradition, it is understood as one of the features of differentiation itself, with *diathige*, contact (for Aristotle, order, *taxis*), and *trope* (assimilated by Aristotle to position, *thesis*). Benveniste notes that Herodotus uses *rhusmos* for the form of letters; thus Lacoue-Labarthe suggests the existence of an ancient tradition that applies *rhusmos* to the configuration of the signs of writing. He evokes Heidegger's comment in his seminar on Heraclitus that Georgiades translates *rhusmos* as *Geprage*: imprint, seal, type, thus character. Thus, he argues, there is an uninterrupted line of filiation that links type to figure, to disposition (*Stimmung*), and character: for Lacoue-Labarthe, it is within the terms of style, incision, and preinscription that one may approach the problem of the subject and autobiography.

He points to Benveniste's emphasis on *skema* as an approximation for *rhusmos*. Thus, *skema*, as it means form or figure, refers to something fixed or stable, while *rhusmos* refers to form as it appears in a mobile configuration, as of the momentary configurations of dance, conditioned by time and difference through repetition. Seen in these terms, rhythm is only secondarily a musical term, defined as such through a "late" theoretical position taken by Plato in *The Republic*. Lacoue-Labarthe pursues his point in showing how music is here presented as an equivalent to *lexis*, enunciation. In *The Republic*, music has a mimetic power: musical form must be adapted to discourse, and its significance lies in its imitation of ethical traits. It renders *ethos* perceptible as simple and "well-behaved" or as heterogeneous, overly complex. Measure and melody are to translate, to be submitted to, the style and speech of a courageous and balanced man. Rhythm, then, is based on diction as it imitates character. Thus, rhythm falls under the categories not only of the musical or figural but also of the ethical, of character. He uses this conception of rhythm to present it as a participating element of character, of subjectivity:

Rhythm is not only a musical category. Nor, simply, is it the figure. Rather, it would be something between beat and figure that never fails to designate mysteriously the "ethical"; for the world (and perhaps already the concept) already implies—at the very edge of what the subject can appear, manifest, or figure itself—the type and the stamp or impression, the pre-inscription which, conforming us in advance, determines us and makes us inaccessible to ourselves. A preinscription that sends us back to the chaos that obviously was not schematized by *us* so that we should appear as what we are. In this sense, perhaps, "every soul is a rhythmic knot." (Lacoue-Labarthe, 202)

Thus, for Lacoue-Labarthe, rhythm is the missing link between the autobiographic compulsion and the "musical obsession"; theorized as figure, or felt as pulsation, as a "repetition marked by a caesura," it translates into a haunting melody that bears the nostalgia of one's origin.

Through the trajectory of his reading of rhythm in terms of an *archi-écriture*, as a prespecular, presubjective element determinative of character and subjectivity that lies behind the enigma of the catacoustic echo, Lacoue-Labarthe approaches the Kristevan perception of the *chora* as "the place where rhythm stops and identity is constituted." It is not surprising, then, that he closes his essay with a section entitled "Maternal Closure" in which he recalls the "maternal voice" (in Nietzsche; in the poem by Wallace Stevens, "The Woman That Had More Babies Than That"; and in several other texts) and wonders whether it is possible to go beyond "maternal closure," asking what other voice can return to us, and by what else we are "rhythmed."

Lacoue-Labarthe's dismantling of the visual metaphor in the theory of the subject in his exploration of the elusive relation between autobiography and the haunting melody makes a place for a better understanding of the role of the auditory in the foundational specular division of the subject. In this context, the myth of Echo and Narcissus takes on a particular resonance. The disembodied voice of Echo speaks of the forgotten role of the acoustic mode, specifically of the feminine voice, in the creation of primary narcissism: before the mirror phase, usually taken as the founding moment of the identity of the subject, occurs the inscription of the maternal voice, the trace of whose echo remains audible within the psyche, though "attainable only through speculation."

Echo figures the peculiar position of women in representation in general: her role is to repeat Narcissus's words and thus figure his desire, her own elided out of representation. The chapters that follow will turn on a study of the feminine voice in certain nineteenth-century representations of extraordinary women singers, material that illustrates this point, for I will show how the seemingly privileged access of these figures to the affective power of the voice, this seemingly Orphic power, is yet underpinned by a romantic preoccupation with the woman's voice as an idealized, constructed object of desire.

Consuelo

High Priestess of Song

> You are the priestess of the ideal in music, and it is your mission
> to spread it, to make it understood, and to lead the reluctant and the
> ignorant to an intuition and a revelation of the true and the beautiful.
> You have something greater to do than to make your reputation and
> your fortune. The one and the other will inevitably be made. But you
> will be concerned with them only as the means to make easy and sure
> the influence of your power and genius on the world. (June 1842)[1]

At the time George Sand wrote these words of admiration and encouragement to her cherished friend, the singer Pauline Viardot, she
was beginning work on *Consuelo*. In this novel and its two companion volumes comprising *La Comtesse de Rudolstadt*, Sand modeled
her heroine on the moral and physical qualities she saw in Viardot
and sought to give form to the ideas about the art of the singer expressed in this letter.

It is not surprising that the figure of Pauline Viardot should have
so fascinated Sand. In his history of opera singers, Rupert Christiansen says that she was one of the most remarkable women of her times,
"a prima donna of intelligence rather than instinct."[2] In an age dominated by such great singers as Catalani, Pasta, Falcon, and her own
mythically famous sister, Maria Malibran, Viardot created for herself a reputation as a thoughtful artist and virtuosic performer.

Pauline García (Viardot was her married name) was born in 1821
into a family of distinguished musicians. Her father, Manuel García,
was the tenor who created the role of Almaviva in Rossini's *Barber
of Seville*. Her brother, also a singer, became a renowned singing
teacher and wrote down the García method in a treatise on singing
that is still respected. Viardot was, however, first known as the little

sister of the meteoric Maria Malibran, whose fantastic career inevitably frames hers. Writing of Pauline's debut, calling her "a star of the first magnitude, and seven-rayed star," Gautier evokes Malibran's fame: "A name that is a halo shone about this young head; the name of Malibran García, so fortunately fallen on the most beautiful day of her life, crushed beneath the flowers and wreaths given by the public, this other Heliogabalus, and raised again in her glory, in Desdemona's white shroud, all white against a golden background, like the divine apparition of whom Dante speaks."[3]

A romantic's romantic, excess was Malibran's trademark on and off the stage: the first time she heard one of Beethoven's symphonies she was carried out in convulsions.[4] The fervent Malibran electrified audiences, "alternating between frenzy and collapse" as Christiansen puts it, until her early death in 1836. His account of her death[5] gives a sense of her characteristic impetuosity: after a bad riding accident (though pregnant, she had purposely chosen the wildest horse available) that left her with spells of depression and blinding headaches, Malibran continued to perform, and in fact threw herself into her activities with even greater intensity. She collapsed after a performance, having insisted on giving an encore, and died a few days later, at the age of 28. Fifty thousand people followed her casket in Manchester. Christiansen lists the admirers who mourned Malibran—Verdi, Liszt, Rossini, Chopin, Mendelssohn—and quotes from the elegy Alfred de Musset wrote for her: "It is your soul, Ninette, and your naive grandeur / It is this voice from the heart that alone reaches the heart / That no other, after you, will ever be able to return to us."[6]

Despite the tone of finality in these words, a few years later Musset was to revise himself in equally hyperbolic terms after attending a recital by her young sister, in his piece "Recital by Mademoiselle García," first published in *Revue des deux mondes*, January 1, 1939. Claiming to have seen a ghost, though not a frightening one, Musset affirms the return of "la Malibran" in her seventeen-year-old sister, though he finds the resemblance more in voice than in features:

It is the same timbre, clear, resonant, bold, this throaty Spanish cry [*coup de gosier espagnol*] with something so harsh and so sweet about it at the same time, and which produces in us an impression something like the savor of a wild fruit. . . . [7] Fortunately for us, Pauline García has her sister's voice; she has her soul as well, and without the slightest effort at imitation, it is the same genius; I do not believe, in saying this, that I either exaggerate or make a mistake.[8]

Musset ends this piece by making a different comparison, one between Viardot and Rachel, the tragedienne and specialist in Racine, finding them, though a study in contrasts, to be sisters of a kind. They are bound by a "sacred kinship," that of genius: "Yes, genius is a gift of heaven; it overflows in Pauline García like generous wine from an overflowing cup; it shines from the depth of Rachel's abstracted eyes, like a spark beneath ash. . . . It is time that truth reign, pure, cloudless, freed of the exaggeration of license and of the fetters of convention. A return to truth is the mission of these two young girls."[9] In comparing Viardot and Rachel in this way, Musset makes an implicit comparison between the singing and dramatic declamation: both are vehicles of vocal expression, and in the adulatory terms Musset employs, both likewise reflect the romantic ideology of genius.

Stendhal has recourse to similarly hyperbolic language in praising the genius of the great singer Giuditta Pasta in his book on contemporary opera, *La Vie de Rossini*:

Without such a palette of breath-taking colour deep within her own being, and without such an extraordinary and compelling natural gift, Madame Pasta could never have achieved the overmastering force of natural expression which we have learnt to associate with her—a miracle of emotional revelation, which is always true to nature, and although tempered by the intrinsic laws of *ideal Beauty*, always alive with that unmistakable, burning energy, that extraordinary dynamism which can electrify an entire theater. . . . Her art appears to be infinitely perfectible; its miracles grow daily more astonishing, and nothing can henceforth stop its power over the audience from growing progressively more binding. Mme Pasta long ago overcame the last of the physical obstacles which stood in the way of the realization of pure musical enjoyment; and her voice today is as fascinating to the listener's ears as it is electrifying to his soul.[10]

Stendhal goes on later in the piece to evoke the "visions of celestial beauty" and the "strange glimpses into the secrets of sublime and fantastic passions" afforded by Pasta's art, as well as "ineffable mysteries, dreams which lie beyond the powers of poetry, vistas unknown, unfathomable, deep-hidden in the recesses of the human heart, which no mere Canova with his sculptor's chisel, no mere Correggio with his painter's brush could hope to reveal to our enquiring souls!" (Stendhal, 369).

That the artists singled out for praise here are women is signifi-cant. Because of the historic developments in opera, the position the woman occupies in general in the romantic imagination, and, as I suggest, the role woman singers in particular play, the fetishistic fas-cination with the feminine voice that we saw in Rousseau assumes a broader aspect at this time, becoming a widespread theme in both social and literary spheres.

In an age when few professions or public creative outlets of any kind were open to women in France, the theater, especially the mu-sical theater, provided a medium, if not always an honorable one, for feminine creativity. In the nineteenth century, for a number of rea-sons, opera flowered as an art form, and in particular as a form in which women occupied a central position—especially in France, tra-ditionally less receptive to castrati than elsewhere. A number of cul-tural motifs are fused in the woman singer: the woman as spectacle, the woman as angel and demon, romantic notions of art and the ideal. It is noteworthy that Musset, in writing of the genius of Rachel and Viardot, should speak of their talent as a "gift of heaven," their art as "pure," and their "mission" as that of ushering in the "reign of truth," and that Stendhal speaks of the "ideal beauty" of Pasta's sing-ing, of her "sublime gifts." These ideas, which Sand seeks to evoke in her heroine Consuelo, are also reflected in Sand's vision of Viar-dot's character and talent.

Though her entry into the Parisian music scene was prepared by the memory of Malibran's brilliance, since initially audiences were eager to see her as Malibran returned, Viardot's singing created a great deal of interest on its own merits, and she was enthusiastically received. Gautier's review of her debut performance was full of praise:

She is endowed with one of the most magnificent instruments one could hear. The timbre is admirable, neither too thin, nor husky. It is not at all a metallic voice like that of Grisi; but the tones in the mid-range have a certain sweet and penetrating something that stirs the heart. Hers is the García method; this says it all. She has all the fullness of voice that puts the listener at ease, freeing him of any apprehension about possible mistakes. Her voice is marvellously trained, the intonation pure and true. Notes are always attacked with great clarity, without hesitation or portamento; this last quality is rare and precious. She is an excellent musician. . . . Mlle. García's success was complete.[11]

Her singing attracted more than just critical acclaim: Musset proposed marriage to her. Sand was already close enough to the García family to be able to maneuver Pauline away from this idea and was instrumental in the match made with her friend Louis Viardot, for a time director of the Théâtre Italien, journalist, and musicologist (he owned the original manuscript of *Don Giovanni*).

In the course of her career, Viardot associated with many of the period's most distinguished artists: Gustave Flaubert and Joseph Ernest Renan were friends of hers. She was called "the woman of the most genius it has been given to me to know" by Clara Schumann, and "illustrissime" by Franz Lizst, who had been her piano teacher (quoted in Marix-Spire, 13). Charles-François Gounod, like Hector Berlioz, was smitten with her; Ivan Turgenev fell lastingly in love with her, following her back to France from Russia to remain in an ambiguous *ménage à trois* with her and her husband until the end of his life. A discerning, conscious artist, as much musician as singer, she continued to grow artistically throughout her life, developing new repertory parts in operas by Saint-Saens, Berlioz, Meyerbeer, Gluck, and Gounod. Christiansen relates that once she sang "a private recital with an audience of two, one of them Berlioz, of the newly composed Love Duet from *Tristan und Isolde*, Richard Wagner taking the part of Tristan: an outstandingly unsuccessful occasion."[12] She gave the first performance of Johannes Brahms's *Alto Rhapsody* in 1870 (when she was almost 50) and extended her patronage to other young composers like Jules-Emile-Frédéric Massenet and Gabriel-Urbain Fauré.

Viardot's career was beset, however, with significant problems. Less attractive, more reserved than Malibran, she was cut out by cabals at the Paris Opera (the director Léon Pillet gave the choice roles only to his mistress, Rosine Stoltz) and had better success abroad during the early years of her career. Marix-Spire shows that her husband's politics, expressed through his journalistic activities, were the source of some of his wife's difficulties, making her especially vulnerable to hostile critics.[13] Viardot, with Sand and Pierre Leroux, was one of the founders of *La Revue indépendante*, which Marix-Spire calls "an opposition journal."

Viardot had some difficulties even during the excitement of her debut in Paris in obtaining desirable roles there: "Yet Pauline limps along" (*Pourtant Pauline piétine*), remarks Marix-Spire, and cites an article Sand published in the *Revue des deux mondes* in 1840 that shows the passion with which she attempted to defend the young singer against a cool public reception. This piece gives a sense not only of Sand's estimation of Viardot's abilities but of her belief in the moral, spiritual bases of Viardot's talent:

We will not analyze here Mlle García's dramatic talent, nor the extraordinary range and power of her voice. This magnificent instrument's quality of timbre would mean little to us if heart and intelligence did not fire it; but it is a prodigy whose honor rises to God, just to see such a rich facility of expression in the service of such a powerful intelligence. This voice comes from the soul and goes to the soul. From the very first sounds she gives forth, we sense a generous spirit, we await an indomitable courage, we feel that a powerful soul is about to communicate with us. . . . She does not merely please. One loves her.[14]

A voice that reaches from soul to soul; a rich gift of expressivity in the service of a powerful intelligence; the generous spirit and indomitable courage of a tempered soul that inspires deep emotion in its audience: these are some elements of the portrait that Sand wished to create of the ideal artist when, several years after writing this encomium to Viardot, she began *Consuelo*. Marix-Spire writes:

In 1840, George Sand sculpted Pauline's statue, but two years later, in the spring of 1842, at the height of her crisis of aesthetic mysticism, the disciple of Liszt and Leroux, convinced of the sacred role of art and of the priestly role of the artist, animates, makes this statue tremble. . . . And at the same time, based on Pauline, emerges the shining figure of Consuelo: an unattractive form transformed by genius, a genius glowing with the loveliest lights of the soul: nobility, greatness, goodness. (Marix-Spire, 43)

Consuelo first appeared as a *feuilleton*, published in the *Revue Indépendante*, beginning in February 1842. *Consuelo* and its sequels, which together constitute the three volumes of *La Comtesse de Rudolstadt*, were published monthly in this serial form through February 1844.

In this immense novel (some 1,550 pages in length) set during the eighteenth century, Sand spins out the story of the Spanish singer, Consuelo. When the story opens, Consuelo is an orphan studying at the school of the church of the *Mendicanti*,[15] whose chorus so enraptured Rousseau during his stay in Venice. In fact, his account of the singers there may very well have served Sand in her invention of Consuelo: like theirs, her wonderful voice is paired with physical plainness. Sand sends her heroine, the virtuosic star pupil of the great Porpora,[16] through a succession of adventures in this meandering work that combines elements of the picaresque, gothic, and historical novels and can be included among the romantic novels of illumination. To sum up the vicissitudes of Consuelo's story: at the brink of success, Consuelo must flee Venice to preserve her virtue, taking refuge in Bohemia at the castle of the Rudolstadt. She becomes caught up with the Hussite heretic Albert, whose seeming madness conceals the wisdom of an initiate of the brotherhood of the "Invisible Ones." In the course of the novel, Consuelo saves a lost Albert in a characteristic élan of compassionate courage, tracking him in high gothic style to his mysterious underground retreat; tramps the open roads disguised as a boy, the young Haydn her companion; performs on the opera stage in Vienna and Berlin; returns to Rudolstadt to fulfill a vow to marry the dying Albert; is thrown in jail; is rescued by a mysterious stranger, with whom she falls in love; renounces her passion during a *Magic Flute*–like initiation into the brotherhood of the "Invisible Ones." Albert is revealed as the romantic stranger, and in a mystic wedding the two consecrate themselves to the creation of a new order of universal love and liberty.

Despite the provisional happy ending of the novel, several epilogues fill the reader in on Consuelo's suffering and the loss of her voice after—and because of—her marriage, though she retains a gypsy freedom, wandering the forests of Bohemia with her children and mad Albert. In these unlikely but fertile inventions, the reader can see something of the romantic flair that made Sand one of the most widely read novelists of her time.

Music dominates the world of *Consuelo*. The novel begins in a music school and takes the heroine to opera stages in Venice, Vienna, and Berlin; many of the characters are musicians or would-be musicians; the author and her characters discuss and comment on music and performance at every turn. It does not seem coincidental that while she was writing *Consuelo*, Sand was living with Frédéric Chopin, whom she called "my third child, in every sense of the term" (quoted in Marix-Spire, 181). Music had, however, always been important to Sand: growing up in a musical family—her father and his parents were all good musicians—she received music lessons from her grandmother. Sand had a good singing voice and improvised at the piano. She also played guitar and harp. In his book *La Musique et les lettres au temps du Romantisme*, Léon Guichard calls Sand the romantic author for whom "music was most alive and most constantly present in the most diverse forms."[17] Marix-Spire develops this rich biographical background for Sand's affinity with music in her book on Sand and music, presenting a vivid picture of Sand's excited arrival in Paris in 1831 (the Paris Walter Benjamin called "the capital of the Nineteenth Century"), at a moment of brilliant literary and musical efflorescence: Marix-Spire suggests that Sand's trademark, her use of male dress, was in fact a way to get in to performances she couldn't otherwise afford:

In this Paris bursting with music, Aurore slips about everywhere and the Théâtre-Italien and the Opéra are the principal reasons for the famous man's suit. Didn't Balzac say that one could not be a woman in Paris on an income of less than twenty-five *livres*, and without them, is one going to deprive oneself of hearing Malibran when any little punk with long hair [*le premier bousingot venu*] can hear her for 2.50 in the orchestra?[18]

The ruse of cross-dressing (*travestissement*) shows up in her novel too: for safety and expediency, Consuelo camouflages herself in male dress during a foot journey. We will see later how this theme of sexual ambiguity comes up repeatedly as well in terms of the voice, not only in Sand's writing, but in that of many others of the period.

In *Consuelo*, music is, above all, the art of singing, and the qualities of the voice, both in speaking and singing, play a prominent role

in Sand's delineation of character. Sand's musical biographer Marix-
Spire has remarked on the importance of voice for Sand in her discussion of Sand's *Rose et Blanche* and points out that Sand's characters distinguish themselves as much by their voices as by their features. She begins this discussion with a telling quote from a letter by
Sand: "There is in the voice . . . a magnetic fluid, a sort of halo, not
visible, but sensitive to the touch of the soul, if I may speak thus,
which acts powerfully on our inmost feelings" (quoted in Marix-
Spire, 246–47).

The association of the voice with the soul is not Sand's alone. In
his chapter on the singer Pasta, Stendhal speaks of the need for the
singer to be free to color an interpretation according to the nuance
appropriate to a given performance, since no particular embellish-
ment can be guaranteed to be what is needed on every occasion:

> It will be glaringly obvious that no specific *mordente*, no particular embel-
> lishment, however excellent *per se*, can be guaranteed to match the voice and
> mood of any given *cantatrice* on any given evening—the 30th of September,
> to take a date at random. This being so, it is flatly impossible for the singer
> in question to stir her audience to the most hidden recesses of their souls on
> the evening of the 30th of September *by means of this particular ornament.*
> (Stendhal, 371)

Stendhal then adds a note in which he repeats an idea he has touched
on earlier: that of the mystic powers of the art of singing. Elsewhere
in his book he calls for the development of a scientific basis for music,
but in this note discussing the voice he indulges in romantic diction:

> The genuinely impassioned lover may often speak a language which he
> scarcely understands himself; there is an intercourse of the spirit which tran-
> scends the narrow physical limitations of vocabulary. . . . I might suggest
> that the art of singing shares this mysterious and inexplicable transcenden-
> talism; but just as in love, *artificiality is repulsive*, similarly in music, the
> voice must be allowed to be *natural*—that is to say, it should be allowed to
> sing melodies which have been especially written for it, in whose company
> it can feel at home, and of whose enchantment the singer herself, deep within
> her being, may be spontaneously aware at the very instant when she sings.
> (Stendhal, 371)

Likewise, Gautier makes an association between the voice and the
soul when he writes: "The voice is the incarnation of the soul, its sen-

suous, evident manifestation. Hearing a voice, I know a soul, and the words it utters do not deceive me about it" (quoted in Marix-Spire, 83). For these romantic writers, the voice is not merely another window of the soul; it is its almost physical manifestation, charged with the power to influence. This characterization of the voice as a "magnetic fluid" provides interesting parallels with the contemporaneous mythology of mesmerism, supposedly based on the "animal magnetism" of its practitioners both real and fictional, such as Mesmer, Caligari, and Svengali, names synonymous with the fascination of danger and a dangerous power of fascination.

In *Consuelo*, as in Sand's other work, voice is thus a touchstone of character. In his essay on music and personality in *Consuelo*, Joseph Marc Bailbé, noting the text's affinities with Goethe's *Wilhelm Meister*, suggests Sand's intent to create a novelistic version of *The Magic Flute*, "rather a return to Mozart who delighted Pauline and G. Sand equally, a sort of *Magic Flute* in a new genre destined to transform the passions of men."[19] In developing his suggestion of Sand's desire to create a novel that could be used as an opera libretto, Bailbé notes the musical sensibility underlying *Consuelo*, which is particularly evident in the importance accorded to the voice as "instrument, feeling and knowledge."[20] He goes on to cite numerous examples of characters' voices serving as their moral signatures.[21]

In fact, Consuelo's voice has a profound effect on all the men who hear her. At the beginning of the novel, when Consuelo is an ungainly fourteen, Count Zustiani hears her voice without seeing her and thinks that she must be beautiful, a real siren. He is shocked to find out who she is: "'Very well,' answered the teacher; 'now I can tell you that your divine singer, your siren, your mysterious beauty, was Consuelo.' 'Her? that awful creature? that ugly little shrimp? Impossible, maestro!'"[22] This passage, with its ironic and shocking disparity between the assumed beauty of the singer and her unappealing true appearance, seems to be lifted from Rousseau's autobiographical account of his visit to the same school where he makes much of the appalling disfigurements of the women there, which provoked in him a definite sexual disappointment. By insisting on the discrepancy between Consuelo's plainness and the loveliness of her voice, Sand works in a different direction, seeking to uncouple the feminine voice from its traditional linking to the erotic and to relocate its resonance on a moral and artistic plane.

At the outset, there is some question about whether a career at the Opera is suitable for such a plain girl. On the occasion of Consuelo's debut among the Venetian aristocrats, she refuses to dress other than in her usual simple fashion, yet when she sings for the composer Marcello, she is transfigured:

A divine fire shone in her cheeks, and the sacred flame sprang from her large black eyes while she filled the vault with that peerless voice and that victorious tone, pure, truly grand, which can only issue from a high intelligence joined to a great heart. After several measures of song, a torrent of delicious tears escaped from Marcello's eyes. The count, unable to master his emotion, cried out: "By all the blood of Christ, this woman is beautiful! She is Saint Cecilia, Saint Theresa, Saint Consuelo! She is poetry, music, faith personified!" (Sand, 74)

When Consuelo goes incognito as "la Porporina" to the castle of the Rudolstadt, Count Albert at first meets her with indifference, absorbed in his religious melancholy. Hearing her sing, however, he throws himself at her feet in exaltation, crying out in Spanish, her native tongue: "'Oh Consuelo, Consuelo! I find you at last!' 'Consuelo?' cried the astonished girl, expressing herself in the same language. 'Why, my lord, do you call me thus?' 'I call you consolation,' responded Albert still in Spanish, 'because consolation was promised to my desolate life, and because you are the consolation that God finally grants to my solitary and gloomy days'" (Sand, 273). Count Albert's response to Consuelo's singing recalls the vocabulary of mystic transport used by Stendhal and Gautier to describe the power of the voice to touch the soul with the qualities of the soul. It is Consuelo's nobility of character and the intelligence manifested in her actions, but more particularly in her voice, that define her as a superior artist and woman and give her a power of spiritual healing.

While *Consuelo* is clearly at one level an extended tribute to the qualities of Sand's friend Pauline Viardot, it is by no means the only work which Sand centers on the theme of the woman singer. She seems to have rehearsed it in several of her earlier works, *Prima Donna* and *Rose et Blanche*, and it serves, in fact, as the focus of the first of her fictional attempts, "L'Histoire d'un rêveur."

The heroine of *Prima Donna*, Gina, is a singer who abandons the stage to marry a duke (like the singer Sontag, "the first of the Victorian nightingales," who married the Sardinian diplomat Count Rossi and stopped singing in opera for twenty years).[23] Based on Malibran, Gina is described as having, like her, "tones by turn burning or soothing, her voice now sweet and resonant, now strong and passionate . . . her eyes shining, 'burning with inspiration'" (Marix-Spire, 233). Her successes are those of Malibran as well: the roles of Anna, Juliet, Ameniada. Retirement causes Gina to languish: on the advice of her doctor, she returns to sing in Zingarelli's *Romeo and Juliette*. Surpassing herself, she dies in Zingarelli's arms at the moment Romeo comes to say farewell.

Rose et Blanche, written the same year, 1831, is the story of a young provincial actress, Rose, gifted with a natural but untutored talent. She detests the atmosphere of the theater and is placed in a convent by a benefactor, where she comes to understand music's true beauty and mystery. Called upon to sing in the choir at the Assumption Mass with the abbé Causcalmon, she feels inadequate to her role but is inspired by him to sing beyond herself:

It was the first time she heard and saw true singing; what a difference between the divine fervor of this priest and the ridiculous simperings of her singing master, between the sonorous purity of this church song and the skilled gurglings that she studied at her piano! Suddenly, she sang: it was a wonder to her; she never understood afterwards how it came about; her eyes misted over, she trembled; yet she did not miss one note of the theme which she did not know, and her voice was strong, full, expansive, vibrant. (Quoted in Marix-Spire, 237)

Rose is struck by a psalmbook hurled by the hostile sister Scholastique and falls to the ground in a faint, overcome. She is caught in the arms of none other than the great Giuditta Pasta, the legendary diva herself, whom Sand seems to have felt no compunction in pressing into service as a fictional character. La Pasta appears again later to reveal to Rose, who has fled the convent, the true path of art: Rose attends a performance of Rossini's *Tancredi* in Paris and, overwhelmed by the beauty of the unknown singer's voice, cries out, disturbing the audience. She is astonished by this revelation of the possibilities of talent: "What a resonant, vigorous voice! what full and rich tones, so velvety and smooth! what majesty shines from this brow still adorned with the naïve graces of childhood, what truth and warmth in all her gestures, and at such a tender age, in a form so delicate, a figure so lithe and so fragile!" (quoted in Marix-Spire, 178).[24] Rose is able to quit the convent after a serious illness and goes on stage. Like Gina, she seems modeled on Malibran, both in terms of the roles she creates and of the warmth and impetuosity of her character.[25]

This theme of the remarkable singer is likewise present, and in a particularly striking form, in Sand's first story, unpublished until 1831. The fledgling author of "L'Histoire d'un rêveur" was markedly influenced by Hoffman, according to Marix-Spire, who shows Sand to have been reading his fiction voraciously during the period she tried her hand at writing. Beginning in 1828, Hoffman's work began to have a popular reception in France, and in 1830, the increasing number of translations and articles about Hoffman contributed to his success among French readers. Sand had an extensive collection of his writings and, like other French romantics, loved Hoffman for his evocations of the realm of the fantastic, the world of dreams.

Elaine Boney points out Hoffman and Sand's shared beliefs in the importance of the artist and in the value of love and simplicity, as well as the dominant role accorded to the imagination in their works, coded in stories about dreams, both waking and sleeping. She points to the influence of Hoffman's sense of the fantastic in works Sand wrote like *Le Drac* and *L'Orco* that feature spirits, one of water, the other of Venice.[26] More to the point here, however, is Hoffman and Sand's common interest in music as a literary subject. Marix-Spire remarks on the musical subject matter in such stories by Hoffman as "Councillor Krespel" and notes Hoffman's special affinity for music, saying, "More than for any of his contemporaries, Jean-Paul, Teick, Wackenroder or even Schopenhauer, music, [in Hoffman] spread everywhere, ringing out or hidden away, expresses the profound life of the world, gives the most satisfying explanation of the universal mystery, lets one touch infinity" (Marix-Spire, 198).

In particular, Sand seems to have been drawn to Hoffman's use of sound to create an atmosphere of mystery. Marix-Spire notes that Sand was obsessed by Hoffman's "Deserted House," in which the sound emitted by a crystal glass struck by accident terrifies two young people who have just met for the first time: one recognizes in the vibration the voice of the mad old woman of the deserted house; the other feels an inexplicable presentiment out of which the action of the story develops (Marix-Spire, 198).

Sand must, however, have been equally influenced by two other, more commonly anthologized tales of Hoffman: "Councillor Krespel" and "The Sandman." In both, a beautiful young woman, a jealously guarded daughter who sings in a high voice with an inhuman quality like that of a bell, a bird, or an aeolian harp, serves as a focal point for the optics of the marvelous. In each, the desirable girl is assimilated to the realm of the inanimate: in "The Sandman" Olympia turns out to be an automaton, while in "Councillor Krespel" the frail daughter who is forbidden to sing becomes identified in a curious way with her father's violin; when she does sing, it is fatal.

In "The Sandman," a young man, Nathanael, becomes fascinated with the daughter of Professor Spalanzini, the lovely, yet strangely rigid and inactive Olympia, on whom he spies through a pair of glasses given him by the malignant optician Coppola, the Sandman. Invited to a reception at which Spalanzini is to present his daughter to the public, Nathanael attends eagerly:

Nathanael received an invitation, and at the appointed hour, when carriages were driving up and lights gleamed in the decorated rooms, he went to the professor's house with palpitating heart. The gathering was large and dazzling. Olympia appeared, elegantly and tastefully dressed. No one could help but admire her beautifully shaped face and her figure. On the other hand, there was something peculiarly curved about her back, and the wasplike thinness of her waist also appeared to result from excessively tight lacing. There was, further, something stiff and measured about her walk and bearing which struck many unfavorably, but it was attributed to the constraint she felt in society. The concert began. Olympia played the piano with great talent and also skillfully sang a *bravura* aria in a voice that was high pitched, belllike, almost shrill. Nathanael was completely enchanted.

Nathanael believes Olympia is looking at him yearningly as she sings, and he yields to an amorous transport: "Her skillful roulades appeared to him to be the heavenly exaltations of a soul transfigured by love; and finally, when the cadenza was concluded, the long trill echoed shrilly through the hall and he felt as if he were suddenly embraced by burning arms. No longer able to contain himself, rapture and pain mingling within him, he cried: 'Olympia!' Everyone looked at him; many laughed."[27]

Nathanael's moment of *jouissance*, his rapturous ejaculation of Olympia's name, represents the acme of his delusion over Spalanzini's "daughter." This scene has its nightmare match in the one in which Nathanael watches in horror as Spalanzini and Coppola tear the wooden doll apart. Nathanael is driven insane by what others regard as a scandalous deceit in introducing a wooden doll into proper tea society.

It is not possible, of course, to evoke "The Sandman" without mentioning Freud's use of the story as the basis for his discussion in "The Uncanny." In developing his definition of the uncanny, he begins by quoting a previous writer on the topic, E. Jentsch, who takes as an instance of the uncanny the impression created by waxwork figures and mechanical dolls and refers to the sense of unease attending doubts about the sentience of an apparently animate being. The mechanical doll thus becomes emblematic of the *unheimlich*, a feeling Freud shows to derive from repression of thoughts about the *heimlich*, the primordial "home," the mother's womb, hence anxiety over sexual difference: the difference of the woman's genitalia.[28] The denial of sexual difference is at the source of the fetishistic obsession with the voice discussed above; the same theme reemerges in a particularly vivid way in Villiers de l'Isle-Adam's work, *L'Eve future,* which places at center stage a female android, and one specially gifted with the intoxicating power of the female voice, deemed sublime.

Even more than in his story about Olympia, the theme of a young girl's heavenly voice is developed in Hoffman's "Councillor Krespel," where it serves as the central focus of the story. The tale begins by setting up in a rather elaborate fashion the eccentricity and genius of Krespel (this motivates the narrator's accusation of murder when Antonia dies at the end, as well as the separation Krespel has imposed on his wife and daughter). When the narrator meets him, a paragraph detailing the strangeness of Krespel's behavior ends in the following way:

Sometimes his voice was harsh and screeching, sometimes it was slow and singsong; but never was it in harmony with what he was talking about. We were discussing music and praising a new composer when Krespel smiled and said in his musical voice, "I wish that the black-winged Satan would hurl that damned music mutilator ten thousand million fathoms deep into hell's pit!" Then, he burst out wildly and screechingly: "She is heaven's angel, nothing but pure God-given harmony—the light and star of song!" and tears formed in his eyes. One had to recall that an hour before he had been talking about a celebrated soprano. (Hoffman, 129)

Krespel had been married to such a celebrated soprano: the volatile Angela, sometimes tender, sometimes treacherous. After she shattered his violin, he threw her out a window. Although she later bore a child and forgave him, Krespel had refused to see her again. At her death, their daughter Antonia, whom Krespel adored, came to live with him. A gifted singer, the consumptive Antonia must not sing.

This information is withheld to create a mystery in the tale over Krespel's autocratic treatment of the gentle Antonia, whom he allows under no conditions to sing, despite the local legend that has sprung up of the marvel of her voice. After Krespel's departure, the narrator's host, "Professor M.," tells of hearing Antonia sing, accompanied by her father playing the violin:

"I must confess that the singing of the most famous soprano I had ever heard seemed feeble and expressionless compared with that voice and the peculiar impression it made, stirring me to the depths of my soul. Never before had I had any conception of such long-sustained notes, of such nightingale trills, of such crescendos and diminuendos, of such surging to organ-like strength and such diminution to the faintest whisper. There was no one who was not enthralled by the magic; and when the singer stopped, only gentle sighs interrupted the profound silence." (Hoffman, 131)

This account of Antonia's violin duet follows shortly the passage in which her name is introduced into the story and in which it is interwoven with mention of her father's marvelous Amati in a kind of chiasmus. The Professor's young daughter asks innocently after Antonia. To distract Krespel from the disagreeable response this question seems about to provoke in him, the Professor asks him about his work with the violins. Krespel brightens and speaks of the "marvelous Amati" which Antonia is to take apart for him. The Professor remarks at what a good girl she is; Krespel agrees, and hastily leaves, near tears. The Professor then explains to the narrator Krespel's odd habit of hoarding old violins which he refuses to play or allow any one else to play: "'As with his own violins, he plays it only once, then takes it apart in order to examine its inner structure, and if he thinks that he has not found what he has been looking for, he flings the pieces into a large chest which is already full of dismantled violins.' 'But what's this about Antonia?' I asked suddenly and impetuously" (Hoffman, 130). In this passage, Hoffman initiates a parallel between Antonia and the violin that becomes progressively more pronounced throughout the story.

Krespel does not dismember the Amati, to which Antonia is very attached; like Antonia herself, it contains a secret:

"This violin," Krespel said when I asked him about it, "this violin is a very remarkable and wonderful piece by an unknown master, probably of Tartini's time. I am completely convinced that there is something peculiar about its inner construction and that if I take it apart I will discover a secret I have been looking for, but—laugh at me if you like—this dead thing which depends upon me for its life and its voice, often speaks to me by itself in the strangest manner. When I played it for the first time, it seemed as if I was but the hypnotist who so affects his somnambulist that she verbally reveals what she is able to see within herself. Do not suppose that I am idiotic enough to attribute even the slightest importance to ideas so fantastic in nature, but it is peculiar that I have never succeeded in convincing myself to dismantle that inanimate and dumb object. Now I am pleased that I have never dismantled it; since Antonia's arrival I occasionally use it to play something to her. She is extremely fond of it—extremely." (Hoffman, 133)

Like the hypnotist who controls his (female) somnambulist, Krespel holds the power of song and silence over Antonia, as he does with his violin.

Singing and the art of violin playing are later specifically compared in a conversation between Krespel and the narrator. The latter, haunted by Antonia's unheard voice, visits Krespel, hoping to induce Antonia to sing, and draws him out about music. Krespel paraphrases the saying familiar to violinists that "to play well, one must sing" (*per ben suonare, bisogna cantare*): "Krespel mentioned that the style of the old masters had been influenced by that of the truly

great singers—Krespel happened just then to be talking about this—
and naturally I commented that the practice was now reversed and
that singers imitated the leaps and runs of the instrumentalists"
(Hoffman, 135). The sexual implication of the parallel is obvious:
one need think only of the familiar phrase that "a woman is like a
musical instrument," with its specific reference to sexual technique
and female orgasm: when Antonia sings, her face becomes suffused
with a deep blush. The oedipal freight of Krespel's restraint of his
daughter's voice is underlined by the threat posed by a visit from her
fiancé, who tempts Antonia to sing. Antonia collapses, unconscious,
and Krespel kicks the suitor out.

Thereafter, Antonia contents herself with not singing anymore,
but living for her father alone. She takes comfort in his playing of the
Amati, and identifies herself with it:

He had barely drawn the first few notes when Antonia cried aloud with joy,
"Why that is me—I am singing again!" In truth, there was something about
the silvery bell-like tones of the violin that was very striking; they seemed to
come from a human soul. Krespel was so deeply moved that he played more
magnificently than ever before. . . . Antonia clapped her hands and cried
with delight, "I sang that very well! I sang that very well!" From this time
on a great serenity and happiness came into her life. (Hoffman, 145)

If the "bell-like" tone of the violin resembles a human voice, the
unearthly purity of Antonia's voice does not resemble anything human. In the passage that describes Krespel's first meeting with Antonia, her voice is compared to the clear, ethereal qualities of a bird
or harp: "The timbre of Antonia's voice was quite individual and
rare, sometimes like the sound of an aeolian harp, sometimes like the
warbling of a nightingale. It was as if there were no room for such
notes within the human breast" (Hoffman, 143). Krespel, at first
transported with delight, begs her to stop, frightened by her consumptive flush. Antonia must not be allowed to sing, "Doctor R."
informs Krespel the next day:

"Whether it results from her having overexerted herself in singing when she
was too young, or whether it results from congenital weakness, Antonia suf-
fers from an organic deficiency in her chest from which her voice derives its
wonderful power and its strange, I might say, divine timbre and by which it

transcends the capabilities of human song. But it will cause her early death; for if she continues to sing, she will live six months at most." (Hoffman, 143)

Like one of the Cremona violins Krespel dismantles, whose extraordinary quality derives from an unusual oblique angle in the placement of its sound post, the "divine timbre" of Antonia's voice is attributed to a similar structural particularity, the fatal "organic deficiency in her chest." Hoffman may have been inspired by the French term for a violin sound post: *l'âme*, the soul. Like that of the violin, Antonia's exceptional tone is a product of a peculiarity of her *âme*.

This assimilation of Antonia to the violin becomes, finally, the crux of the fantastic element of the story. She dies after a last visit from the suitor and a final song rising to a "shattering fortissimo" that plunges Krespel into an incomprehensible state, "for an appalling fear was combined with a rapture he had never before experienced." When Antonia dies, the Amati "dies" with her: "'When she died,' [Krespel] said very solemnly and gloomily, 'the sound post of that violin broke with a resounding crack and the soundboard shattered to pieces. That faithful instrument could only live with her and through her; it lies beside her in the coffin; it has been buried with her'" (Hoffman, 137). Antonia's soul and the *âme* of the violin shatter together. With Antonia's death, the secret of the violin reveals itself at the same time that the secret of her "deficiency," her illness, becomes known to the narrator obsessed with hearing her fabulous voice that haunts his dreams, "like a gentle, consoling light."

Hoffman's use of musical voices as a springboard to the fantastic parallels and probably directly inspired Sand's early fictional attempt in "L'Histoire d'un rêveur," where, like the bell-like voices of the marvelous Antonia and Olympia, an exquisite, inhuman voice belonging to a supernatural creature fascinates a young man, with fatal results, again as in the Hoffman stories.

"L'Histoire d'un rêveur" tells the adventure of a young visitor to Italy, Amédée, who sets out against the advice of his host to climb Etna alone at nightfall, intending to see the volcano at dawn. He hears a mysterious voice of miraculous beauty: it is in a strange register, too silvery and smooth to be male, too full and sonorous to be female, a voice that combines the qualities of bass, contralto, and tenor. Responding to the song's enchantment, he answers in kind, when suddenly he sees a delicate youth in a red mantle appear and leap to the summit of a heap of volcanic rock. Amédée follows him and encounters him in the spot known as the "philosopher's hole" next to the crater.

Amédée is struck by the pallor and suffering expressed on the youth's face, and speaks to him. He hears no response but the sound of the aeolian harp, the harp of the winds. Bewitched, he begs the youth to take him with him to the land of phantoms. The youth seems to consent, and suddenly the volcano erupts, and smoke and fire boil out of the quaking volcano. Amid the savage harmony of the violent eruption, the words "temporale, temporale" drift in the air. Amédée approaches the brink, and the spirit seizes him by the hair and drags him to a rock above the volcano. He feels himself embraced, and sees the youth transformed into a ravishingly beautiful woman. She leaps, he follows, and the story ends with the hero waking up.

This little tale, with its transparently Freudian overtones of ambivalent sexuality, already contains elements later to be developed in *Consuelo*: the motif of a transcendently beautiful voice of a woman, who transports her hearer—in this case literally—to another world; and that of sexual ambiguity. It is telling that Sand should evoke an androgynous figure symbolic of creative expressivity in this early effort to find a narrative "voice": in transforming herself from Aurore Dudevant, frustrated wife, to George Sand, writer, she herself took on a male persona to gain the mobility she needed. Although her use of it was colored by her own struggles toward autonomy and creative work, Sand was far from being the only writer during this period to explore the motif of voice, rendered at once feminine and ambiguous in gender.

The Bird of Artifice

Singers, Angels, and Gender Ambiguity

In *La Vie de Rossini*, less a biography of Rossini than a series of essays about the music and opera of his time, Stendhal meditates on the
appeal of the human voice in Chapter 35, "Concerning the Various
Qualities of the Human Voice":

A hunting horn, echoing over the hills of the Scottish highlands, can be heard
at a considerably greater distance than the human voice. In this respect, *but
in this respect only*, art has outdistanced nature: art has succeeded in increasing the *volume* of sound produced. But in respect of something infinitely
more important, namely inflexion and ornamentation, the human voice still
maintains its superiority over any instrument yet invented, and it might even
be claimed that no instrument is satisfactory except in so far as it approximates to the sound of the human voice.

Stendhal attributes the particular charm of the voice to two causes,
one of which lies in its function as the vehicle for speech, hence its
ability to stimulate and guide the audience's imagination. The other
stems from its emotive power, "the suggestion of passion,"

which . . . inevitably colours anything which is sung by living man or
woman. Even the least impassioned of *prime donne*, le Signore Camporesi,
Fodor, Festa, etc., whose voices express no positive emotion, still radiate a
kind of indeterminate *joy*. I make a half-exception only in favor of Mme.
Catalani, whose prodigiously beautiful voice fills the soul with a kind of astonished wonder, as though it beheld a miracle; and the very confusion of
our hearts blinds us at first to the noble and goddess-like impassivity of this
unique artist. Sometimes, in an idle moment, I like to imagine a creature who

combined the voice of Signora Catalani with the impassioned soul and dramatic instinct of la Pasta—a fond, sweet chimaera, whose dream-like quality
leads only to sadness and regret for a thing which *is not*; and yet, whose very
possibility leaves one convinced that music sways a greater power over the
soul than any other art.[1]

It is telling that, writing of the affective intensity of the voice, of its
power to evoke a certain indefinable joy, Stendhal should cite women
singers like Catalani and Pasta as emblematic of the art.

Why would Stendhal and other writers of the period like Gautier,
Musset, and Sand, when speaking of the affective power of song,
think of women singers first and foremost? Initially, the question
leads to the role played by women in the opera of the period. Perhaps
surprisingly, though, one finds a curious blurring of gender distinctions when one begins to investigate representations of operatic
voice, which leads finally to a subversion of the kind of opposition of
nature and artifice that emerges from the Stendhal piece.

Stendhal and his contemporaries frequently used scenes involving
opera and singing in their novels; one can recall numerous scenes at
the opera in Stendhal's work and that of Balzac, Flaubert, and Gautier. The opera was a particularly rich source of material for Sand.
As we have seen, she makes a point of Consuelo's plainness, which
at first seems to pose an obstacle to her career in the theater. Despite
her lack of beauty, however, Consuelo electrifies all the men who hear
her, herself transfigured by her art. Writing of the singer Giuditta
Pasta, Stendhal refers several times to the celestial power of her singing to move listeners' souls.[2] Sand herself once wrote in a letter:
"There is in the voice . . . a magnetic fluid, a sort of halo, not visible,
but sensitive to the touch of the soul, if I may speak thus, which acts
powerfully upon our inmost feelings."[3]

The interest of writers like Sand, Stendhal, and Gautier in the
voice, and in the female voice in particular, has historical determinants in the popularity of the opera in Restoration Paris and in certain changes that took place in the bel canto of the period, giving
women an expanded and very singular role in the romantic opera.
Writers discussing the reception of opera in Paris in the 1830's and
1840's generally point out the link between the social and political
transformations of the time and the changes in musical taste: the old

opera seria form, with its aristocratic patronage, gave way to a different kind of musical spectacle, one more closely attuned to the tastes and sensibility of the new bourgeois audiences that began flocking to the opera houses. Herbert Lindenberger points out that the opera box was as much a place for people to define themselves socially and to be seen in luxury, as to listen to the music.[4] (One thinks of the careers made and unmade, the intrigues staged, in the plush opera boxes in Balzac's novels.)

The account Jane Fulcher gives in her recent book *The Nation's Image: French Grand Opera as Politics and as Politicized Art* is more powerful. Fulcher argues that opera was employed by the tension-fraught governments of the Restoration and after to promote the legitimacy and political stances of these regimes. Beginning with the Revolutionary public's emerging sense of itself as a nation, French audiences looked to opera for representations of national identity, while successive regimes appropriated opera "as an image to associate 'the popular spirit' with [themselves]."[5] Thus, opera became an interpretive ground of contestation as various groups interpreted the new libretti based on historical subjects according to their conflicting visions of national and political identity. Her thesis is reinforced by aspects of Benedict Anderson's *Imagined Communities*. Anderson defines the sense of nationality as collectively imagined community. The rise of the sense of nationality after the eighteenth century was linked to the secularization of languages and governments, the interrelated spread of capitalism and print culture—newspapers and novels—and a new sense of time that accompanied these conditions: an experience of simultaneity within "imagined communities." An example Anderson gives of this is the singing of national anthems on national holidays. Singing "The Star-Spangled Banner" or "La Marseillaise" makes people feel joined to others in a temporal experience of simultaneity within a nation.[6] Attending an operatic performance in nineteenth-century France would ideally have conveyed such an effect of communal experience. Despite the ambiguities and failures in staging of operas that Fulcher elaborates, the opera seems to have served as a theater, bitterly contested, for rituals to confirm and reinforce national and political identity.

Paradoxically, the music that served notions of what French national opera ought to be was largely imported: the vivid, spectacular sound of Meyerbeer, German born but Italian trained; but also and especially the Italian music of Bellini, Rossini, Donizetti, and the bel canto style with its attendant innovations in dramatic subject matter and vocal style, its new palettes of power, vocal coloring, and range. With Italian singing setting the standard, it is not surprising that in *Rossini* Stendhal finds it impossible to describe singing techniques in French and breaks into Italian for the terms, as for entire descriptive passages.[7]

Several changes in operatic style in the nineteenth century created a more important role for women. One of these was the gradual phasing out of the castrato voice, which had dominated Italian opera until then. The castrati had been associated with opera since its inception: in the first performance of Monteverdi's *Orfeo*, the first opera, the role of Euridice was played by a castrato. In his history of the castrato, Angus Heriot writes: "Italian opera was, till the late eighteenth century, almost synonymous with the castrati, and . . . Italian opera was the opera that mattered."[8] Heriot states, in fact, that "it has been computed that, in the eighteenth century, seventy per cent of all male opera singers were castrati" (Heriot, 31). The hegemony of the castrati can be attributed to several factors: their superior musical education, which made them the best musicians; a certain taste for the artificial during the period that tolerated, better, appreciated travesty; and the apparently remarkable suppleness, agility, and singular tone the castrati voices were capable of achieving. To give some idea of their effect, Heriot quotes the impressions of the music historian Enrico Panzacchi, who heard one of the surviving castrati in the Vatican chapel late in the nineteenth century:

What singing! Imagine a voice that combines the sweetness of the flute and the animated suavity of the human larynx—a voice which leaps and leaps, lightly and spontaneously, like a lark that flies through the air and is intoxicated with its own flight; and when it seems that the voice has reached the loftiest peaks of altitude, it starts off again, leaping and leaping still with equal lightness and equal spontaneity, without the slightest sign of forcing or the faintest indication of artifice or effort; in a word, a voice that gives the immediate idea of sentiment transmuted into sound, and of the ascension of a soul into the infinite on the wings of that sentiment. . . . Here, all my being was marvellously satisfied. Not the least mark of the passage from one register of the voice to the other, no inequality of timbre between one note and another; but a calm, sweet, solemn and sonorous musical language that left me dumbstruck, and captivated me with the power of a most gracious sensation never before experienced. (Heriot, 36–37)

This impression of something *unheard of* in the castrato voice emerges as well in the anecdote Heriot includes of Emma Calvé's reaction to the singing of the castrato Mustafà:

Emma Calvé heard Mustafà when in Rome . . . and was particularly impressed by "certain curious notes he called his fourth voice—strange, sexless, superhuman, uncanny." She took lessons from him, and learnt the secret of these tones. "They are," says Mr. Desmond Shaw-Taylor, "presumably, the very high floating notes which Calvé could suddenly produce, as though from nowhere, and sustain for an extraordinary duration." (Heriot, 22)

The castrato voice is typically heard as both sexless and inhuman; in one case it is compared to the sound of a flute or a bird, in the other called uncanny.

Heriot explains that the preference for the castrato voice in the seventeenth and early eighteenth centuries was associated with a concomitant prejudice against the tenor and bass voices. This taste resulted in a downplaying of male voices in serious opera: tenors sang roles of old men, while basses were often reserved for special effects, like the pronouncements of Neptune's oracle in *Idomeneo*. Only in comic opera did these voices have much play. Oddly enough for our sense of heroic type, the roles of heroes, kings, and warriors were the domain of the castrati. Thus the castrati were not, as one may think, substitutes for female voices but were heard as the appropriate voice for the principal roles, male or female. Moreover, women sometimes played the same roles as castrati, taking male parts in travesty, while men (the so-called male soprano) sang feminine roles (especially in Rome, where women were forbidden to perform on stage). There was thus a certain fluidity of gender-role attribution in seventeenth- and eighteenth-century Italian opera. Heriot notes that in one performance of Scarlatti's *Pompeo* in 1684, "out of eleven characters, four were sung by castrati, three by natural male voices, and four by women. Of the women, however, three were singing male roles,

which in another performance might equally have been sung by castrati" (Heriot, 33).

There seems to have been a definite appreciation for sexual and
vocal reversals in the opera of the seventeenth century: travesty was
an important element of the plots, and sometimes quite perverse
twists were introduced in the writing for the voice and casting to cap-
italize on its possibilities:

In Monteverdi's *L'Incoronazione di Poppea*, the parts of Nero and Ottone
are for soprano, while Ottavia and Poppea were sung by female contraltos:
thus, the male characters actually sang in a higher voice than the female,
though these were played by women. Even more eccentric, Cavalli's *Eliogabalo* has the parts of Eliogabalo, Alessandro, and Cesare for sopranos, and
Zenia (a woman) for the tenor voice. . . . For the opening of the San Carlo
in 1737 . . . [in] Metastasio's *Achille in Sciro*, Achilles is supposed to be disguised as a woman during most of the evening, but to throw off his feminine
trappings at the end and reveal his real sex. Unfortunately the singer chosen
for the title role was a woman, the famous Vittoria Tesi, which made the
whole thing rather absurd. In comic opera, too, the same sort of thing went
on, and we find tenors taking the parts of decrepit old women, etc. (Heriot,
33–34)

Heriot concludes that such practices, what he calls the "taste for peculiar sexual and vocal reversals," did not arise out of necessity, but
rather that "such ambiguities were valued for lending a spice of
double-entendre, even to the most tragic situations." He recalls to the
reader the practices of Elizabethan drama, quoting the passage from
Shakespeare in which "Cleopatra fears to see 'some squeaking Cleopatra boy my greatness i' the posture of a whore,'" sure to get a big
laugh from an audience watching a squeaking boy speak the lines.
Operatic pleasure was thus very much at this time associated with
the theatrical game of *travestissement*, a pleasure taken in play with
role reversals and gender ambiguities.

Over time the castrati and the particular florid, agile vocal style
for which they were famous began to decline, partly because of
Gluck's reforms, partly because the disruption of order in Italy during the Napoleonic wars created a permanent shortage in the supply
of these rare creatures. Consequently, the soprano and tenor voices
assumed greater importance: in the first part of the century, the lead

male part was increasingly handed over to women, or else the part was transposed for tenor. Eventually, the soprano and tenor voices took on their familiar prominence, and the baritone voice emerged as a vocal role. These modern vocal categories were not codified as we know them until the end of the eighteenth century, according to some; Heriot puts it as late as the 1820's with the recognition of the baritone.

In the new dispensation of romantic bel canto, the soprano voice took on particular importance, replacing the castrato voice as operatic "high point"—in both senses—and as the subject matter of romantic opera placed the figure of the woman in a new and central position. In his book *L'Opéra ou le cri de l'ange*, Michel Poizat writes:

The Italian opera, which had built its fortunes on the trans-sensical voice of the castrato, now reinvested its appetite for vocal jouissance in the double, sexually divided figure of the soprano and the tenor, the soprano voice carving out the lion's share here, as though it were somehow felt that for want of the castrato, the soprano voice might constitute the privileged site where music lovers were most likely to find what they were after.[9]

Thus, late in the game, the soprano moved to the focal point previously occupied by her old rival, the castrato. The arias written for women in the bel canto of Bellini and Donizetti then pushed the female voice higher and higher into the operatic stratosphere.

Just as the woman's voice became foregrounded musically, so did the dramatic importance of the roles played by women increase markedly. Rupert Christiansen emphasizes that while they generally played victims, "in many of these operas women become genuinely heroic, put in positions of power and made agents of their own destinies: Beethoven's Leonore or Bellini's Norma and Cherubini's Medea . . . are notable examples of this. Opera provided the strongest image of woman in any romantic art form. . . . Nowhere else was a woman put so firmly at the structural centre."[10] Others writing about the opera, such as Lindenberger, Poizat, and Catherine Clément have taken a different view and remark instead on the persistence with which opera marks out its heroines for fatality. Clément's book, *L'Opéra ou la défaite des femmes*, points out the obsessive insistence with which romantic opera portrays women as suffering exquisitely, then dying: it is a cavalcade of women done in by tuberculosis, plunges, stabbings, poisonings, or by simple collapse under unbearable pressures.[11] Lindenberger remarks that

the process by which operatic heroines move towards death is as oppressive as that in any Christian martyr play. The plot mechanisms that any particular opera uses are important, above all, for their capability of effecting the most powerful possible martyrdom. . . . Among the operatic characters who die, whether or not by violent means, the men are surely as numerous as the women. Yet in the vast majority of tragic operas the burden of pathos is carried by a woman.[12]

In his piece reviewing the debut of Pauline Viardot, Musset praises the "angelic purity" of Desdemona in Rossini's *Otello*, and says, "In the opera, a terrible, inexorable fate rules. From the moment the action begins through its finish, the victim is offered up in sacrifice."[13] Such a portrayal of women as martyrs in romantic opera is congruent with ideas about the representation of women in literature of the period that emerge in such studies as Mario Praz's classic *The Romantic Agony*, with its focus on the persecuted and fatal woman of the romantics,[14] and Nina Auerbach's *Woman and the Demon*, where she argues for the dual polar image of women as angels and demons in the Victorian mind. Of special interest here is her demonstration that in traditional Christian angelology, angels were by definition masculine. It was only in the nineteenth century that angels became identified with the feminine—the Victorian angel in the house—in a process parallel to the one taking place in opera.

In her heroine Consuelo, Sand presents an individualistic, unusually active, but recognizable avatar of the romantic angel/woman. Her qualities of chastity, piety, material disinterestedness, and self-sacrifice, together with the intense purity of her voice, locate her explicitly on the side of heaven: she is too good to be true. Described as a "celestial virgin" by her singing master, Consuelo resists the loose *moeurs* of her profession, energetically protecting her virginity at all turns. In melodramatic style, threats to her virtue fuel the narrative motor: each time she flees, and her flights structure the plot development.

Consuelo's nobility of character is highlighted in other ways as well. She always achieves recognition through her innate superiority, never participating in cabals or allowing competitive feeling to affect her behavior. In *La Comtesse de Rudolstadt* she exerts herself without rancor to obtain help for her rival, who appears at the home of Consuelo's host, pregnant by Consuelo's erstwhile fiancé, begging for help. Consuelo arranges for the canon to take her in and even persuades him to raise the child.

In accordance with the romantic association between artistic creativity and sexual continence, Consuelo's unmarried state is in the logic of the novel the condition of her artistry. At the outset of her career, her master Porpora tries to induce her to give up not only her faithless fiancé but any marriage:

You will replace it with a greater idea, a more pure and life-giving one. Your soul, your genius, your whole being will no longer be at the mercy of a weak and disappointing form; you will contemplate the sublime ideal stripped of this terrestrial veil; you will leap into the sky, and you will live in a sacred marriage with God himself. . . . Whatever you do and wherever you are, at the theater as in the cloister, you can be a saint, a celestial virgin, the betrothed of the sacred ideal. . . . You must have solitude, absolute freedom. I wish for you neither husband, nor lover, family, passions, nor any bond of any sort. . . . The day you give yourself to a mortal will be the day you lose your divinity.[15]

The visionary Albert also expresses this sense of her high destiny: "'Music and poetry are the highest expressions of faith, and the woman gifted with genius and beauty is their priestess, sibyl and initiatrix'" (Sand, 385). Consuelo's combination of artistry and saintliness makes her, like the angels, a mediator with heaven.

In her essay "Le Mythe de la femme dans *Consuelo*," Simone Vierne discusses Sand's use of the romantic antinomy between the angel and the siren. She suggests that Sand casts Consuelo as angelic but imbues her also with elements taken from the siren figure to redeem in an active, affirmative figure the essentially masculine myth of woman as "daughter of fire" or "daughter of ether." Borrowing this distinction from Pierre Barbéris's work on certain feminine characters in Balzac, she lays out the familiar polarities between purity and sinfulness, calm harmony and spicy allure, naive ignorance and worldly calculation, the angel's victimized passivity and the siren's vampirism, corruption and redemption.[16] Vierne points out, of course, that the perspective constructing this opposition is masculine. The hero is content to commiserate with the angel, whose happiness usually lies in a self-sacrifice of which he is the beneficiary, and to blame the siren, who seeks her own satisfaction, not his. If the angel does lose her virginity, she recuperates her noble purity as "sublime mother," while the siren can only possess the "cold majesty of the sterile woman."

For Vierne, Consuelo's lack of beauty enacts one revision of the convention, while the intense magnetism of her voice, despite this, constitutes another. Like any siren, Consuelo creates devastating passions, but does it involuntarily, while she sings, chaste.[17] Sand, then, borrows some of the qualities of the siren to give her heroine a more affirmative cast than that of the usual angel. Pure, self-sacrificing, inspiring, but also active and clear-sighted, Consuelo is a supercharged angel, able to act positively, and in consequence, to some extent free.

A more conventional version of the romantic angel appears in Nerval's "Sylvie," one of *Les Filles du feu*. As in the Rousseau material, nostalgia for a lost past merges in the narrator's mind with the memory of a feminine singing voice. Or rather, in this curious story in which the narrator's imagination creates a network of associative relays between three women, Aurélie, Sylvie, and Adrienne, he associates several feminine voices with love and lost youth. As Tzvetan Todorov has shown, Nerval sets up at the outset a system of oppositions between the present and the past, Paris and the narrator's childhood home in the Valois, theatrical illusion and reality, art and nature, the real woman and the imaginary one. In the course of the story, Nerval breaks down these neat antinomies, problematizing the categories. In particular, the women and their significance are overlapped and metonymically linked in the narrator's mind.

The theme of longing for an impossible love is framed in the theater proscenium at the beginning. The narrator describes watching a performance of the actress with whom he is infatuated; that he does not mention her name, Aurélie, until later is appropriate enough, given the manner in which he identifies her with theatrical artifice and with all other women. She is simply an actress, exemplar of a type. He is content to feel that she performs for him alone, an illusion compounded with the pleasures of the theater: "For a year, I had never yet thought to find out who she could be besides; I was afraid to disturb the magic mirror that sent her image back to me; at most I had lent my ear to some idle talk about the woman, not the actress." After summing up the turbulence of the era, the aspirations and rosy-tinted poetry of the romantics, the narrator professes his preference for women who do not disturb dreams with reality: "Seen up close, the real woman disgusted our naïveté; it was necessary for her to appear to be a queen or a goddess, and above all, not to come too near." And, learning that his actress is the mistress of another, he conceals his disappointment, saying, "It is an image I pursue, nothing more."[18]

The figure of the actress is initially contrasted with the memory of a young girl from his provincial childhood in the Valois. The chance sight of a poster advertising a "Regional Festival of Flowers" brings back the memory of Adrienne in a series of "tableaux" (memory being itself already theater): in the company of another girl, Sylvie, the one he loved devotedly then, he attended such a rural festivity and saw Adrienne, heard her perform. Having been paired with her by the dance, it was his part to kiss her. At the contact with her, he felt stirred, "an unknown turmoil took hold of me." His memory of her hinges on her singing, however:

The beautiful girl had to sing to have the right to return to the dance. Everyone sat around her, and right away, in a fresh and penetrating, yet slightly husky voice, like those of the girls in this misty country, she sang one of those ancient melodies so full of melancholy and love. . . . The melody ended at each stanza with those quavering trills that show off young girls' voices so nicely, [one sees they are] imitating the trembling voices of their grandmothers with a carefully modulated quiver. (Nerval, 134)

The emotion left by the girl's song in the narrator's memory is composed of an amalgam of impressions: the bucolic setting, the archaic flavor of the dance, his awakening sexuality, the charm of the girl's fresh voice attempting to imitate the uncontrolled vibrato of older voices. A mood of enchantment holds the circle still as the girl continues to sing after nightfall: "We thought we were in Paradise." Paradise lost, in Nerval's text, is loss enshrined in memory. The narrator

crowns her with a wreath of living laurel and comments on her resemblance to Dante's Beatrice, "who smiled at the poet wandering at
the edge of the sacred dwelling place." Despite the jealousy Sylvie dis-
plays, Adrienne will remain a distant image, a "mirage of glory and
beauty" in the realm of the ideal symbolized by the comparison to
Beatrice: the narrator reports that he learned sometime later that she
has been sent to become a nun.

The actress and the nun are curiously assimilated to one another
in the narrator's imagination: the memory of Adrienne provides a key
to his love for the actress. He shifts immediately after to the present:
"Everything was explained to me by this half-dreamed memory. This
vague and hopeless love, conceived for a woman of the theater which
took hold of me every night at bedtime, had its germ in the memory
of Adrienne, flower of the night blooming in the pale clarity of the
moon, pink and blond phantom floating over the green grass half
bathed in white mists" (Nerval, 135). The later love resembles the
earlier one as a copy of a master drawing resembles its original, Nerval writes, and underlines the correlation: "To love a nun in the guise
of an actress! . . . and if they were one and the same! It is enough to
drive one mad. It is a fatal urge that drags you along to where the
unknown beckons like a will-o'-the-wisp over the rushes of a dead
pool. . . . Let us regain our footing in reality" (Nerval, 136). The
truth is a provisional one, at one level, for the narrator's search for
his authentic lost love makes him turn immediately to the thought of
Sylvie, "the sweet reality," and later to a liaison with Aurélie herself.

At another level, the logic holds. As Ross Chambers has shown,[19]
a certain family resemblance links the figures of actresses, angels, and
automata one finds in romantic fictions and later. Chambers cites a
number of the texts that concern us here: "Sylvie," the Hoffman tales,
L'Eve future. In what he calls the "myth of the actress," he notes a
common fascination with illusion, an emblematic use of figures that
provoke nostalgic reverie for a lost paradise. The actress, for Chambers, assimilates to herself various avatars: the doll, the angel, the
artificial woman, and the messenger from the beyond. Within the figure of the actress, signifier of illusion, one finds the contaminant of
"these two embodiments of absence, the angel and the automaton."[20]
Chambers's account significantly draws in the notion of these figures

as masculine constructions, of the identity of the beloved and the work of art; the net cast by this articulation of the theme covers much of the ground of the present study. Chambers invokes, for example, the Pygmalion myth and the myth of Orpheus and Eurydice, "the dead one who speaks," that offer themselves, perhaps inevitably, for consideration in a discussion of these figures, irresistibly so in the case of Villiers's automaton. He anticipates also the argument I make for the role of Baudelaire's aesthetic in the taste for artifice. His central thesis, of the woman as signifier for absence or lack, is especially useful in its homology with Poizat's argument about the function of the angelic feminine voice in opera, to which we will return below.

Of particular interest here, however, is Nerval's use of the feminine voice in this system of nostalgic reminiscence and desire. The framing of the woman in performance and the posing of the woman as spectacle form part of the "myth of the actress" but also serve to frame the stance of the singer. While Sylvie, who belongs to nature and reality, cannot replace the actress in Nerval's relay, the actress declaiming her part is also, as are both Adrienne and Sylvie, denoted by a common characterizing term, her voice.

In "regaining a footing in reality," the narrator's first thought is of Sylvie; his first thought of her is of her voice. His memory of her recalls her window, brightly decorated with roses and a cage with singing birds. This frame encloses a snippet of her singing, italicized in the text: "*the beautiful girl was sitting / by the flowing brook*" (Nerval, 136). The thought of rustic Sylvie, poor, still waiting for him perhaps, is the impetus for his impulsive nocturnal journey back to the Valois. The actual Sylvie is a disappointment, however: no longer poor, no longer even a peasant, she is a glove-maker, a bourgeois marvel, "an industrious fairy, spreading abundance around her." In accordance with her new status, she reads novels and is up on the newest opera melodies, though he wishes her to sing one of the "old airs." To his displeasure, when she does sing for him, he finds her voice has lost the appeal of its simplicity: "Sylvie modulated some measures from a modern opera aria. . . . She was *phrasing*!" (Nerval, 156). If Sylvie no longer signifies provinciality and nature to the narrator, she is equally unable to stand in for Adrienne, to replace a haunting memory of her singing at Châalis:

Then I made the mistake of telling about the apparition at Châalis that had remained in my memory. I led Sylvie into the very room of the castle where I had heard Adrienne sing. "Oh, I understand what you want". . . . "For your dear voice to resonate through these vaults and chase away the spirit that torments me, either divine or fatal!"—She repeated the words and the song after me: *Angels, descend quickly / To the depths of purgatory!* "That's pretty sad" she said to me. "It is sublime. . . . I believe it is by Porpora, with verses translated from the sixteenth century." "I wouldn't know," Sylvie answered. (Nerval, 156)

Shortly after, he dismisses Sylvie as too much like a sister, and his thoughts shift back to Aurélie. Sylvie, too limited (despite her bourgeois accomplishments she does not catch the reference to Porpora), too real, finally, cannot occupy the place left vacant by his experience of hearing the nun Adrienne perform at Châalis, where the coach pauses en route. He recalls stopping before at the château there with its medieval charm, its figures of saints and angels, to attend an allegorical performance, a kind of mystery play. The costumes in misty half-tones recall the crepuscular ambiance of the fête, and again he hears Adrienne:

The scene took place among the angels, on the splendors of this dead globe, and the angel of death explained the causes of its destruction. A spirit mounted from the abyss, holding a flaming sword in one hand, and summoned the others to come admire the glory of Christ, conqueror of hell. This spirit was Adrienne transformed by her costume, as she had been by her vocation. The halo of golden cardboard she bore on her angelic head seemed quite naturally to us a circle of light; her voice had gained in force and range, and the infinite fioritura of Italian song embroidered the severe phrases of a pompous recitative with the warbling of bird song. (Nerval, 147)

The narrator recalls this performance as if it were a dream. It is a dream, parallel to his dream of Aurélie, and occupies the same space of theatrical magic. Art and artifice are pleasurably joined: Adrienne, distant, costumed as an angel and rendered as asexual as one by her vocation, produces the rich eroticized trill of Italian song, the birdlike sound which the all-too-real Sylvie cannot match. Where Sylvie merely "phrased," the angel performed to the unforgetting memory of Nerval's romantic lover.

*

The romantic topos of the woman as angel is central to the argument that Michel Poizat makes about the voice in opera. In the context of the progression he traces from intelligible word toward pure "cry" in opera, Poizat argues that operatic taste developed in favor of the highest, most piercing voice. Like Heriot, Poizat ascribes the dominance of the castrato voice to the interdiction against women singing in the church. Out of the need for high, clear voices to fill what he calls the "angelic function" in the liturgy emerged the practice of making castrati. The advent of opera naturally entailed use of these unnatural singers: they were the most accomplished musically and possessed the qualities Poizat identifies as desired in its principal singers: a voice of sexual indeterminacy that soars to the heights. This voice of the angel is what made for the operatic amateur's delectation in the voice as erotic object. Poizat underlines the metaphoric association of emotional or spiritual height and the vocal "height": angels, children, birds, and castrati share in common their purity, their sexlessness, their essentially "*inhuman*" quality.

The highest voice, traditionally that of the principal role, once the domain of the castrato, becomes in romantic opera divided between that of the soprano and tenor voices, with a marked preference given to the soprano voice. For Poizat then, "operatic romanticism establishes Woman as the last avatar of the Angel, makes her the privileged ground of the quest for the vocal object" (Poizat, 132). The voice of the angel becomes that of the woman, and of the woman dedicated to sacrifice and death.

In romantic opera and its reflections in the literature of the period, then, the woman singer with her particularly intense affective power occupies a privileged position. She seems in part to owe this special role less to any transparently natural power of the human voice—as in the Stendhal citation quoted above—than to something more complex, even paradoxical: the castrato's legacy of the fundamentally erotic pleasure (for the "music lover") to be had from a voice not merely ambiguous in gender quality but even sexless—the inhuman voice of the angel.

If the castrato voice seemed sexless, the castrati themselves were not and were, in fact, very popular with the ladies. Their appeal lay to some extent in the star status that wealth and public acclaim brought them. A second reason was that, as Heriot explains, "their embraces could not lead to awkward consequences" (Heriot, 55). Lasting liaisons were not uncommon, and Heriot mentions several poignant accounts of castrati who tried unsuccessfully to obtain permission to marry women they lived with (papal law would not sanction such inevitably barren marriages).

Among other forms of discrimination to which they were subject, however, was castigation as evil creatures who led men into homosexuality. Heriot provides several stories by Casanova to lend color to the statement that there were indeed homosexual castrati. Casanova writes that in 1745

an abbé with an attractive face walked in [to a café]. At the appearance of his hips, I took him for a girl in disguise, and I said so to the abbé Gama; but the latter told me that it was Bepino della Mamana, a famous castrato. The abbé called him over, and told him, laughing, that I had taken him for a girl. The impudent creature, looking fixedly at me, told me that if I liked he would prove that I was right, or that I was wrong.

Casanova gives another bemused description of a castrato who resembled a woman in an account of a trip to Rome in 1762. This singer took prima donna roles and was the *mignon* of Cardinal Borghese:

In a well-made corset, he had the waist of a nymph, and, what was almost incredible, his breast was in no way inferior, either in form or in beauty, to any woman's; and it was above all by this means that the monster made such ravages. Though one knew the negative nature of this unfortunate, curiosity made one glance at his chest, and an inexpressible charm acted upon one, so that you were madly in love before you realised it. To resist the temptation, or not to feel it, one would have had to be cold and earthbound as a German. When he walked about the stage during the *ritornello* of the aria he was to sing, his step was majestic and at the same time voluptuous; and when he favoured the boxes with his glances, the tender and modest rolling of his black eyes brought a ravishment to the heart. It was obvious that he hoped to inspire the love of those who liked him as a man, and probably would not have done so as a woman. . . . Rome the holy city, which in this way forces every man to become a pederast, will not admit it, nor believe in the effects of an illusion which it does its best to arouse. (Heriot, 54–55)

Heriot points out that Rome was famous for its tradition of carnival, and travesty, like other topsy-turvy goings-on, was part of it: such a person as this would perhaps not have seemed as extraordinary there as elsewhere. Women, moreover, as Casanova points out, could not appear on the stage in Rome. This story shows an interesting parallel with that of Balzac's *Sarrasine*, whose factual origins Heriot accepts:

> Others, again, refused to believe that the travestied castrati were not in real-ity women, and among many anecdotes is that of the French sculptor "Sar-rasin," who pursued the castrato Zambinella with his attentions in the conviction that he was a woman, until the singer's protector, Cardinal Cicognara, had the importunate Frenchman assassinated; this story was afterwards written up by Balzac. Consolino, another castrato, was able to carry on an affair with a society woman under her husband's nose, by the simple expedient of arriving in one of his stage costumes; and it was not un-common for castrati to go about in women's clothes all the time. (Heriot, 27)

The ambiguous gender of a singer who is the object of an intense erotic focus drives Balzac's *Sarrasine*, brought to critical attention through Roland Barthes's detailed reading of it within the framework of his five narrative codes in *S/Z*. The narration of the sculptor Sar-rasine's unfortunate passion for the castrato soprano Zambinella, whom he believes to be a woman, is framed in a double sense: first, by the outer narrative of another failed seduction, that of the narra-tor/dandy of the woman whom he is trying to interest by recounting the tale; second, by the sexually indeterminate painting of a sleeping Adonis that fascinates the young lady. The encounter initiates the storytelling rendezvous that will explain, in a multiple stroke, the or-igin of the painting, the source of the wealth of the Lanty family whose party the young lady and her friend attend, and the identity of the strangely effeminate Methuselah who hovers like a ghost among the guests.

This painting flags the preoccupation with gender ambiguity that structures and drives the narrative, and encapsulates in the oscilla-tion between masculine and feminine the history of its own making. The narrator reveals to his listener at the end that Zambinella was the model for the painting and had survived to become the unsettling creature she had seen, whose secret tale he offers her. The relay of copies encapsulated in its image of Adonis began in Sarrasine's sculp-ture of Zambinella as a woman. The narrator explains: "'Madame, Cardinal Cicognara took possession of Zambinella's statue and had it executed in marble; today it is in the Albani Museum. There, in 1791, the Lanty family found it and asked Vien to copy it. The portrait in which you saw Zambinella at twenty, a second after having seen him at one hundred, later served for Girodet's *Endymion*; you will have recognized its type in the Adonis.' "[21] Thus, the subject of the painting, originally the male *musico* Zambinella, had become successively feminine, as the statue, somewhat questionably male again, as Endymion, then the Adonis the young woman looks upon with the evaluative eye of a rival:

"Does such a perfect creature exist?" she asked me, after having, with a soft smile of contentment, examined the exquisite grace of the contours, the pose, the color, the hair; in short, the entire picture.

"He is too beautiful for a man," she added, after an examination such as she might have made of some rival. (Balzac, 231–32)

Too beautiful to be a man, too perfect to be true, indeed: this ironically marveling doubt (she can't know how right she is) points directly to the essential question of Zambinella's deceptive status as love object: "she" is a woman only in Sarrasine's imagination. It is Sarrasine's illusion about Zambinella's sex that sets him up for his singular disappointment (not unlike Nathanael's disappointment over Olympia) and brings about the confrontation that causes his death.

Zambinella is an imaginary woman: references to "her" in the story are throughout couched in terms of the artificial, the constructed, the imaginary. At the beginning of the piece, Balzac enters on an extended description of an old man, "this strange creature," who is revealed at the end to be the octogenarian Zambinella. This Methuselah, seemingly barely alive, corpselike in his skeletal stiffness and silence, attaches himself to a lushly beautiful young woman, alarming her: "Thereupon, she gathered up enough courage to look for a moment at this creature for which the human language had no name, a form without substance, a being without life, or a life without action." The sense of the mechanical quality of this "strange body" is reinforced a few lines later: "A feeling of profound horror for mankind gripped the heart when one saw the marks that decrepitude had left on this fragile machine" (Balzac, 229).

This description of the withered appearance of the old creature continues for another page with typical Balzacian zest for detail, insistently detailing his artificial, inhuman aspect: "Some old people have presented more hideous portraits; what contributed the most, however, in lending the appearance of an artificial creature to the spectator which had risen before us was the red and white with which he glistened." The red and white refer to the old man's incongruous makeup. The "feminine coquetry of this phantasmagorical personage" makes him resemble a statue: "this sort of Japanese idol" is "silent and motionless as a statue" (Balzac, 230). Even in movement, he seems less alive than animated: "Although the old man turned his eyes toward the crowd, it seemed that the movements of those orbs, incapable of sight, were accomplished only by means of some imperceptible artifice; and when the eyes came to rest on something, anyone looking at them would have concluded that they had not moved at all" (Balzac, 236). Finally, the young woman touches "le phénomène" and screams, creating a scene.

This event sets up the scene in which this person and her escort, the narrator, having retired to a quiet room, look at the painting of Adonis, the second-to-last refraction in the infinite regression of images of Zambinella (the final taking place in the narrator's tale). The detailed juxtaposition of opposites that has generated the descriptive grid so far (the drawing room with hot and cold currents, juicy young ladies and the desiccated old creature, etc.) continues in this evocation of another effeminate male figure, this time, though, a youthful, erotic one: Adonis stretched out on a lion's skin.

The characterization of the aged Zambinella as artificial and a statue is paired with a different kind of distancing in the painting "of" Zambinella that ascribes to him/her a hybrid "perfection": "Does such a perfect creature exist?" is the young lady's response to the image. Barthes notes that perfection belongs to what is excessive or extreme:

Thus, La Zambinella is Super-Woman, essential perfect woman (in any theology, perfection is the essence, and Zambinella is a "masterpiece"), but at the same time, by the same impulse, she is sub-man, castrated, deficient, definitively *less*; in her absolutely desirable, in him absolutely execrable, the two transgressions are united. This confusion is warranted because transgression is actually a *mark* . . . ; it enables the discourse to engage in a game of equivocations: to speak of the "supernatural" perfection of the Adonis is also to speak of the "sub-natural" deficiency of the castrato. (Barthes, 72)

Zambinella, at once superwoman and woman *manqué*, is assigned an inhuman status.

Pygmalion's statue is also at once a perfect woman, too good to be true, and also less than a woman, not even real. An identification of Zambinella with Pygmalion's statue emerges in the tale the moment that Sarrasine sees Zambinella performing for the first time. The narrator evokes the Grecian beauty of Zambinella, comparing "her" qualities to the "wonders of those images of Venus revered and rendered by the chisels of the Greeks." The artist admires the details of the singer's feminine beauty:

This was more than a woman, this was a masterpiece! In this unhoped-for creation could be found a love to enrapture any man, and beauties worthy of satisfying a critic. With his eyes, Sarrasine devoured Pygmalion's statue, come down from its pedestal. When La Zambinella sang, the effect was delirium. The artist felt cold; then he felt a heat which suddenly began to prickle in the innermost depth of his being, in what we call the heart for lack of any other word! (Balzac, 238)

Sarrasine's passion finds form in giving form to the woman he desires: once at home alone, he sketches her in endless drawings in a multitude of imaginary poses. Barthes remarks on the aptness of the topos of the "reassembled body" in Sarrasine's response to the sight of Zambinella as fragmented object, and on its relation to the Lacanian theme of the "partial object" or "fetish object" (Barthes, 111). Artistic fantasy and erotic phantasm fuse in Sarrasine's obsession.

Sarrasine's delusion explodes when, having abducted Zambinella to his studio, he confronts the singer, who confesses to the deception. With the trembling castrato at his feet, Sarrasine glances to the statue of Zambinella, the idealized woman he has made of him:

"I shall forever think of this imaginary woman when I see a real woman." He indicated the statue with a gesture of despair. "I shall always have the memory of a celestial harpy who thrusts its talons into all my manly feelings, and who will stamp all other women with a seal of imperfection! Monster! You who can give life to nothing. For me, you have wiped women from the earth." (Balzac, 252)

The facts turn Sarrasine's earth angel into a celestial harpy. Zambinella is a construction, even—and especially—in the fabrication of his voice. Sarrasine receives an initial glimmer of the truth about Zambinella in a conversation with a certain prince Chigi. Seeing him in male dress at a private recital, Sarrasine speculates to Chigi that "she" must be so dressed in consideration for the clerics present:

"She? What she?" asked the old nobleman to whom Sarrasine had been speaking. "La Zambinella." "La Zambinella!" the Roman prince replied. "Are you joking? Where are you from? Has there ever been a woman on the Roman stage? And don't you know about the creatures who sing female roles in the Papal States? I am the one, monsieur, who gave Zambinella his voice. I paid for everything that scamp ever had, even his singing teacher. Well, he has so little gratitude for the service I rendered him that he has never consented to set foot in my house. And yet, if he makes a fortune, he will owe it all to me." (Balzac, 250)

The irony of the prince's "he will owe it all to me" takes its pungency from the very mixed blessing of the procedure he arranged for the singer—implicit in all he says here: for it was the "little knife," as the operation was known, not the music lessons as such, that gave Zambinella his voice. The castrato's voice is itself an artifact.

This voice is one that Barthes characterizes as an erotic substance, itself asexual, but penetrating, orgasmic. He observes that Italian music is above all a vocal art and makes (well before Poizat) the connection between the asexuality of the castrato and the erotic power of his voice:

Italian music, an object well defined historically, culturally, mythically . . . connotes a "sensual" art, an art of the voice. An erotic substance, the Italian voice was produced *a contrario* (according to a strictly symbolic inversion) by singers without sex . . . as though, by selective hypertrophy, sexual density were obliged to abandon the rest of the body and lodge in the throat, thereby draining the organism of all that *connects* it. (Barthes, 109)

He reminds the reader of the erotic hysteria that would overcome audiences listening to the "star castrati" and cites Stendhal's account of the fad of women hanging little portraits of their favorite stars on their arms, around their necks, and on their shoe buckles. Barthes identifies this musical voice with a specifically sexual property:

This music's erotic quality (attached to its *vocal nature*) is here defined: it is the power of *lubrication*; *connection* is a specific characteristic of the voice; the model of the lubricated is the organic, the "living," in short, seminal fluid (Italian music "floods with pleasure"); singing (a characteristic generally ignored in aesthetics) has something coenesthetic about it, it is connected less to an "impression" than to an internal, muscular, humoral sensuality. The voice is a diffusion, an insinuation, it passes over the entire surface of the body, the skin; and being a passage, an abolition of limitations, classes, names . . . it possesses a special hallucinatory power. Music, therefore, has an effect utterly different from sight; it can effect orgasm, penetrating Sarrasine. (Barthes, 110)

Although Barthes associates the erotic influence of the musical voice with semen, there is nothing necessarily masculine about the qualities of "lubrication" and "diffusion," which could apply equally well to sexual qualities that are specifically feminine. More interesting than an assimilation of the erotic power of the voice to the phallic would be a reading that respected the inherently ambiguous, "slippery" nature of the musical voice Barthes describes. Erotically *double*, the voice is (to use Barthes's own vocabulary) at once penetrating, fluid, and diffuse; it abolishes limits, passes through the skin; it is linked to an internal sensualism, it provokes orgasm. It is pleasure, and pleasure is not a specifically masculine property by any means: it is dual, hermaphroditic. The act of listening is not analogous to the gaze, assimilated in the Freudian system to phallic power. Listening must be both active and passive, since hearing implies a receptive state, a stance usually coded as feminine. The pleasure Barthes describes is not necessarily that of a male subject but may as easily be female pleasure. If Zambinella's sexuality is ambiguous, so, in listening to him/her, is Sarrasine's. Similarly, Consuelo's singing is both feminine in tonality and penetrating, powerful, that is, phallic, in its effect. In a certain sense, the "magnetic fluid" that is the idealized voice escapes gender identification by participating in qualities of both.

This notion of a voice that is sexually double forms the subject of the poem "Contralto" by Gautier. It was first published in the *Revue des deux mondes* on December 15, 1849, and is included in his collection of poems, *Emaux et camées*, the first edition of which came out in 1852. The poem, written in octosyllabic quatrains rhymed *abab*, evokes the image of the Louvre sculpture, the *Sleeping Hermaphrodite*, to celebrate the pleasure afforded by the contralto voice. He begins with the statue's appearance:

> On voit dans le Musée antique,
> Sur un lit de marbre sculpté
> Une statue énigmatique
> D'une inquiétante beauté.
>
> Est-ce un jeune homme? est-ce une femme,
> Une déese, ou bien un dieu?
> L'amour, ayant peur d'être infâme,
> Hésite et suspend son aveu.
>
> Dans sa pose malicieuse,
> Elle s'étend, le dos tourné
> Devant la foule curieuse
> Sur son coussin capitonné.
>
> Pour faire sa beauté maudite
> Chaque sexe apporta son don.
> Tout homme dit: C'est Aphrodite!
> Toute femme: C'est Cupidon!
>
> Sexe douteux, grâce certain,
> On dirait ce corps indécis
> Fondu, dans l'eau de la fontaine,
> Sous les baisers de Salmacis,
>
> Chimère ardente, effort suprême
> De l'art et de la volonté,
> Monstre charmant, comme je t'aime
> Avec ta multiple beauté![22]

[In the ancient Museum one sees / On a marble bed / An enigmatic statue / Of a disquieting beauty.

Is it a youth? Is it a woman, / A goddess, or a god? / Love, afraid to seem vile / Defers his confession.

In her malicious pose, / She stretches out / On her padded cushion / Her back to the curious crowd.

To make her cursed beauty / Each sex brings its gift. / Every man says: She is Aphrodite! / Every woman says: He is Cupid!

Doubtful sex, certain grace, / One would say this undecided body / Is melted in the fountain's water / Beneath Salmacis's kisses.

Ardent chimera, supreme effort / Of art and will, / Charming monster, how I love you / With your multiple beauty.]

The text's editor, Claudine Gothot-Mersch, notes that Gautier had two sources of inspiration for the poem. The first was the theme of the hermaphrodite itself, which Gothot-Mersch calls a "theme of the period." She points to several other contemporary writings in which it appeared: Henri de Latouche's 1829 novel *Fragoletta* and Balzac's *Sarrasine*. One might add Gautier's own *Mademoiselle de Maupin* to the list.

The second source was personal, according to Gothot-Mersch, who states that "Contralto" was Gautier's gesture of homage to his mistress, the singer Ernesta Grisi (sister of the dancer Carlotta Grisi). In the eighth strophe, Gautier shifts the focus of the poem from the visual register to the auditory, proposing the contralto voice as the statue's equivalent in sound:

> Rêve de poète et d'artiste
> Tu m'as bien des nuits occupé,
> Et mon caprice qui persiste
> Ne convient pas qu'il s'est trompé.
>
> Mais seulement il se transpose,
> Et, passant de la forme au son,
> Trouve dans sa métamorphose
> La jeune fille et le garçon.
>
> Que tu me plais, ô timbre étrange!
> Son double, homme et femme à la fois,
> Contralto, bizarre mélange,
> Hermaphrodite de la voix!

[Dream of poet and artist / For many nights you have preoccupied me, / And my persistent caprice / Does not admit to error.

It is only transposed, / And, passing from form to sound, / Finds in its metamorphosis / Both the girl and the boy.

How pleasing you are to me, oh strange timbre! / Double sound, man and woman both, / Contralto, bizarre mélange, / Hermaphrodite of the voice!]

The shifting sexual identity of the singer, source of intrigue in *Sarrasine*, becomes in this poem a doubled gender within the singer's voice itself. The five strophes that follow enumerate a series of figures that are either sexed opposites posed in unity or twinned mirror images. The first two give a sense of the rest:

> C'est Roméo, c'est Juliette,
> Chantant avec un seul gosier;
> Le pigeon rauque et la fauvette
> Perchés sur le même rosier;
>
> C'est la châtelaine qui raille
> Son beau page parlant d'amour;
> L'amant au pied de la muraille,
> La dame au balcon de sa tour.

[It is Romeo, it is Juliet, / Singing with a single throat; / Raucous pigeon and warbler / Perched on the same rosebush;

It is the lady of the manor who mocks / Her handsome page talking of love, / The lover at the foot of the wall / The lady at her tower balcony.]

One among these is interesting, since within it recur the terms of the angel and the voice compared to a bell, familiar now from the discussion of the Hoffman stories and the Sand material:

> L'ange qui descend et qui monte
> Sur l'escalier d'or voltigeant;
> La cloche mêlant dans sa fonte
> La voix d'airain, la voix d'argent.

[The angel who descends and climbs / Fluttering, about the golden stairway; / The bell blending as it melts / The bronze voice and the silver.]

Gothot-Mersch informs the reader that this strophe borrows its metaphor from a poem by Victor Hugo, "Ecrit sur la vitre d'une fenêtre flamande" (1837), in which figure also the elements of a bell and a celestial dancer who dances on its crystalline melody.[23] Gautier had already used this same metaphor once before, in a piece on Carlotta Grisi published in his *Histoire de l'art dramatique en France*, where he wrote, "Carlotta is, in fact, the aerian dancer whom the poet sees descending and mounting the crystalline stairway of melody in a mist of sonorous light!"[24]

In the final strophes of the poem, the poet enumerates a series of opera roles, alternately masculine and feminine, which belong to the contralto repertoire or to that of a singer whose range includes the contralto range. Here are three of the five last strophes:

> Sur le pli de sa jupe assise,
> Ce soir, ce sera Cendrillon
> Causant près du feu qu'elle attise
> Avec son ami le grillon
>
> Demain le valeureux Arsace
> A son courroux donnant l'essor,
> Ou Tancrède avec sa cuirasse,
> Son épée et son casque d'or
>
> Desdemona chantant le Saule,
> Zerline bernant Masetto,
> Ou Malcolm le plaid sur l'épaule;
> C'est toi que j'aime, ô contralto!

[Sitting on the fold of her skirt, / Tonight it will be Cinderella / Talking with her friend the cricket / Beside the fire which she stirs

Tomorrow, valorous Arsace / Giving scope to his anger, / Or Tancredi with his armor, / His sword and his golden helmet

Desdemona singing the Willow Aria, / Zerlina fooling Masetto, / Or Malcolm, a plaid thrown over his shoulder; / It is you I love, Oh, contralto!]

All these are roles from works by Rossini, except for Zerlina, from Mozart's *Don Giovanni*. Gothot-Mersch notes that Malcolm was one of Ernesta Grisi's great roles. Intriguingly, she includes Jean Pommer's observation that this list, and the order of its elements (Arsace, Tancrède, Malcolm), is the same as the series of roles Gautier had imagined for Pauline García in 1839, on the occasion of her debut, as future proof of the sureness of her lower register.[25] Perhaps Gautier was thinking as much of Pauline Viardot as of his companion Ernesta Grisi in his homage to the contralto. After all, the range described in this passage outdoes the "hermaphroditic" quality of a contralto, since Viardot's vocal range seems to have embraced with equal facility the tenor voice and the soprano. On this singer, then, whom many considered one of the foremost female singers of her time, Gautier projects a shadow image of the double-sexed hermaphrodite, echoing the fantasy operative in *Sarrasine* and other fictions and summing up in an explicit way the curious slippage of gender identity in opera voice and its literary representations.

It is an interesting coincidence that the singer whom Gautier arguably had in mind in writing his contralto piece is the same Pauline who served as the model for Sand's heroine. In the novel, Sand also dresses her character in travesty: Consuelo travels happily in drag during an adventure that lasts for about one third of volume 2 of the novel. Vierne notes the freedom Consuelo thus enjoys, and the echo of androgyny to be heard even in her name: "To a French ear, the name Consuelo can cause confusion: it sounds masculine. Only Anzoleto sometimes calls her 'Consuelita,' and a neighbor in Venice, 'Consuelina.' When she calls herself Porporina, she makes reference to her master, the paternal and masculine figure of Porpora. Beneath her boy's clothing, Consuelo sketches out a possible form of 'liberation.'"[26] Although Vierne goes on to say that Sand rejects the provisional solution of travesty in favor of an image of unity provided by the couple, the observations she makes here about the possible gender confusion coded in Consuelo's names support certain suggestions of her androgyny offered in the text. At the very least, travesty suits Consuelo to a T.

When Consuelo undertakes her self-transformation, she is able to effect it with elegance and pleasure:

Retiring behind the rocks . . . she proceeded immediately to transform herself. The spring served as a mirror for her when she left her retreat, and it was not without a certain pleasure that she saw appear there the prettiest little peasant boy the Slavic race had ever yet produced. Her waist, lithe and slender as a reed, swam inside the wide belt of red wool; and her leg, slender as a doe's, showed modestly a bit between the ankle and the wide folds of the pants. Her black hair, which she had steadfastly resisted powdering, had been cut during her illness, and curled naturally about her face. She tousled her locks with her fingers to give them the true rustic neglect suitable to a young shepherd boy, and carrying her costume with an ease learned at the theater, knowing even, thanks to her mimetic art, how to give right away an expression of wild simplicity to her features, she felt so well disguised that courage and a sense of security returned to her on the spot. Just as it happens with actors, as soon as they put on their costume, she felt her role, and even identified with the character she was to play, to the point of feeling in herself something like the insouciance, the pleasure of an innocent roaming, the gaiety, vigor and bodily freedom of a boy playing hooky. (Sand, 122)

Although the narrator attributes Consuelo's ease in travesty to her theatrical experience, the vocabulary of the passage appeals largely as well to Consuelo's native qualities. Her unpowdered hair, already cut short, curls naturally around her face; her slender form easily assumes a boy's apparel. Even the similes used to describe how Consuelo looks in the costume: "Her waist, lithe and slender as a reed," "her leg, slender as a doe's," with their appeal to earthy, rustic images, subtly echo a second sense of her appearance as natural, instinctively fitting as well as attractive: "This transformation made Consuelo extraordinarily more beautiful, and at the same time, it lent her a totally different aspect in the young musician's imagination. . . . The change in dress, so *successful* it seemed like a true change in sex, suddenly changed the young man's frame of mind as well" (Sand, 122–23). Consuelo's transformation into a boy releases Haydn from the tension he has felt traveling in the company of a woman.

If Consuelo and Haydn are able to relax into a comradely fraternity of the road, others are drawn to Consuelo as to a charming boy. At one point, they take refuge with a group of peasants who offer them their hospitality: "They looked closely at Consuelo, who seemed to them to be a very pretty boy, and who pretended, in order to play well her role, to look straight at them with a pair of very bold and wide-awake eyes" (Sand, 132). The passage continues in a firm feminist vein, for while Sand has Consuelo experience a pang of nostalgia for their time-honored ways, it resolves in a movement of revulsion toward the lot of these women:

But looking at these poor women standing behind their husbands, serving them respectfully, and then gaily eating their leftovers, some nursing a baby, the others already instinctively the slaves of their young boys, taking care of them before thinking of their daughters and themselves, she no longer saw in all these good farmers anything but victims of hunger and need, the males chained to the earth, servants to the plow and to beasts; the females chained to the master, that is, to the man, cloistered in the house, servants into perpetuity, condemned to work without respite amid the sufferings and troubles of motherhood. (Sand, 132)

In this vignette of rural life, the women fare worse than their men. Sand speaks through her character, who contemplates the feminine role with distaste, rejoicing that her profession gives her a ticket to freedom like the one she enjoys in disguise:

She said to herself that it was better to be an artist or a bohemian than lord or peasant, since along with the possession of land or even of a sheaf of wheat goes either unjust tyranny or the dreary subjection to greed. *Viva la libertà* she said to Joseph, to whom she expressed her thoughts in Italian, while the women noisily washed and put away the dishes, and one crippled old woman turned her wheel with the regularity of a machine. (Sand, 132–33)

Consuelo's voice plays its part in her travesty. In suggesting to Haydn that they work up some duets to earn money and dispel suspicions that they are thieves, Consuelo maintains that by keeping her voice in the contralto range, she will be able to sustain the illusion that she is a boy: "'My voice, if I keep it entirely in contralto, can pass for that of a young boy whose voice is changing'" (Sand, 148). In their itinerant performances, Consuelo thus plays the part of a musically talented young boy, with the kind of sweet voice such boys were castrated to preserve. At one point, another traveler, taken in, advises her to learn to play the fife: "'—Well, before the year is out, you will be singing like a little frog, and there is no guarantee that you will become a nightingale again afterwards. The transition from childhood to youth is an uncertain trial for a boy. Sometimes sprouting a beard means losing one's voice'" (Sand, 151). During her travesty episode, then, Consuelo merges the role of the angel/woman with that of the angel/boy. Consuelo's contralto voice is thus, in some sense, hermaphroditic, like the contralto voice of her model Viardot, shadowed also in Gautier's poem.

This play of gender ambiguity through the voice is particularly evident in the episode involving the aged, music-loving canon who shelters Haydn and Consuelo. The old man is taken with her and has a sleepless night after Consuelo performs for him:

Never had music made such an impression on the mind of the canon, even though he had been a passionate lover of music his whole life. Never had a human voice so shaken him to the core as did Consuelo's. Never had features, language, or manners exerted such a fascination over his soul, as had the face, the bearing and the speech of Consuelo for the last thirty-six hours. Did the canon guess the sex of the so-called Bertoni or not? Yes and no. How to explain? (Sand, 268)

Sand explains the innocence of the old celibate, in love with a woman he takes to be a boy: "In that respect he was completely mistaken, and in all the naïveté of his heart, he took Consuelo for a boy. . . . At the cathedral in Vienna, he had seen any number of beautiful youths there studying; he had heard voices that were silvery, clear and practically female for their purity and suppleness; that of Bertoni was a thousand times more pure and supple" (Sand, 269). Loyally plugging for the superiority of a fine feminine voice over those of boy singers, Sand is implicitly arguing Consuelo's superiority over the castrati here; this canon's predicament parallels that of Sarrasine with Zambinella, with the gender error inverted. At the same time she is cashing in on the freedom from the restricting definitions of gender determinations made available through the game of travesty, the kind of pleasure Judith Butler evokes in her idea of "gender parody."[27]

While she insists on the chaste, paternal nature of this old man's emotion, through this very disclaimer Sand suggests something more confused. More than paternal emotions are involved in the canon's white night: he is agitated by "a singular emotion"; "amazed at what was taking place within him, he convinced himself of a thousand things besides the truth" (Sand, 270). Like Sarrasine, the old canon is in the throes of a paradoxical passion: he has mistaken his object. Indeed, the particular charm of each in both cases comes from what makes them impossible by their nature.

The topos of the angelic singer, ambiguously gendered, is not confined to French narrative. The heroine of George du Maurier's novel *Trilby*, published in 1894, provides a final instance of this figure, although the subject is self-consciously enough suited to the novel's Parisian setting and artistic milieu.[28] Trilby begins as a hearty, sweet English girl who lives a Bohemian life as an artist's model. She is not merely statuesque (or "Olympian in scale"); she is almost masculine, but also angelic. Du Maurier introduces her to the reader in the following way:

Suddenly there came a loud knuckle-rapping at the outer door, and a portentous voice of great volume that might almost have belonged to any sex (even an angel's!) uttered the British milkman's yodel, "Milk below!" and before any could say "Entrez" a strange figure appeared. . . . It was the figure of a very tall and fully developed young female. . . . [S]he would have made a singularly handsome boy.[29]

Trilby is a down-to-earth, generous young person with no pretensions to artistry. Despite her "immense" voice and a presence that fills any room she enters, she sings laughably out of tune until she falls under the influence of the unscrupulous musical genius, Svengali. Hypnotized by him, she becomes the world-famous singer La Svengali.

Like Honorine, his first pupil, she is a contralto. Here again, the contralto's voice is compared to that of an angel; in this description, Little Billee, the British painter who falls in love with Trilby, listens to Honorine sing: "And before everything else, he had for the singing woman an absolute worship. He was especially in thrall to the contralto—the deep low voice that breaks and changes in the middle and soars all at once into a magnified angelic boy treble. It pierced through his ears to his heart, and stirred his very vitals" (du Maurier, 61). The pleasure Little Billee experiences in listening to the "angelic boy treble" is like that of the old canon in Sand's novel, that expressed by Gautier in his poem, or that of Balzac's Sarrasine.

In du Maurier's description of La Svengali's last and greatest performance, Poizat would recognize the piercing cry of the angel, the voice *hors-sens* (a voice beyond hearing or beyond thought). During this performance, Trilby's "infinite voice" astonishes her old friends who have come to hear her: "Every phrase is a string of perfect gems, of purest ray serene, strung together on a loose golden thread. The higher and shriller she sings, the sweeter it is, and sweeter than any woman had ever sung before" (du Maurier, 330). Following this, du Maurier embarks on over three pages of imagery evoking the delight and tender nostalgia provoked by her singing. The passage ends with references to glowing reviews of La Svengali by such distinguished critics as Berlioz and Gautier, the latter supposedly having written an article called "Madame La Svengali: Ange ou Femme?" (du Maurier, 355).

Trilby, though, is a divided being. Unhappily prevented from marrying her true love, she has become Svengali's creature. Trilby herself knows nothing of her singing; hypnotized, she takes on a new identity, La Svengali. Trilby, the artist's model, the Galatea of painter Durien's would-be Pygmalion, has become a living statue molded by Svengali. At the end, Svengali's violinist protégé Gecko explains:

There were two Trilbys. . . . He had but to say "Dors" [sleep] and she suddenly became an unconscious Trilby of marble, who could produce wonderful sounds—just the sounds he wanted and nothing else—and think his thoughts . . . love him with a strange unreal factitious love . . . *un écho, un simulacre, quoi, pas autre chose* [an echo, just a simulacrum, nothing else] . . . . Trilby was just a singing machine, an organ to play on, a Stradivarius, a flexible flageolet of flesh and blood, a voice and nothing more. (du Maurier, 457–58)

The marvel of Trilby's voice is the result of her strangely denatured state as Svengali's mesmerized puppet. In her way, La Svengali is as artificial, as constructed, as La Zambinella or Olympia.

In these fictional representations of singers, a particular pattern emerges of a feminine singer who yet combines qualities of both genders, or who is in some sense beyond sexuality yet inspires an intense response of pleasure and desire in others. While Barthes turns to a sexual model to account for the pleasure available in the sung voice, Poizat employs a specifically psychoanalytic one. He points to the role of the voice in Lacanian theory as object of primary erotic pulsations:

From the Lacanian perspective, it is as object of a drive (the "invocatory" drive) that the voice is inserted into an eroticizing system, which, like all systems built around the drives, consists of the object's source (structured as an orifice, as a rim: in this case, the ear); its goal—a satisfaction; and its "impetus"—the tension it engenders by being sought, its characteristic circular trajectory ("to make itself heard"). (Poizat, 105)

Without rehearsing the material developed earlier, it will be useful to recall here the importance of the voice for Vasse and Anzieu in their separate discussions of psychic formation, on the one hand, and on the other, the work of both Kristeva and Lacoue-Labarthe which revises the visual Lacanian model on which the theory of subjectivity (the famous "mirror stage") has been based in favor of another, one that postulates the anteriority of the acoustic and rhythmic modalities in the constitution of subjectivity. While Poizat and Vasse share a Lacanian perspective rejected (at least) to some extent by the others, they all accord the pulse of the voice a key function at the ground of experience.

Poizat looks to this notion of the voice as primal object to account for the erotic appeal of the ambiguously gendered voice:

The eroticization of the voice follows from its elevation to object status according to modalities that I have attempted to describe and has little to do with its role as a mark of sexual difference. . . . In fact, the voices considered most erotic, those that hold the greatest fascination for the listener, whether male or female, are voices that may be called trans-sexual—the deep voice in a woman (think of Kathleen Ferrier, or Marlene Dietrich, the "blue angel"), the high voice in a man (the castrato, the tenor). (Poizat, 150)

One could add to Poizat's list the character of Dil in the film *The Crying Game*, or for that matter, Michael Jackson. He thus argues that the feminine voice, identified with the angelic and positioned outside of the human sphere, takes its origin not from any essentially feminine quality but from an effect of its positioning as such, and perhaps from the very blurring of difference. Poizat appeals to the Lacanian notion of woman as lack to account for the angel-woman placed *hors-sexe*, beyond sex (or "trans-sexual" as Arthur Denner translates it) in cultural representations. He draws from Lacan's characterization of the *fin'amor* of courtly love as placing the woman in the position of an impossible object of desire, hence as a kind of absence. Illustrating his discussion with examples from *Turandot* and Wagner, he shows the continuation of this function of the woman as signifier of absence in opera narratives, noting how it informs the pleasure of the opera lover:

The neurotic avatar of masculine desire described by courtly literature is especially apt to underpin the quest for the Voice as opera structures it. The woman may be a stand-in for "nothingness," for that which, like Euridice, immediately disappears when exposed to the human gaze or to the light of day; or her Absolute Beauty, which is supposed to satisfy man's every desire, at the cost of the death of his desire or quite simply his death, may make her a stand-in for the divine. In either case, The Woman, thus fantasized, incarnates the "lack of lack," the emblematic figure that is supposed to bridge the gap that causes desire. For Woman, imagined as Voice, is ever elusive, whence the intensification of desire ad infinitum. (Poizat, 150)

This argument, which holds that the woman articulates the place of Lacanian lack, is congruent with the readings by Grosrichard and

Marin of Rousseau's fetishistic preoccupation with the voice. Freud's *unheimlich* Olympia may likewise be seen as working under the same regime: the function of the fetish object is the same, simultaneously representing and denying what the woman "lacks." It will be useful when we look at the overdetermined figure of Villiers's future Eve. Yet the angelic voice also resonates with the infinite: an echo to which we will return in closing.

From one perspective, then, we can think of the tradition of the castrato voice in opera as giving rise to a literary topos, that of the pleasure offered by a sexless voice, produced by a singer whose gender may be ambiguous or occluded, a reading that may suggest an instability in the terms of gender structure. From a slightly different perspective, another pattern emerges in these stories. Beyond the gesture that renders ambiguous the gender of the singers is a sense of the perfect singer as sexless in another sense: of neither sex, possessing qualities or implicated in identifications that make her in some way inhuman, with a voice comparable to bird song, bells, crystal, violin music, and so on. The simple romantic story of the charming singer, on closer examination, tells a different story, one of the pleasure of the artificial, of the desire for an object rendered inhuman. Beginning with Baudelaire, one finds a progressive identification of women in romantic texts with the modernist theme of artifice. When notions of the artificial become imbricated with romantic theories of art through representations of women as cold, artificial, and statuelike, we may hear nothing new. The artificial singer's song carries another, multiple, message: along with the thread of a "sweet fragile voice," the archaic ground-note of infancy, one may hear as well echoes of a theme that anticipates and expresses modernity with its technological surprises and ambivalent pleasures.

Baudelaire and the Painted Woman

A fascination with women singers who are presented as being in some way constructed, artifacts even, whose voices are curiously inhuman in their beauty, drives the fictions discussed in the preceding section. The curious appeal of the artificial expressed in these texts seems to diverge from the kind of association of women, voice, and nature one might expect from nineteenth-century writers and that seems to hold in Stendhal's writing on music, for example, where he maintains the natural superiority of the voice over man-made instruments. This simple antithesis breaks down, however, in the light of Poizat's argument about the voice in opera, where he shows that the most prized voices in Italian opera to have been the "unearthly" voices of the castrati. As we have seen, this privileged place was progressively given over during this time to an "inhuman" female soprano voice.

This taste for the artificial appears to run counter to the mainstream of romantic valuation of nature and, where it bears on the representation of women, the deeply inscribed cultural assimilation of woman to nature. At the same time, however, both the artificial woman and the woman as nature are equally reified, or, in Heideggerian terms, seen as *physis*, in opposition to *technē*. We have seen how Goux has suggested that Western metaphysics distributes gender through these categories, linking the feminine with the former as matter, the masculine with the latter as spirit. Within the context of romanticism, a definite shift nevertheless takes place. Later we will consider the text that most emblematically depicts the woman as artificial, Villiers de l'Isle-Adam's *L'Eve future*, where it reaches its most explicit development and its most elaborated form of the era. I suggest that this apparent contradiction in fact articulates the shift to modernity and modernism. The new phantasmal projection of woman as artifice, as simulacrum, appears in French letters through the writing of Baudelaire, whose work is well known to be the flash point in France for the transition to the modern.

The preferred rendition of the woman as statue, of artifice as the desirable woman's most important fashion accessory, is adumbrated already in Baudelaire's praise of makeup in *Le Peintre de la vie moderne*. In these essays, he intervenes in the tradition dating to antiquity that censures women's use of "paint," affirming instead the value of artificiality and linking it specifically with ideas of modernity. While the painted woman has long been a metaphor for the seductions of representation, I will argue that the artificial woman enacts a metafiguration of the technologies of the mechanical reproduction (to borrow Benjamin's phrase) of human presence that transformed the culture of the late nineteenth century: the brilliance of electricity, the instantaneity of telegraphy, the capture of the warmth of the human voice in the phonograph, the advent of cinema. Villiers's sterile mechanical singer sings of ambiguous marvels, of the machines that repeat human presence, of the ghost finally caught in the machine.

My argument is parallel in this regard, once again, with certain points of Kittler's discussion of the transition from romanticism to modernism, his shift from the "discourse network" of 1800 to that of 1900. Kittler argues that in 1800, the woman was identified with nature, in 1900, no longer: "If the phantasm of woman arose in the distribution of form and matter, spirit and nature, writing and reading, production and consumption, to the two sexes, a new discourse network cancelled the polarity."[1] Kittler somewhat optimistically goes on to say that the singularity of Woman gives way to pluralism of women, no longer subjects of love, "Ariadnes, Bettinas, Abelones, and thus women's discourses." My own view is somewhat less sanguine.[2] More convincingly, Kittler recalls both Benjamin and Marshall McLuhan, when he states that "a medium is a medium is a medium," and that "the ability to record sense data technologically shifted the entire discourse network circa 1900."[3] That is, the invention of mechanical means of production, of mechanical means of reproduction of the senses with the phonograph, the cinematograph, and, centrally for his discussion, the typewriter, radically changed the production of discourse, revolutionizing literature and art. Among the effects of these recording machines he discusses are the unleashing of the associative process, Freud's "flight of ideas," and a new grounding of art in the materiality of the producing forms, whether literary, phonographic, or filmic.

This last notion of materiality resonates interestingly with Jean-François Lyotard's notion of the avant-garde's work within the space of the material itself of the work of art, an idea I will discuss in the context of my closing chapter. Where Kittler alludes to *L'Eve future* as a signature text of this transition and mentions Edison's talking dolls and Berliner's writing angels as markers of this shift, his argument meets and supports my own.[4] This is material I take up as well in my discussion of the Android in "Edison's Recorded Angel." For while the topos of the female automaton likewise long precedes Villiers's text, only in the late nineteenth century does it become associated with the idea of the modern and the new modes of representation and artistic reproduction suddenly made both possible and problematic.

The inhuman woman carries forward the ancient topos of the automaton so prevalent in German literature of the period at the same time that she expresses one aspect of the dominant romantic image of the fatal woman as Praz has described it,[5] and the icy, expressionless symbolist woman Kermode isolates in his discussion of the dancer figure in romantic imagery.[6] As an early champion of Wagnerism Baudelaire was a key figure in the importation of the *Frühromantik* aesthetic impulses from German to French artistic circles. Baudelaire's writings on modernity and art are closely articulated through his ideas on women and artifice.

The essays that comprise *Le Peintre de la vie moderne* were first published in *Figaro* in three parts from November 29 to December 3, 1863, and were later collected in *L'Art romantique* in 1868. Intending to create a public for the sketches of his friend Constantin

Guys, who was in financial difficulties because the Parisians were apparently not receptive to his work, Baudelaire interprets his drawings for the reader and in the process articulates a matrix of figures and ideas that will strongly color the stance and attitudes of the symbolists, the decadents, and others who follow him. As Benjamin has shown in his essay on Baudelaire in *Illuminations*, "On Some Motifs in Baudelaire," he here outlines the types of aesthete who embody for us the Paris of the time and their world of values: the *flaneur*, connoisseur of crowds, and the dandy, whose cold demeanor and disciplined attention to detail in dress and manner reveal and mask his service of a hidden ideal; the paradoxical junctures of the momentary and the eternal, the passage from *spleen* to *idéal*; the scorn of nature in favor of the artificial; and the new italics placed on the word *modernity*.[7]

Among these pieces are three in which Baudelaire considers women: "La Femme," "Eloge du maquillage," and "Les Femmes et les filles." In his simultaneously extolling and intensely disparaging paean to women, one can trace an anticipation of the terms Villiers adopts to characterize the desired beauty, his own bitter terms of endearment. Common to both writers is the kind of nineteenth-century fantasy of the femme fatale that Praz shows to be pervasive in romantic writing and that Bram Djikstra finds typical in the visual representations of women in the late nineteenth century: a vision of the woman as seductive, perverse, and infinitely dangerous.[8]

Baudelaire begins the first of these pieces, "La Femme," with what resembles an invocation of the woman as muse, in a sentence whose long periodic cadence sounds extolling. It opens by calling her the being who is the source of the most lively happiness of men, toward whom all their efforts tend, that being "as terrible and incommunicable as the Deity."[9] Baudelaire explains parenthetically that this is probably because she has nothing to communicate. According to Claude Pichois, Baudelaire rather perversely misquotes Joseph de Maistre, attributing to him the statement that the woman is a "graceful animal whose beauty enlivened and made easier the serious game of politics; for whom, and through whom, fortunes are made and unmade, for whom, but above all, *through whom* poets and artists create their most exquisite jewels" (*Painter*, 30). Pichois interestingly points out that rather than relegating woman to the animal order, de Maistre emphasizes the dignity that gospel confers on her, calling the Christian woman "a *supernatural being*, because she is raised up and sustained by it in a state which is not *natural* to her (because of the stain of Eve's sin)."[10] Baudelaire does seem to have read de Maistre, but he appropriates, perverts, one might say, the thesis of woman's "supernatural" status for his own ends: the arguments he puts forward in "Eloge du maquillage" are curiously similar.

Baudelaire continues with a denial of the thesis of his factitious citation: woman is not merely an animal. For the artist, woman is not merely "the female of Man":

Rather, she is a divinity, a star, which presides at all the conceptions of the brain of man; a glittering conglomeration of all the graces of Nature, condensed into a single being; the object of the keenest admiration and curiosity that the picture of life can offer its contemplator. She is a kind of idol, stupid perhaps, but dazzling and bewitching, who holds wills and destinies suspended on her glance. (*Painter*, 30)

Bringing into his discussion the old antinomy of ancient and modern, Baudelaire claims that neither the severe meditations of the sculptor nor the art of Winckelmann can really suffice to explain the woman's "mysterious and complex spell." The moderns come closer, in the portraits of Reynolds or Lawrence.

Baudelaire finally discloses to his reader the source of the woman's charm: its secret lies in the magical luxury of her adornments. All the touches that enhance and ornament her beauty are part of her, and one must make no effort to think of her as separate from them:

Everything that adorns woman, everything that serves to show off her beauty, is part of herself. . . . No doubt Woman is sometimes a light, a glance, an invitation to happiness, sometimes just a word, but above all she is a general harmony, not only in her bearing and the way in which she moves and walks, but also in the muslins, the gauzes, the vast iridescent clouds of stuff in which she envelops herself, and which are as it were the attributes and the pedestal of her divinity; in the metal and the mineral which twist and turn around her arms and her neck, adding to the fire of her glance, or gently whispering at her ears. What poet, in sitting down to paint the pleasure caused by the sight of a beautiful woman, would venture to separate her from her costume? Where is the man who, in the street, at the theater, or in the park, has not in the most disinterested of ways enjoyed a skilfully composed toilette, and has not taken away with him a picture of it which is inseparable from the beauty of her to whom it belonged, making thus of the two things— the woman and her dress—an indivisible unity? (*Painter*, 30–31)

What matters, then, is not the woman herself, her particular quali- ties, but what she becomes when transformed by a system of well- conceived beauty aids. When she and her dress form an indivisible totality, she becomes a successful construction for the production of aesthetic pleasure, an artistic artifact.

Despite the charming style of the passage, there is no doubt of the misogyny of its underlying message: where women are concerned, it is better not to look too closely. The editor notes that Mme Aupick mistook this piece as a tribute to women. Baudelaire quickly dis- abuses her of this idea in a letter written a few days after the article was published: "I am very sorry to shatter your illusions about the passage where you thought to see a eulogy of this famous sex. You have completely misunderstood it. I believe there has never been any- thing as harsh as what I said in the *Delacroix* and in the *Figaro* ar- ticle. But this does not concern the *woman/mother*."[11] The passage to which Baudelaire refers his mother for a truer picture of his con- ception of the woman paints a much less charming portrait than a surface reading of the piece "La Femme." The following is the extract Baudelaire had in mind from "La Vie et l'oeuvre de Delacroix":

He considered woman as an object of art that is delicious and suitable to stimulate the mind, but a disobedient and disturbing object if it opens to itself the door of the heart, [it then] gluttonously consumes one's time and energy. I remember how once, in a public place, when I pointed out to him the face of a woman of an original beauty and a melancholy character, he was quite ready to savor her beauty, but said to me . . . "how can you expect a woman to be capable of melancholy?" Hinting thereby, no doubt, that in order to know the feeling of melancholy, there is a *certain essential some- thing* missing in woman.[12]

The idea that a woman's beauty is an artistic object, a synthetic cre- ation, into which one should not look too closely, is taken up and elaborated in horrific manner in *L'Eve future* in the section devoted to Mr. Anderson's fall at the hands of the "charming creature," Miss

Evelyn Habal. No longer actually young and beautiful, she conceals her age and staleness behind what is revealed to be an initially deceptive but in fact nauseatingly coarse screen, a concatenation of wigs, dusty costumes, greasepaint, perfumes, mysterious prostheses, and repulsive contraceptive devices, all of which, curiously, is described in the book through the narration of a kind of film (predating its actual invention) shown to Ewald by the inventor Edison. Thus, the same attitude, the same bitterness reflected in the derisive comment Baudelaire attributes to Delacroix about women's spiritual incapacity, is mirrored in a basic element of the plot of Villiers's novel: the burden of Ewald's complaint about his mistress is her lack of a certain quality of feeling. The vulgarity that renders her intolerable is essentially her failure to feel as he wishes, her inability to reflect the quality of refined melancholy he desires. One must also think inevitably here of the significance in the psychoanalytic lexicon of this "lack of a *certain essential something*" that flaws the woman so profoundly, rendering her so displeasing. As in the joke about the famous "nobody I met on the road—I met him again today," we have met with this significant lack at every turn during the course of this study.

Baudelaire's sense that the woman lacks "something essential" is not surprising, given the weight of the metaphysical tradition dating back to Plato that identifies the woman as lacking, in fact, an *essence*. In "Making Up Representations: The Risks of Femininity," Jacqueline Lichtenstein points out the way this tradition informs the metaphors of makeup and seduction prevalent in the seventeenth-century arguments between the partisans of Rubens and Poussin over the primacy of color versus design in painting, metaphors reflected in rhetorical references to the proper and improper relations of femininity and ornamentation. Lichtenstein fittingly heads her piece with an epigraph from Baudelaire: "What is art? Prostitution."

While affirming a view of the classical period as one of widespread admiration for the discriminating acuteness of feminine reason, almost as a "feminist" age, Lichtenstein cites a text by Jean de La Bruyère that criticizes the dishonesty of women who "paint" themselves, a text that Baudelaire perhaps had in mind when writing his own piece:

For a woman to paint herself red or white is, I admit, a smaller crime than to say one thing and think another; it is also something less innocent than to disguise herself or to go masquerading, if she does not pretend to pass for what she seems to be, but only thinks of concealing her personality and of remaining unknown; it is an endeavor to deceive the eye, to wish to appear outwardly what she is not; it is a kind of "white lie." We should judge of a woman without taking into account her shoes and head-dress, and, almost as we measure a fish, from head to tail.[13]

This passage from La Bruyère provides an interesting counterpoint to Baudelaire's "Eloge du maquillage," presenting as it does the same question of the judgment of a woman in terms of her adornments but affirming opposing values.

Lichtenstein notes that in these remarks La Bruyère participates in a long rhetorical tradition that associated ornamentation with femininity and united aesthetic with moral judgment in condemning at once the deceptions of women and the excesses of overly orna-mented styles of representation:

From antiquity to the classical age, the seductions of makeup were thought to correspond, in the hierarchy of representations, with the aberrations of femininity. It was as if the luster added to appearances could only be thought through categories designating a sex whose essence, it was said, consists pre-cisely of the deprivation of essence—since its nature, ontologically deficient, is necessarily exhausted in its simulation of appearances. *Makeup, woman*: two terms signifying the same substance, or rather the same absence of sub-stances—as La Bruyère wrote, 'a kind of white lie.' (Lichtenstein, 78)

If the woman is defined as "ontologically deficient," literally lacking that "essential something," then not only can she be identified with her adornments and her makeup, but "dressed up" in this way, she becomes metonymically identified with adornment and makeup in general and comes to stand for excess of ornament and its consequent damage to truth and nature. Lichtenstein shows that the analogy uses the feminine to articulate the relation between ornamentation and truth: some is needed for beauty, perhaps, but the tradition holds that too much ornament distorts truth:

We can summarize thus an aesthetic principle, current until France's classical period and still shaping our own discourse. This principle implies an essential distinction that constitutes all metaphysical aesthetics, allowing one to separate the wheat from the tares: a distinction between ornament and makeup, between a regulated and unregulated use, between lawful employment and abuse. Used to excess, ornament becomes makeup, which conceals rather than elucidates truth. This distinction, the secret of cosmetics as taught in the schools of metaphysics since Plato, was applied in the same manner to language and to the image. (Lichtenstein, 78)

She develops this point, showing how the Latin rhetorical tradition characterized excessive ornamentation through metaphors of femininity: for Cicero, a clear, simple style was like a natural beauty; for Dionysius of Halicarnassus, overly ornamented style was like a shameless prostitute who takes over the house, booting out the pure Attic bride.

Such metaphors, which equated a dissolute style with a dissolute woman, came to be used in painting as well, where the metaphor of "painting" took on a particular resonance because of the very nature of the medium itself:

Coloring, when applied to painting—the preeminent and essential cosmetic art, consisting of both "staining" (*teindre*) and "feigning" (*feindre*)—became . . . sensible, tactile, and visible, made of paste and ointments, genuine pigments like those used in women's cosmetics. The seductive artifice of the coloring praised by the colorists partook of the courtesan's and prostitute's allures. Here, love is not very different from art; in both cases, cosmetic illusion must be seen as a promise of illicit pleasures. (Lichtenstein, 79)

Lichtenstein extends this observation to show the correlation of color and instability (as opposed to the structure implied in design) in writing on painting since Plato. Makeup and color, then, both belong to what is ephemeral, heterogeneous, and qualitative: a range of terms negatively associated with the feminine. Thus, in the rhetorical tradition Lichtenstein traces from the ancients to classical French culture, and in the metaphysics that underpins it, the marked use of artifice has been identified with the feminine through the metaphors of makeup and its excesses. At the same time, the image of the painted woman, the woman who resorts to artifice, has been central to writers' efforts to speak of representation itself. If in this tradition the excessive use of ornamentation, the too obvious recourse to art, has been most often negatively valued, equated with what is immoral and undesirable, and set up as foil to natural beauty, this is not the case in Baudelaire's "Eloge du maquillage," where he sets out deliberately to invert this scale of values.

In this piece, Baudelaire attacks the association of beauty and virtue with nature in order to relocate them in the realm of art and artifice. Taking as his point of departure a line from a popular song, "Nature Embellishes Beauty," which he corrects as meaning "Simplicity embellishes Beauty" and reduces to "Nothing embellishes Something," Baudelaire criticizes the eighteenth-century moral conception of nature as the source and type of the beautiful and sees the denial of original sin as being much to blame for the "general blindness" of the period.

Rather, Baudelaire excoriates nature as the source of crude constraint and evil (he himself preferred evil in a more refined form). Far from being a source of virtue and beauty, nature pushes mankind to every crime, and it is only what lifts man outside of nature that furthers what is good: "I ask you to review and scrutinize whatever is natural—all the actions and desires of the purely natural man: you will find nothing but frightfulness. Everything beautiful and noble is the result of reason and calculation. Crime, of which the human animal has learned the taste in his mother's womb, is natural by origin" (*Painter*, 32).

Baudelaire thus places virtue and good on the side not simply of religion and philosophy but of what is specifically artificial: "Virtue, on the other hand, is artificial, supernatural, since at all times and in all places gods and prophets have been needed to teach it to animalized humanity, man being powerless to discover it by himself. Evil happens without effort, naturally, fatally; Good is always the product of some art" (*Painter*, 32). Just as the good is a product of art, the fruit of a rejection of nature, so the beautiful and the desire for beauty emerge from the desire to rise above nature. Baudelaire applauds the "savage" who demonstrates through his self-adornment the nobility of his aspiration. Likewise, the vicissitudes of fashion are to be taken as a sign of a thirst for the ideal: "Fashion should thus be considered as a symptom of the taste for the ideal which floats on the surface of all the crude, terrestrial and loathsome bric-à-brac that the natural life accumulates in the human brain" (*Painter*, 31–32). This paradoxical logic allows Baudelaire to strike one of the essential themes of *Le Peintre de la vie moderne*: the revelation of the transcendent in the transitory.

Speaking of fashion leads Baudelaire metonymically to the subject of women and makeup, the heart of his "Eloge du maquillage." If virtue is "surnaturel," then it becomes the woman's duty to make herself up, not to imitate natural beauty or to "heighten" her good features but to appear as artificial as possible:

Woman is quite within her rights, indeed she is even accomplishing a kind of duty, when she devotes herself to appearing magical and supernatural; she has to astonish and charm us; as an idol, she is obliged to adorn herself in order to be adored. Thus she has to lay all the arts under contribution for the means of lifting herself above Nature, the better to conquer hearts and rivet attention. It matters but little that the artifice and trickery are known to all, so long as their success is assured and their effect always irresistible. By reflecting in this way the philosopher-artist will find it easy to justify all the practices adopted by women at all times to consolidate and as it were to make divine their fragile beauty. (*Painter*, 33)

For Baudelaire, then, the woman is at her best by making herself appear "supernatural," and the thoughtful artist might take a page from her issue of *Elle*. In this way, Baudelaire puts a spin not only on the discourse on art and representation summarized by Lichtenstein (by promoting art as artifice against art as truthful representation) but on Christian values as well. Recall the de Maistre passage cited above, which states that the gospel exalts woman is exalted to a "supernatural" state by raising her from her fallen nature. Baudelaire follows de Maistre in accepting woman as carrying forward Eve's original sin but rewrites him by proposing that what raises woman to a supernatural state is her ability to transform her appearance through the illusory magic of dress and makeup. She rises above nature by looking unnatural. Clearly one can correlate this somewhat revisionist version of Christian doctrine (of the redemption of Eve's fallen nature through the arts of Jezebel) with the image of Villiers's future Eve, the ideal supernatural woman, fabricated by a scientific wizard and makeup artist supreme.

In Baudelaire's very particular lexicon, the notion of the supernatural associates the spiritual not only with the artificial, with art in the broad sense, but with modernity as well. In his introduction to the Garnier Frères edition of the *Spleen de Paris*, in a chapter titled "Modernité et surnaturalisme," Henri Lemaitre insists on this aspect of Baudelaire's aesthetic. He quotes the famous reference, also from *Le Peintre de la vie moderne*, to the artist as a man of the crowd, who becomes drunk from his contact with "the fascinating union of the strange and the real" at the heart of the most mundane modernity. Lemaitre continues, "For Baudelaire's modernity is poetic only because curiosity 'spiritualizes' itself as passion and fascination: through the multiple play of fascination, modernity—far from contradicting it—becomes merged with supernaturalism. And the prose poems offer themselves as the concentrated mirror for this supernaturalist modernity's fascinations."[14]

Jean-Paul Sartre proposes as the source of Baudelaire's spiritualistic antinaturalism—of such decisive influence on the symbolists and decadents, as well as on Villiers—not the Christian writings of Joseph de Maistre but the influence of the utopian Saint-Simonian movement, one of many that swept England, France, and America during the nineteenth century. Sartre suggests that around 1848 what he calls the "dream of an anti-nature" came into being as a result of the combined actions of the Saint-Simonians, the positivists, and Marx. He points out the invention of the expression "anti-nature" by Comte and the incidence of the term *antiphysis* in the Marx-Engels correspondence. Thus, while their systems may have differed, both looked to a similar ideal: the creation of a human order that would correct the blind forces and ills endemic to the natural order through the introduction of a new factor, and which distinguished it from Kant's "City of ends," which was also opposed to a strict determinism:

The new factor was work. Man no longer imposed order on the Universe by the pure light of Reason; he did so by work and, oddly enough, by industrial work. The Industrial Revolution of the nineteenth century and the advent of machinism played a far more important part in the origin of this antinaturalism than the obsolete doctrine of grace. Baudelaire was carried away by the movement. True, he was not much interested by the worker; but work interested him because it was like a *thought* imprinted on matter. He was always attracted by the idea that things are thoughts which have been objectified and, as it were, solidified. In this way he could see his own reflection in them.[15]

Sartre no doubt found attractive the idea that Baudelaire was interested in Saint-Simonism and Marxism; how directly he may have paid attention to these movements is questionable. Still, it is undeniable that Baudelaire too felt the disturbing and transforming groundswell of change created in the wake of the Industrial Revolution and that he expressed its influence in his own fashion. This response to industrialism sheds an interesting light on his specific association of modernity with the artificial. Baudelaire invented the modern because he saw it happening around him. Others responded with utopian reformist fervor; he assumed a pose of dandyist ennui.

For Baudelaire, an important element of modernist decor was feminine beauty enhanced by artifice. He begins the last of the three pieces on women in *Le Peintre de la vie moderne*, "Les Femmes et les filles," by saying, "Having taken upon himself the task of seeking out and expounding the beauty in *modernity*, Monsieur G. is thus particularly given to portraying women who are elaborately dressed and embellished by all the rites of artifice, to whatever social station they may belong" (*Painter*, 34). It is their specifically artificial beauty that renders the women drawn by Guys specifically modern. Baudelaire pushes his endorsement of adornment further than a praise of simple makeup. In fact, he prefers the woman to look as unreal as possible. In the section "Eloge du maquillage," he insists that

anyone can see that the use of rice-powder, so stupidly anathematized by our Arcadian philosophers, is successfully designed to rid the complexion of those blemishes that Nature has outrageously strewn there, and thus to create an abstract unity in the colour and texture of the skin, a unity, which, like that produced by the tights of a dancer, immediately approximates the human being to the statue, that is to something superior and divine. (*Painter*, 33)

The appeal Baudelaire affirms in the "abstract unity" that makes a woman appear like a statue is characteristic of his predilection for the cold, the barren, the artificial in all realms. Sartre points out Baudelaire's frequent recourse to "hard, sterile forms of minerals" in his poetry, his preference for the metallic: "For him metal and, in a general way, minerals reflected the image of the mind. . . . Thus Baudelaire's horror of life led him to choose materialization in its purest form as a symbol of the immaterial" (Sartre, 105). One can find a direct echo of this preference for "paradis artificiels" in Villiers's novel, where he depicts an artificial underground garden created by Thomas Edison, a Disneyland of mechanical birds and elegantly factitious blooms. Edison descends with his young visitor to a subterranean hall by means of an "artificial tombstone," and Ewald finds himself beneath a concave vault illuminated by an electric lamp shedding blue light:

The half-circle which formed the rear of the room opposite the entry rose on either side in elegant slopes like gardens; and there, under the caress of an imaginary breeze, swayed thousands of tropical vines and Oriental roses, Polynesian flowers with their petals drenched in perfume, their pistils luminous, their leaves gleaming like green jewels. The allure of this Niagara of flowers was overwhelming. A flock of birds from Florida and the southern states of the Union chattered away throughout this artificial garden; a rainbow of clear colors seemed to rise over this part of the hall, and to radiate beams of light through prisms, from the height of the circular walls to the base of a great alabaster fountain at the center, within which an elegant plume of snowy water rose and fell in glittering drops.[16]

Associated with Baudelaire's affinity for the inorganic is his preference for cold or unconscious women, what Sartre calls Baudelaire's projection of frigidity into the other, his "resorting to artificial methods of refrigeration" with women, as in his seeking out an affair with Marie Daubrun, who adopted the coldest possible manner with him, in preference to more accessible women. Sartre notes his dream of the "frigid angel" evoked in the poem "Une nuit que j'étais près d'une affreuse Juive":

> Je me pris à songer, près de ce corps vendu
> A la triste beauté dont mon désire se prive . . .
> Car j'eusse avec ferveur baisé son noble corps
> Si quelque soir, d'un pleur obtenu sans effort
> Tu pouvais seulement, ô reine des cruelles!
> Obscurcir la splendeur de tes froides prunelles.

[Beside this prostituted body, I began to dream / Of the sorrowful beauty my desire denies itself . . . / For I would have ardently kissed her noble body / If some evening, by an effortless tear, / You had only, cruel queen! / Been able to hide the splendor of your cold pupils.] (Quoted in Sartre, 117)

Baudelaire's preference for icy indifference in women does not stop short of necrophilia, as Sartre points out. Analyzing the fantasy that lay behind *Ivrogne* (documented in "Les Notes d'Asselineau"), where Baudelaire recounts a scene in the proposed work in which a drunkard kills his wife, then violates her body, Sartre comments that

the insensibility, the sterility and the inaccessibility of the frigid woman are interpreted here in their extreme sense and are fully realized: in the end the frigid woman is the corpse. It is in the presence of the corpse that sexual desire assumes its most criminal and its loneliest form. What is more, disgust at this dead flesh will at the same time fill him with a profound sense of the void, will make him more the master of his actions, more artificial and will, so to speak, "cool him down." (Sartre, 127)

The icy absence of the statue or dead woman is related to Baudelaire's project of dandyism (a dandy is, after all, chilled out, a cool guy) and evokes the atmosphere of stasis and death toward which it tends, and which one finds in works of writers influenced by Baudelaire, like Joris-Karl Huysmans's *A rebours*, *L'Eve future*, and Stéphane Mallarmé's *Hérodiade*.

Baudelaire's preoccupation with the woman as frigid statue can be enrolled in the catalog of masochistic fantasies of the fatal woman Praz finds typical of a certain strain of romantic erotic pathology, anticipating or suggesting the symbolist's privileged image of the "cold majesty of the sterile woman." At the same time, it might also remind one of the way Balzac's Sarrasine perceives Zambinella as Pygmalion's statue come to life, of Hoffman's story of Nathanael's passion for the wooden doll Olympia, and of his tale of Antonia, the instrument maker's daughter who becomes herself a violin. One can, in fact, think of the image of the woman as cold statue as a late expression of the literary theme of the automaton.

The *topos* of the artificial woman belongs, in a broad sense, to the tradition of the automaton. In *L'Automate et ses mobiles*, Jean-Claude Beaune traces the automaton back to ancient Greece and Alexandria, to the school of Alexandria and the works of Hero, who wrote a treatise on the operation of a theater of automata, Philo, who wrote on pneumatics, and Ctesibios, who is said to have invented a drinking cup in the form of the Egyptian god Bes that played a trumpet as the wine poured. Beaune also writes of traditions of automata among the medieval Arabs and Chinese, as well as of the appearance of automata in the literature of the European Middle Ages: Lancelot's battle with two bronze warriors; Tristan seeing the animated image of Isolde after his defeat of Moldagogg; Albert the Great's talking human robot, which he destroyed on the advice of Saint Thomas that it was diabolic and blasphemous.[17] One cannot speak of the early history of automata without making reference also to the figure of the Golem, the servant made of clay, and to the efforts of the alchemists to create the "philosopher's son" without the participation of a woman: instead, the alchemist would bury his sperm in a dung heap; the homunculus would emerge, the product of reproduction without sexuality, without contact with the female body.[18]

In seventeenth-century Holland and Italy, gardens of noble houses displayed animated human figures and hydraulic automata. Beaune, who calls the automaton a "metaphysical machine" that occupies the "center of frictions between logical categories" (Beaune, 10),[19] writes that the history of automata took a new turn with the rationalism of Descartes and Leibniz. He examines Descartes's philosophical preoccupation with automata on the one hand and the practical efforts of Leibniz and Pascal to construct calculating machines on the other. Informing all these philosophical uses of the model of the machine is the prestige of the clockwork-mechanism metaphor of the universe that lay close to the surface in this period and affected ideas of social and even political function, as Otto Mayr has demonstrated in *Authority, Liberty and Automatic Machines in Early Modern Europe*.[20] Beaune shows how Descartes used the automaton as a model for his theory of animals as machines as well as for his epistemological reduction of the body to a mechanism. Descartes had been since his youth fascinated with automata and had dreamed of constructing fantastic machines.

From the time of his *Experimenta*, Descartes had employed automata and the illusions they create as images in his writing. Descartes sought to ground his double dualism of man/animal and soul/body in the heuristic model that the simplicity of the automaton provided. Speaking about how the "animal spirits" become distributed to parts of the body, making them able to move "without being guided by the will," Descartes goes on to say,

This will not seem at all strange to those who know how many kinds of automata, or moving machines, the skill of man can construct with the use of very few parts, in comparison with the great multitude of bones, muscles, nerves, arteries, veins and all the other parts that are in the body of any animal.

For they will regard this body as a machine which, having been made by the hand of God, is in incomparably better order than any machine that can be devised by man, and contains in itself movements more wonderful than those in any such machine.[21]

Beaune stresses another such passage to the effect that the body is like a machine:

I suppose that the body is nothing other than a statue or machine made of earth that God forms on purpose in order to render it as similar to us as possible; so that not only does he give it outwardly the color and the shape of our limbs, but he also places inwardly all the necessary parts such that [this statue or machine] can walk, eat, breathe, and finally, imitate all those of our functions that can be imagined as proceeding from matter and not depending on anything but the placement of the organs. (Quoted in Beaune, 184–85)

An even stronger vision of the human body as functioning according to the mechanical principles of automata can be seen in the following passage from Descartes's *Traité de l'homme*:

You will have seen how, in the grottos and fountains found in the gardens of our kings, the force created by the water alone as it emerges from the spring is enough to give movement to various machines and even to make them play instruments or speak words, according to the particular placement of the pipes into which it feeds. And truly, one could quite easily compare the nerves of the machine I am describing to you to the pipes of these water machines; its muscles and its tendons to the various other springs and engines that serve to move them; the heart is, then, the spring, and the hollows of the brain are the glances. (Quoted in Beaune, 185)

For Descartes, then, automata can resemble human beings, while humans may seem like automata. Elsewhere, Descartes remarks that the people he sees "passing in the street might, under their cloaks and hats, be nothing more than automata" (quoted in Beaune, 10). If Descartes considered animals as machines, while making use of mechanical imagery to create an epistemologically convenient model of the functioning of the body, his follower, Julien Offroy de la Mettrie, took this model to its materialist limit in his *L'Homme-Machine*, where he compares man, as the title suggests, to a machine. The prestige of the mechanistic Cartesian model has been, of course, far reaching and has persistently affected ways of thinking of the body, remaining implicit beneath modern images of robots and androids.

An example of the persistence of this mechanical model of the body with a definite misogynist cast occurs in a passage Beaune points out from Stendhal's *Le Rouge et le noir*, in which M. de Renal says of his wife, who is unwell, "There is always something going wrong with these complicated machines" (quoted in Beaune, 9). Similarly, Condillac's famous statue is in a certain sense a philosophical descendant of the statue described by Descartes. Annette Michelson, in fact, speaks of Villiers's Android as a "philosophical toy" based on Condillac's statue, as we will see later. In fact, the Cartesian problematic of mind and mechanics continues to have some force in the context of contemporary arguments, as may be seen in the philosopher Keith Gunderson's recourse to an analysis of Descartes's arguments in his discussion of the logic behind the arguments for artificial intelligence.[22]

The above reference from Descartes to words spoken by automata reflects the rage in the seventeenth and eighteenth centuries for automata that could make music and imitate speech. Advances in the watchmaker's art paved the way for a number of mechanical musical instruments of all kinds. These were sometimes adorned with human heads whose movements could be regulated with the expulsion of air, as in the giant statue of Saint Pierre that blessed the people from above the organ at the cathedral at Beauvais, or the Saint Cecilia created by Gallmayr in 1753 that was agitated by the pedals of the organ. At about the same time Jacques de Vaucanson, Pierre Jaquet-Droz, and Henri Maillardet made automata that actually played their instruments. Jaquet-Droz's elegant clockwork harpsichordist, draftsman, and writing child have been restored several times and still exist.

There was also the hope of making automata that would imitate speech. A contemporary of Descartes, the scientist and musician Marin Mersenne, attempted to categorize the sound elements that make up vowels, and sought, with Leibniz, to develop a form of universal writing. He also dreamed of developing a machine that could produce these sounds, a miniaturized orchestra in the form of a pocket-organ. In 1635, he wrote:

I am now working on finding a way to make organ pipes pronounce syllables. I have already come across the vowels "a," "e," "o" and "u," but "i" is giving me a lot of trouble, but then I have found the syllables "vê" and "fê." . . . I am now trying to make an organ which one could carry anywhere in one's pocket; I will see if this can work, but it requires five keyboards to make the pipes speak such that one can make the four upper parts. And if one adds the play of viols and lutes, which is easy, then one will have a panharmonic that contains everything. (Quoted in Beaune, 165–66)

Although Mersenne did not succeed in his efforts to invent a kind of Walkman, the dream did not go away and was taken up with more success several centuries later by Charles Cros and Thomas Edison. Other attempts to develop technical correspondences to vowels were made by the Abbé Mical, C. G. von Kratzenstein, and Wolfgang von Kempelen in the eighteenth century. The latter took the prize offered by the Academy at Saint Petersburg in 1779 for Kempelen's Talking Head, a machine that perfectly pronounced the word "exploitation." Disembodied talking heads will reappear in our text in a later connection.

Kempelen was also the creator of the famous Turk: a supposedly mechanical chess player that toured the courts of Europe, baffling all, first in Kempelen's hands, then in those of Johann-Nepomuk Maelzel and other later owners, participants in a secret shared at a high price. Many suspected but were unable to see the system of mirrors that concealed a small man inside the Turk (a homunculus, as it were). Edgar Allan Poe was among those who examined the chess player, animated during his time by one Schlumberger, who was often seen around the Turk but who professed a total ignorance of chess. Poe wrote a well-known article called "Maelzel's Chess Player," published in the *Southern Literary Messenger* in 1836, in which he concluded that the Turk must not be a real machine because of Maelzel's refusal to claim outright that it was. He also thought that if it were a real machine, it would always win, which it did not. Poe's interest in the chess player is interesting in the light of his well-known influence on Villiers.

The artificial woman has had a long history of her own. Classicists are familiar with the tradition of the false Helen sent to Troy, the real Helen to Egypt. In her article "Le Fantôme de la sexualité," speaking of Helen's slippery status as object of desire, of Helen as lack or mirage, Nicole Loraux evokes the references to Helen doubled by an *eidôlon* in the poetry of Stesichorus and in Euripides' *Helen*, where she is called a *mimèma*, imitation, and an *agalma*, a jeweled treasure in the form of a statue.[23] The familiar tale of Pygmalion itself centers on a sculptor who falls in love with the statue he has created (a theme dressed in modern garb by George Bernard Shaw in *Pygmalion*, itself to become *My Fair Lady*).

A reverse Pygmalion theme emerges in the eighteenth century in an early work of Jean Paul, *Simple, yet well-intended biography of a new and pleasing woman of pure wood, whom I long ago fashioned and married*. Klaus Theweleit writes that Jean Paul "had no trouble explaining in detail why nothing would be lost if flesh-and-blood women were replaced by wooden ones. What would the real difference be, after all?"[24] Hoffman's wind-up doll Olympia, of course, bears kinship with both Jean Paul's wooden woman and the perfected model of the artificial woman conceived by Villiers de l'Isle-Adam. Interestingly, one of the early uses made of the phonograph was as a voice for a series of talking dolls in whose manufacture Edison was induced to participate. Although these nineteenth-century Chatty Cathy dolls didn't catch on, they were known in Europe, since the English enthusiastically exploited this idea, which had its moment roughly at the same time as Villiers's writing of *L'Eve future*.

Images of automata have been shown by Lieselotte Sauer to be central to the problems of German romanticism. Sauer demonstrates how the essentially optimistic metaphor of the machine widespread among post-Renaissance and Enlightenment philosophical writers undergoes a shift in romantic literature to become a negative literary image. In German literature, the motif emerges in numerous literary texts by Jean Paul, Clemens Brenanto, Achim von Arnim, Hoffman, and others, while in English literature, Sauer finds it appearing mainly in metaphoric terms, as in Mary Shelley's *Frankenstein*, as well as in works by authors such as Ambrose Bierce, Edward Bulwer-Lytton, Samuel Butler, and others. Sauer argues that these texts show an ambivalent response to the Industrial Revolution and that in them "the central problems and questions of romanticism are touched upon in the context of metaphors and motifs connected with artificial man."[25]

The image of the artificial woman that emerges in French writing may be seen in part as reflecting the influence of German romantic imagery, or perhaps more accurately, as expressing some of the same uneasy responses to the technological transformations taking place during the period. At the same time, this image fuses with the motif of the fatal woman that Praz argues to be a major topos of romantic erotic pathology in his chapter "La Belle Dame sans Merci" in *The Romantic Agony*. Praz shows that while the romantic imagery of the first decades of the period was dominated largely by passive, suffering women and their cruel persecutors, latter-day sons of "the Divine Marquis," a shift took place that reversed these roles toward the middle of the century:

The function of the flame which attracts and burns is exercised, in the first half of the century, by the Fatal Man (the Byronic hero), in the second half by the Fatal Woman; the moth destined for sacrifice is in the first case the woman, in the second the man. It is not simply a case of convention and literary fashion: literature even in its most artificial forms reflects to some extent aspects of contemporary life. It is curious to follow the parabola of the sexes during the nineteenth century: the obsession for the androgyne type towards the end of the century is a clear indication of a turbid confusion of function and ideal. The male, who at first tends towards sadism, inclines, at the end of the century, towards masochism. (Praz, 216)

Praz follows this summary of his argument with an extended analysis of the fatal woman image in the works of Gautier, Flaubert, and Algernon Swinburne. Among the examples Praz gives are Gautier's

Cleopatra in "Une Nuit de Cleopatra," who kills her lover, like a praying mantis; his bloodthirsty Nyssia in "Le Roi Candaule"; Flaubert's demonic and serpentlike courtesan Marie in *Novembre*; Moreau's Helen; Swinburne's cold Mary Stuart in *Chastelard*; and his vampire woman, Faustine. The type of the sexually cannibalistic woman is characteristic of the period and culminates in the figures of Herodias and Salome near the end of the century. Writing of the frequent use of Salome as a figure of the cruel "lynx-eyed" enchantress in numerous texts, Praz notes the dominance of this type in the series of novels called *Cruel Women* by Sacher-Masoch, who "gave his name to the sexual tendency illustrated in this chapter" (Praz, 300, n. 120).

If these women are cast as feral, demonic, or vampiristic, demanding the submission of hapless young lovers to their insatiable and bloody passions, they also are called cold, statuelike in their pallor and cruel indifference in a way that recalls Helen, the jeweled *agalma*, or the female automaton: when Gyges begs release from Nyssia's order to kill her husband, Gautier describes her thus: "The hand holding that of Gyges was cool, delicate and soft; yet those slender fingers squeezed hard enough to bruise it, just as the fingers of a bronze statue animated by some marvel could do" (quoted in Praz, 218). Praz points out the similarity of this image with Prosper Mérimée's *Venus d'Ille*, who "suffocated in her arms of bronze the young bridegroom, who—according to an old legend of the Middle Ages—had committed the imprudence of placing a wedding ring on her finger" (Praz, 218). Another such comparison of the femme fatale with an automaton may be seen in Swinburne's Faustine, who, like his ghostly Venus (*Laus Veneris*), is eternal, a frightening "love-machine with clockwork joints of supple gold" made for the destruction of her lovers (Praz, 240). Other characterizations of the fatal woman portray her as frighteningly pallid, like a statue (like Balzac's Jane la Pâle), or beautiful and dead (like Very, seven years dead, in Heinrich Heine's "Florentine Night") (*Salon*, iii). The attraction of necrophilic amours closes the circle back to Baudelaire.

Kermode treats some related material in *Romantic Image* where he discusses the motif of the masklike dead face of the dancer. He places it, however, in the different context of the romantic artist's effort to forge a defining figure for the poetic image. In the chapter "The Dancer," Kermode studies the symbolic importance of a certain type of self-contained feminine beauty for W. B. Yeats and other late romantic poets. Women—like artworks—should not "think" but be beautiful. In the citation Kermode offers from Yeats to support his argument, one sees an echo of the motif of woman as statue, as a spiritually remote or absent but artistically constructed object:

The body of a beautiful woman is a constant element in the emblematic equivalents Yeats finds for the symbol, the Romantic Image. Writing, in the 'twenties, of Maud Gonne, he said, "her face, fused, unified and solitary, the face of some Greek statue, showed little thought, her whole body seemed a masterwork of labouring thought, as though a Scopas had measured and calculated, consorted with Egyptian sages, and mathematicians out of Babylon." (Kermode, 55)

In Kermode's terms, the beauty of a woman thus becomes an emblem for the work of art, or "Image." In particular, the figure of a woman in movement, a dancer, takes on this symbolic aspect in Yeats, Walter Pater, and others.

Kermode extends his discussion through an examination of the cult of the woman with a "dead" or masklike face in John Keats, D. G. Rossetti, Pater, and Yeats, typified by Pater's influential piece on the "Mona Lisa" where he calls her the "symbol of the modern idea" (quoted in Kermode, 67). For the decadents, the figure of the enigmatic dancer exerted a special fascination, turning up in Huysmans, Moreau, and Oscar Wilde: Kermode points out that Moreau's painting of Salome dancing ("her face closed, solemn, almost august") is the focus of a detailed description in *A rebours* and that Des Esseintes contemplates the same painting later, Mallarmé's *Hérodiade* open in front of him. The passage offers an evocation of the pathological fascination of the dancer motif fused with a manifesto of symbolist art.

In the course of his discussion of the special importance of the dancing Salome as an emblem for the costs of art, Kermode recounts the following anecdote:

When Richard Strauss heard Elisabeth Schumann sing, he expressed a great desire to hear her in the role of Salome; and when she protested the apparently obvious unsuitability of her voice, he explained that what the part needed was not some heroic soprano . . . but precisely the transparent, even girlish quality of her tone. Unhappily nothing came of the proposal, but it seems clear that Strauss was not talking eccentrically, and that he had recognized in Mme. Schumann's voice the possibility of her achieving some vocal equivalent for that unemotional, disengaged quality—Yeats's word might be "uncommitted"—which Wilde gave his Salome, and which, despite the ridicule of critics, was fundamental to his conception of her. There should be an innocent, totally destructive malice; beauty inhumanly immature and careless cruelty. That is the type. (Kermode, 74).

Kermode goes on to show the connection between the vitality of the Salome emblem and the masked, inhuman women in certain of Yeats's Noh-inspired plays (*At the Hawk's Well, The Only Jealousy of Emer*). To conclude, he calls the concept of the dead face and the dancer the central icon of Yeats and of the whole romantic tradition he has surveyed.

   This anecdote provides an interesting point of convergence between the image of the dancer with a dead face as Kermode describes her and the motif of the inhuman singer. It may be useful to remember that dance during the nineteenth century had developed into a highly artificial, stylized form, and it is interesting that at that time, operas were performed with popular balletic intermezzi between the acts. The topos of the fatal woman, icy, cruel, and statuelike, that Praz shows to be dominant in romantic texts, and that of the remote dancer Kermode argues to be emblematic of late romantic and symbolist aesthetic theory are both affiliated with the new valuation of artificiality as a defining term of modernity first given form by Baudelaire in the influential writings discussed above.

   Just as the painted woman earlier served as a metaphor for an undesirable visibility of the artistic gesture of representation, after Baudelaire, the woman posed as artificial, as inhuman singer or dancer, became a figure for art as a modern, willed construction. In certain of the texts Praz and Kermode cite, a secondary sense of her as a diabolically clever artistic construction emerges at times, a motif that comes to the fore in the Villiers novel to which we will next turn our attention. Within the image of the inhumanly cold woman appears as well the features of the automaton, a figure of long tradition brought forward with a new uneasiness in German romantic texts. In Villiers's novel, all these elements are framed with the modern seductions and terrors offered by technological wonders. The inhuman woman of the romantics is thus a hypostasis of self-reflective images of masochistic romantic sexual pathology, of its aesthetic theory with its newly valued art for art's sake, and finally, of the ancient dream—or nightmare—of an uncanny artificial being: Helen as jeweled statue.

Edison's Recorded Angel

"I offer you, myself, a venture into the ARTIFICIAL and its untasted delights!" This curious proposition is made by a fictionalized Thomas Edison to the despairing Lord Ewald in Villiers de l'Isle-Adam's 1886 novel *L'Eve future*. What "Edison" is offering to his young friend is an artificial woman. A perfect copy of Ewald's beautiful but vulgar fiancée, the Android will substitute for her as the Eve of an ambiguous technological paradise.

Because of its remarkable staging of the female body as a spectacle, fusing as it does certain traditional misogynist themes with concerns about technology that link it to the next century, *L'Eve future* has in recent years lent itself to some interesting critical studies, such as those by Annette Michelson and Raymond Bellour. Michelson explores the connection between Villiers's novel and previous traditions of the representation of women in her piece "On the Eve of the Future: The Reasonable Facsimile and the Philosophical Toy," where she elaborates the parallels between Villiers's Android and the erotic detailing of women in the poetry of Fontainebleau, Clemente Susini's anatomical "Venus," and Condillac's statue.[1] Bellour's study in *Camera Obscura* reads the text in terms of his hypnosis model of the cinema.[2] Neither of these discussions, however, considers one of the novel's most interesting features: the striking predominance of the voice in the text and the accompanying foregrounding of the phonograph as instrument of technological and social transformation. If one follows the text's own emphasis and considers the phonograph, not the cinema, as the key to the novel, then the aptness of Villiers's choice of Edison as presiding genius becomes clear: it was when his name became associated with the phonograph, "the Miracle of the Nineteenth Century," that the prolific inventor Edison became known worldwide as the Faustian inventor of a new era. The importance of the phonograph in Villiers's novel reveals much about its role in the history of the times and about the cultural reception of technological innovation. One also gains a better understanding of the nature of the Android if one sees the significance of the phonograph as paradigmatic of her equivocal being: her paradoxical status as the artificially incarnated bearer of a disembodied voice.

Villiers's *L'Eve future* is haunted by disembodied voices. The text is structured largely through extended dialogues between Edison and Ewald about Woman and her several representatives in the text (Alicia Clary, the mistress, Hadaly, Sowana, and Miss Evelyn Habal, a revolting prostitute) and long metaphysical passages attributed to Edison as soliloquies. The spoken voice, however, is foregrounded in a myriad of other ways in the text and circulates through it prominently.

The book begins with an evocation of Thomas Edison as the inventor of the phonograph, the machine that separated the human voice from the body. Villiers identifies Edison primarily and repeatedly as the creator of the phonograph, rather than, for instance, as the inventor of the incandescent light bulb (which Edison interrupted his first round of work on the phonograph to perfect). Villiers opens his novel by describing Edison's residence in New York: "This is Number One Menlo Park; and here dwells Thomas Alva Edison, the man who made a prisoner of the echo."[3] The second chapter of the book is titled in English as "Phonograph's Papa."

In the first chapters of the novel, Villiers shows the reader the solitary Edison reflecting alone, or speaking, Prospero-like, with voices summoned like spirits; thus Villiers presents him as the Faustian "Wizard of Menlo Park." Other characters first appear in Edison's study as detached voices heard through such Edisonian apparatuses as microphones and telephones. At the close of section 3, the voice of a young woman interrupts Edison's extended meditation on the phonograph, which constitutes the initial part of the book: "Suddenly a soft whisper, the voice of a young woman murmuring very gently, was heard close by—Edison?" (*Eve*, 11). The next section introduces this character, Sowana. She speaks to Edison about Hadaly, establishing a metonymic link that will eventually shade into a kind of identity. The passage extends the sense of mystery about this voice that seems to come from nowhere: "The voice of the being called Sowana—laughing over its last word—seemed to come, always quietly and discreetly, from a pillar supporting the violet curtains. In fact it was a sounding box and reverberated in response to distant whispers carried by electricity—one of those new condensers, invented barely yesterday, by which the individual syllables and tone of the voice are distinctly transmitted" (*Eve*, 12).

The voice of Villiers's otherworldly, Ligeia-like character Sowana, suspended in a hypnotic sleep, ushers in an atmosphere of mystery not meant to be dispelled by the disclosure that an electrical apparatus is the secret to her absent presence, for in Villiers's novel science becomes suffused with and eventually becomes the marvelous. Sowana's speech here in turn introduces the Android, speaking of "her" as if she were a sleeping girl. Sowana eventually transports her spirit supernaturally into the shell of the Android's body, as she here transmits her voice electrically. One of the final images of the novel is of Sowana's corpse lying on her couch, in her dead hand the "electrophone" that served as her medium of transcendence.

After several sections in which Edison resumes his reflections about the phonograph, the next human voices with whom Edison converses are likewise brought into the room by artificial means: first that of his assistant Martin, to whom he speaks through a phonograph hooked to a "telephone"; then that of one of his children, whose voice he hears transmitted from elsewhere as if coming from a piece of furniture. When Lord Ewald appears in chapter 11, he, too, is introduced as a voice detached from a body (obscured behind a door). The embedding of these conversations in Edison's soliloquy on the novelty and power of his invention foregrounds both it and the voice which the phonograph (along with the telephone, microphone, and megaphone) newly isolated at that historical moment.

Edison's meditation on history and its moments of greatness lost in time extends through seven of the brief initial chapters of the book.

He daydreams about what he could have recorded had he been present at the beginning of time, now that his "cylinder" can collect "sound waves from a distance." His reflections resonate with the book's title, announcing the themes of Edison's Promethean or Faustian ambitions, ironically renounced, to record the voice of God at creation: "We needn't pretend to that life-creating cliché, *Fiat lux!*, a phrase coined approximately seventy-two centuries ago (and which besides, according to immemorial tradition—perhaps invented, perhaps not—could never have been picked up by any recording machine)" (*Eve*, 9).

After reflecting on Eden, Edison passes to the "Oracles of Dodona" and the "chants of the Sibyls," evoking all the "important speeches of men and gods." Edison regrets those mythical or historical moments that founded the world and have been forever lost. Villiers puts into Edison's speech a view of the passage of time and history as *sound*: "Dead voices, lost sounds, forgotten noises, vibrations lockstepping into the abyss, and now too distant ever to be recaptured! . . . What sort of arrows would be able to transfix such birds?" (*Eve*, 10). He wishes to capture even the unheard, or the unhearable, the Fall of Rome, treating literally the cliché of the voice of the conscience and punning (untranslatably) on the name of the Milky Way, the *Voie [voix] lactée.*

This fantasy kindled by the capacity of the phonograph to evoke *dead voices* offers in condensed form a sense of the phonograph's potent appeal to the imaginations of Villiers and his contemporaries: the miraculous capacity to preserve the human voice, which always had seemed to be utterly fleeting by nature, compounded of duration, sound, and human presence, all bound to time's arrow and extinguished in its passage. The phonograph can thus be seen as a Proustian machine, a precursor and analogue to the project that would be *A la recherche du temps perdu*: a disembodied voice that brings back the past. As Jacques Perriault writes in his *Mémoires de l'ombre et du son*, a study of the inventions that led to film and recording, "This is actually the first technology that seeks actively to cast out death: it allows us to keep a living memory of those who have passed away, that of their voices. The astonishment at the freshness of the preserved voice a month or a year after its recording, comes, to my way of thinking, from the same certain unconscious anxiety."[4] Perriault is referring to an article published in the *Semaine du clergé* in 1877, the year of the invention of the phonograph, explaining the nature of this new instrument as a "casting out of death." The phonograph thus promised its astonished hearers a way to cheat time and death.

In 1874 Villiers published a piece that seems to have given form to a version of this dream, before the advent of the phonograph. Entitled "Appareil pour l'analyse chimique du dernier soupir,"[5] it was a sketch for what became "La Machine à gloire" (another story whose premise is a machine, this one for producing canned applause in a theater). "L'Appareil" is a fantasy advertisement for a new invention that would spare the heirs the trouble and pain of grieving personally at the deathbed of a loved one, allowing them to capture his dying breath and preserve it scientifically in a luxurious little box: "the soul is at the bottom!"[6] Playing on the ancient association of life with breath, the piece anticipates the theme of the recorded voice as soul in *L'Eve future*.

Villiers may have been influenced by Charles Cros's story "La Science de l'amour" (also from 1874), which features an apparatus built to measure amorous intensity. Cros may also have suggested the conception of *L'Eve future* through his piece in verse called "La Machine à changer le caractère des femmes," performed in 1875 at Nina de Villard's salon. In this humorous skit, grumpy, unpleasant types would enter a kind of booth and exit sweet tempered: the "machine" in question was merely a screen behind which the characters ducked to drink champagne. Finally, Cros's name must be evoked in association with Villiers's novel since he was himself one of the inventors of the phonograph. Cros had conceived of the phonograph at around the same time as Edison, but having no money he was only able to deposit a written description of his idea with the French Academy of Science—three months before Edison went public with his invention in the fall of 1877.

Paul Charbon writes in *La Machine parlante* that Cros, like Alexander Graham Bell, had become interested in the mechanisms of sense perceptions through his work with the deaf. In a kind of extension of Cartesianism, Cros seems to have become absorbed in thinking of sense perception as mechanical. Noting that the sense organs are by nature "veiled," he turned to the idea of using "kinetic models" to reproduce the effects of sense perceptions on people. In 1871, he describes a "vision machine" and imagines a "hearing machine." Charbon states that it was "a thought process that sought to 'mechanize' human perceptual systems"[7] that led Cros to his version of the phonograph. In 1879, he constructed a battery intended to demonstrate the absolute identity between electrical current and the phenomena of the human nervous system. Villiers was evidently aware of Cros's work to make physical traces of the voice and responded to this conception of the materiality of the voice.

The desire to make a material record of the voice is an endeavor characteristic of the nineteenth century, with its passion for documentation and analysis. While experiments in several fields eventually united to realize the phonograph, the *desire* to have such a thing fueled its invention, for as Perriault remarks, the concept of the phonograph preceded its construction. Before it existed, people longed for something like it. As early as 1856, the photographer F. Nadar was already dreaming of the phonograph in fairly specific terms, in a form modeled, however, on photography: "Everything is now possible, and I have not the slightest doubt in the world that an inventor might present tomorrow, for example, to the Academy of Sciences something like an ACOUSTIC DAGUERREOTYPE, that would reproduce as faithfully as you like any sound submitted to its objectivity. Haven't you often dreamed, as I have, of that instrument whose need is so generally felt?"[8] Nadar wrote this passage in 1856, some twenty years before Charles Cros did exactly what he had imagined, by submitting his idea for a "paleophone" to the Academy. The word "phonograph" itself crops up in an article by Nadar dated some eight years after the passage quoted above, in which Nadar imagines a family listening to a recording of an opera they had been unable to attend.

I amused myself, some fifteen years ago while daydreaming, by writing in an obscure corner (it was probably in the *Musée franco-anglais*) that one must not put anything beyond man, and that one of these days someone would show up to bring us the Daguerreotype of Sound—the phonograph—something like a box in which melodies would be fixed and retained, just as the black box surprises and fixes images.—So that a family, I suppose, unable to attend the premier of the *Force of Destiny* or [some other opera] would only have to deputize one of its members, armed with the phonograph in question. And on his return:—How did the overture go?—Here it is!—It's very good. And what about the finale of the first act, so talked about in advance?— There!—And the quintet?—Here you are. Marvelous. But don't you think the tenor screams a little too much?[9]

This fantasy was shared by Stendhal, who years earlier dreamed of a way of obtaining perfect "portraits" of singers to preserve their art: operatic pleasure is linked to a yearning to record the voice.

As Nadar put it, it was an age in which all seemed possible. The notion that the human voice could be captured may be seen as one of the offspring of scientific positivism that transformed the latter years of the nineteenth century, a time when technological marvels of all kinds were appearing on the scene: photography, the telegraph, electricity, eventually the electric light. The quantification of the world demanded by positivism led to increasingly rigorous and radical technological endeavors. Yet this was also the period of credulous beliefs in such "scientific" experiments as spirit photography and earnest attempts to calculate the substance of the soul by weighing the newly dead: in the sweep of the desire to render the immaterial material, the unseen seen, the boundaries between science and scientism were often blurred. Kittler points out the relationship between the invention of telegraphy and the fashion of table turning:

And the tapping specters of the spiritistic séances, with their messages from the realm of the dead, appeared quite promptly at the moment of the invention of the Morse alphabet in 1837. Promptly, photographic plates—even and especially with the camera shutter closed—provided images of ghosts or specters which, in their black-and-white fuzziness, only emphasized the moments of resemblance. Finally, one of the ten uses Edison predicted (in 1878, in the *North American Review*) for the recently invented phonograph was to preserve the "last words of the dying."[10]

This fusing of the scientific with the scientistic, the interest in spiritual phenomena and the supernatural, is characteristic of the period; Villiers's own scornful fascination with technology appears in this light as representative of an ambivalence and confusion shared by many of his contemporaries about the inventions of the phonograph and the cinema. Kittler interprets these new forms that can store and reproduce acoustic and visual data—and with them, time—in terms of writing:

Ear and eye have become autonomous. . . . What was new about the storage capability of the phonograph and cinematograph—and both names refer, not accidentally, to writing—was their ability to store time: as a mixture of audio frequencies in the acoustic realm, as a movement of single picture sequences in the optic realm. Time, however, is what determines the limits of all art. The quotidian data flow must be arrested before it can become image or sign. . . . Texts and scores were Europe's only means to store time. Both are based on writing; the time of this writing is symbolic (in Lacan's terms). This time memorizes itself in terms of projections and retrievals—like a chain of chains. Nevertheless, whatever runs as time on a physical or (again in Lacan's terms) real level, blindly and unpredictably, could by no means be encoded. Therefore all data flows, if they were real streams of data, had to pass through the defile of the signifier. Alphabetic monopoly, grammatology.[11]

Kittler's discussion of the invention of the phonograph places it within his larger argument about the turn to an intensified materiality of the "discourse network of 1900" effected by these turn-of-the-century technologies.

Such an emphasis on the phonograph's tie to writing is supported by its prehistory because, curiously enough, one path to the phonograph led through writing, ordinary writing. Perriault's account of the chain of research and invention that produced the phonograph shows that it resulted on the one hand from the meeting of the telegraph and electricity, and on the other from a line of development stemming from attempts to capture sound as writing.

The phonautograph was one outcome of researches conducted by Léon Scott on a means of transcribing the human voice into an inked line, a "series of signs" on material wrapped around a cylinder. With a mechanic named Rudolph Koening, Scott constructed the phonautograph, which consisted of a horn that ended in a sensitive membrane on which a stylus, agitated by the human voice, made a mark, a continuous line. Charbon notes that the physician F. C. Donders used a phonautograph to record the "voice" of Henry Sweet, the linguist who served as the model for Shaw's *Pygmalion*. The concept of a natural stenography of the voice stymied certain attempts to progress on these lines, but the elements of the apparatus—horn, stylus, cylinder—provided the nucleus of what would eventually become Edison's phonograph.

Another line of work led to the phonograph from a different kind of writing—the telegraph—through the telephone. The development of each led to the next: in the mid-1870's, Alexander Graham Bell, a teacher of vocal physiology who married a deaf woman, was researching ways of using the telegraph to transmit the voice. He developed a telegraph system that would use electrical current to produce a vibration on a membrane, doing on a wire what the voice does through the air, thus stumbling on the basic principle of the telephone. Bell's invention was improved through the work of Elisha Gray, Comte Théodore du Moncel, and Thomas Edison—himself hard of hearing.

Edison invented the phonograph as a by-product of his attempts to create a repeating telephone, a kind of early phone-answering machine, that would record and relay telephonic messages. During the course of his work on the telegraph, he had noticed that paper soaked in paraffin would clearly retain the imprint of a needle. He replaced the paper with sheets of copper or other metals. Like the Native Americans, he had also noticed that the telegraph "sang."

Perriault observes that Edison, absorbed in the theory of the telephone, became involved with the storage and reproduction of the human voice without fully realizing what he was onto. Initially (in July 1877), he still sought to improve the telegraph, but by November 1877, Edison had filed his patent for a design of a functional phonograph, a device to record and reproduce the human voice.

The idea of an artificial production of the voice was, moreover, once again in the air, several centuries after Mersenne and Kempelen had worked on similar projects. Edison became involved at the same time in a project with George Baker, a professor at the University of Pennsylvania, to produce vowels mechanically. A number of French scientists were involved as well in the problem of a synthetic production of vowels, a project that dates back to the seventeenth century. Edison was interested in the work of one of them, Dr. René Marage, who created a pneumatic apparatus designed to emit vowel sounds. This path led nowhere, but it shows something of the fertile atmosphere of investigation of ideas for distilling, projecting, magnifying that newly isolable commodity, the voice.

In fact, there were some quite astonishing experiments, by our conception of the times, conducted during the period when the phonograph was being worked out. Perriault describes efforts made in the 1880's to transmit the voice stereophonically to people at the Opera listening with earphones to concerts played over a telephone system, a diversion not uncommon at the time. Another such experiment was the "photophone," an effort to transmit the voice using light rays. This didn't work only because they needed a kind of ray that wasn't within their reach at the time: the laser. There was also the "motophone," a long-distance phonograph, as well as Edison's attempt to transmit images through the telephone using the sensitive properties of selenium. A final curiosity was the suggestion Eadweard Muybridge made to Edison in 1888 that they collaborate to join the phonograph to the image to create a talking image. This idea did not come to immediate fruition, although Edison was definitely interested himself in combining the young cinema with the phonograph. In fact, he wanted to film opera but was unable to coordinate sound with moving images: the technical means were simply lacking.

On the other end of the spectrum is the line of talking dolls that Edison and his collaborators developed and began to seek markets for in 1887, close to the time *L'Eve future* was published. Perhaps Edison was himself a source for Villiers's idea for an android: Perriault reports that in 1877 Edison had constructed a voice-activated mechanical doll for his daughter. It was based on a mechanism that employed a funnel to channel the sound of a yell into a vibrating diaphragm, which turned a gear and a pulley to make a little man saw wood. According to Perriault this toy created a furor in France in 1877 and 1878: numerous contemporary accounts feature explanations of Edison coming on his idea by talking through his hat. Thus, Edison was early associated in the public mind with voice and mechanical dolls, and the French were aware of Edison's work on the phonograph at that time.

In a novel whose protagonist is a fictional version of the inventor of the phonograph, it is not surprising that the human voice should be privileged, nor that in its female characters the voice should be of primary importance: Alicia Clary, the model for the Android, is a singer, and Hadaly's own voice takes on special significance in the text since she *is*, essentially, a phonograph. The relay of women who compose the Android are brought together in her as voice. A key element of Alicia Clary's beauty is the quality of her voice, and it is that as much as her physical form that is taken from her to create a perfect copy. When Ewald first describes his mistress to Edison, he begins with the harmony of her overall appearance, including her resemblance to the Venus de Milo, and catalogs her individual attributes: her hair, the shape of her face, her mouth, her hands. He begins with the qualities most closely associated with her individuality, her eyes, her perfume, building to and closing with the quality of her voice: " 'When she speaks, the resonance of Miss Alicia's voice is so penetrating, the notes of her singing are so vibrant and so profound, that whether she is reciting a tragic passage in noble verses or singing some magnificent aria, I am always amazed to find myself trembling with an admiration the like of which, as you shall see, I've never known before [*d'un ordre inconnu*]' " (*Eve*, 30).

The beauty of Alicia's voice is a promise at once of erotic bliss and transcendent spirituality: Ewald's horror of his predicament derives from his sense of an absolute discrepancy between the angelic promise of Alicia's beauty and his judgment of her as mediocre. Her unforgivable failing is to be an ordinary woman—one with some personal ambition as a singer—instead of an angel. Edison's gift to Ewald is an artificial angel to replace the disappointingly real woman: "In a word, the present gorgeous little fool will no longer be a woman, but an angel; no longer a mistress but a lover; no longer reality, but the IDEAL!" (*Eve*, 54). To evoke the happiness his mechanical angel will bring to Ewald, wandering with him like a mysterious sleepwalker in the solitude of his own estate, Edison describes his pleasure when Hadaly sings for him: " 'There her angelic singing, in that voice which is dear to you, accompanied by the organ or whenever you choose by a splendid American piano, will spread through the majestic autumn evenings, rising above the whispering of the breeze. Her accents will deepen the charm of summer evenings and explode across the beauty of the dawn, mingled with the song of the birds' " (*Eve*, 78). The hauntingly beautiful voice of the Android will blend a seductive feminine charm with the strange fascination of a transcendently inhuman being.

Basic to the novel is the contradiction implied in Ewald's desire for a woman he knows to be artificial (like the fetishist as O. Mannoni describes him, he "knows," yet does not know: his desire is ruled by bad faith, for he desires an object he knows to be false). The paradox that creates the condition for his surrender develops from the conflation of voice and being implied by Sowana's curious act of spiritual ventriloquism as she animates the form of Hadaly, thus endowing her with a supernatural presence. Villiers's essential hostility to positivism emerges in this replacement of Hadaly as scientific artifact with Hadaly as angelic being of mystery, the artificially incarnated bearer of a voice that animates the Android with a disembodied supernatural presence.

In the fetishistic vision of the ideal woman as android/phonograph, one may recognize certain essential similarities to the erotic fantasy of a contemporary of Villiers de l'Isle-Adam, Sacher-Masoch in his *Venus in Furs*. In his *Présentation de Sacher-Masoch*, Deleuze stresses the importance of spoken rituals between the "cruel" Wanda and her "submissive" victim and draws a comparison with Sade:

It seems that, for Masoch as for Sade, language assumes its full value in acting directly on sensuality. Sade's *The One Hundred-Twenty Days* is organized according to the stories the libertines have the "*historiennes*" tell them; and no initiative of the hero, at least in principle, should get ahead of the stories. For the power of words peaks when he commands the bodies' practice, and the "sensations communicated by the organ of hearing are the most pleasing and provide the most intense impressions." For Masoch . . . it is necessary that love be fixed by *contracts* which must be spoken, promised, announced, carefully described before being performed.[12]

Deleuze discusses the importance of education in the relations between the "victim" and his "tormentor," for the victim must teach and persuade the tormentor to form an alliance with him for his pleasure. The contract between them thus reveals the victim to be in fact the partner essentially in control, since, as "educator," he defines the terms; thus the "tormentor" is essentially passive: "The masochistic hero seems to be educated, formed by the authoritarian woman, but at a deeper level, it is he who forms and costumes her, he who whispers to her the harsh words she addresses to him. It is the victim who speaks through his torturer, without restraining himself" (Deleuze, 22).

Ewald's idyll with his perhaps somewhat rigid Android would resemble Masoch's rituals with his obdurate mistress also in the repetitiveness of the scenes: "This dialectic does not involve simply a circulation of speech, but transfers or displacements of this sort, which work such that the same scene is played out simultaneously at a number of levels, according to the doublings and reversals in the distribution of roles and language" (Deleuze, 22). In the same way, Edison tells Ewald of the "role" he will play; Edison argues that the same words will always be different, that the charm of Hadaly's company will always be fresh since her response will never be the same, even if the words repeat, since Ewald's own expectations and mood will alter their meaning:

"With the future Alicia, the real one, the Alicia of your soul, you will no longer have to endure these sterile and bitter frustrations. The word that comes will always be the *expected* word; and its beauty will depend entirely on your own suggestive powers! Her 'consciousness' will no longer be the negation of yours, but rather will become whatever spiritual affinity your own melancholy suggests to you." (*Eve*, 133)

If Hadaly is designed essentially as a moving statue, Wanda's role demands that she strike certain fixed poses. Deleuze writes of the "frozen cascade" of scenes in the *Venus*; Masoch's narrative art depends on a string of moments of suspension: "The torturer-woman takes fixed poses that identify her as with a statue, a portrait, or a photograph" (Deleuze, 31). Common to both the masochistic scenes of the *Venus* and Ewald's projected life with the Android are repetition, stasis, and ritual, fundamental elements of fetishistic sexuality.[13] Deleuze writes that the fetish is "like a fixed and frozen shot, an arrested image, a photo to which one always returns to cast out the tiresome results of movement" (Deleuze, 29). The Android, like the masochist's cruel mistress, is a fetish object. As fetish objects, they express the idealizing impulse common to both texts. In Deleuze's account there are three moments in fetishization: the denegation of the female lack of the penis, followed by a defensive neutralization that effectuates a kind of suspension of an acknowledgment of the state of things, and last an idealizing, protective neutralization: "For in its way the belief in a feminine phallus is itself felt as asserting the rights of the ideal against the real, the better to nullify the attacks which the knowledge of reality bring against it" (Deleuze, 29).

If the movement toward the ideal in Masoch is marked by a pressure toward narrative suspension in Deleuze's analysis, it is matched in Villiers's novel by the static sublimity toward which tends the enactment of the Android's creation and Ewald's acceptance of her, as well as by the heavy use of the vocabulary of sublimity. Descriptions of Hadaly are repeatedly couched in such terms as "sublime," "celestial," and "transcendental," and her very name is supposed to mean "ideal" in Persian. Deleuze points to a similar pattern in the _Venus_:

In the pedagogic project of Masoch's heroes, in the submission to the woman, in the torments they undergo, in the death they know, there are as many moments of ascension toward the Ideal. _The Divorcée_ has as a subtitle: _The Calvary of an Idealist_. Séverin . . . develops his doctrine, the "supersensualism," and takes for his motto the words of Mephisto to Faust: "Go on, suprasensual, sensual seducer, a little girl leads you by the nose." (_Übersinnlich_, in this text by Goethe, is supersensible, it is "suprasensual," "supracarnal," in conformity with a high theological tradition in which _Sinnlichkeit_ means _flesh, sensualitas_.) (Deleuze, 21)

Like Villiers, Masoch was touched by the idealism of a popularized Hegelianism becoming intellectually fashionable during the last quarter of the century.

This movement of idealization of the woman in both texts makes a place for a markedly theatrical intensification of the kind of fetishization of the feminine voice that recalls Marin's and Grosrichard's demonstrations of a similar fetishistic investment by Rousseau in the voice. It parallels _Sarrasine_, where the centrality of the ambiguity of the singer's gender points up the underlying term that structures fetishism: the denial of sexual difference, the effacement of female specificity in favor of a revised image of the female that mirrors male desire. The notion of the theatricality of the "masochist _jouissance_" implicit in a fetishistic investment in the singing or declamatory voice has been described by Lacoue-Labarthe writing of musical catharsis in "L'Echo du sujet." He describes the source of musical pleasure in terms of a mimetic reenactment of the pain of originary loss and the sense of mortality. This implicit gesture of representation, met by a corresponding act of identification in the listener, evokes what Lacoue-Labarthe calls "that specifically theatrical and tragic form of pleasure that Freud will define as 'masochistic.'"[14] The particularly intense pleasure that male figures in these texts derive from the female voice thus may be seen in the light of a fetishistic mise-en-scène of an artificially produced voice.

The most arresting fact about the Android, the key to the space of ambiguity invested in her, is her essential status as phonograph. Fittingly, Ewald's first meeting with her occurs in an artificial underground Eden remarkable for its luxurious appointments and the pervasive iconography of death that imbues it: to arrive there, one descends on a kind of tombstone; the walls are of such polished minerals as might line a tomb; there is no furniture. The voices of mechanical parrots animated by the recorded voices of people and birds enliven the scene; there, her unfinished being shrouded in heavy veils, Hadaly approaches "in her disquieting beauty," one hand on a dagger at her waist, and speaks to Ewald in muted tones "in a voice deliciously grave." She hands him a metallic golden flower, and he shudders at her remote, melancholy voice; later incarnated as Alicia, Hadaly will also assume her voice, leaving behind this first one.

At a later meeting, the emblems of death and the supernatural are once again invoked. The gentlemen arrive in Hadaly's subterranean chambers to find her waiting to perform, as if with the practiced composure of a salon singer: "Beside a pillar Hadaly, still heavily veiled, was standing erect, resting one hand on the case of a grand piano; lighted candles were reflected from its polished surface" (*Eve*, 92). This simulacrum of a recital is reinforced by a cacophonous din of human voices, male and female, issued by a crowd of mechanical birds that greets the arrival of the human visitors. Edison calls them "winged condensers" and comments that he felt it better to substitute human for bird voices, the recording art being superior to the poor imitative ability of birds: "I thought it might be fun to catch on the phonograph a few admiring or curious phrases spoken by my occasional visitors, and then to install them in these birds by means of electricity—thanks to one of my still-undisclosed discoveries" (*Eve*, 93). The birds provide a chorus to back the unearthly voice of Hadaly, reinforcing the exotic atmosphere of artificiality.

Hadaly sings for Ewald; he is captivated by her voice accompanied by a piano played as if by unseen hands:

And the gentle voice of the Android began to sing to this accompaniment, her voice coming from beneath the veil with intonations of supernatural voluptuousness:

> All hail to you, young man without a grief!
> Love cries her curses on me through the skies
> And woeful Hope berates me for a thief.
> Flee me then! Get you gone! Shut . . . your eyes
> And spurn me as you would a withered leaf!

Listening to this unanticipated song, Lord Ewald felt himself overwhelmed by a kind of fearful amazement. (*Eve*, 94)

The paradoxical seductiveness of her song urging him to spurn her doubles in its message her own ambiguity (is she or is she not sentient?): she is herself an oxymoron. Ewald's shock is a moment of sublimity, in the manner of Poe, whom Villiers openly emulated, as A. W. Raitt has shown.[15]

In a gesture reminiscent of Poe, Villiers evokes the voice of the Android as a voice from a supernatural beyond. Fittingly, Hadaly is persistently garlanded by the iconography of death. She travels, for example, only in her own satin-lined coffin. An interesting curiosity to note here is that the Edison Standard Phonograph was marketed in a wooden box that looks very much like a little sarcophagus; perhaps the sight of wooden boxes that contained preserved voices suggested this to Villiers. Further, she can administer death with her little electrified knife to any man who approaches her unwisely; she "lives" in a tomblike underground vault. Her voice, the sign of breath and life, also seems to belong to the realm of death. In a section of his book in which he discusses the experiments of Mersenne and Kempelen to create automata that would produce artificial speech, Beaune could be writing about Villiers's Android:

Dissecting the human voice and putting it back together is a technical matter, but one cannot help thinking that perhaps someone strange—and certainly malevolent—speaks through this voice, the voice of the automaton. A voice necessarily inhuman and from beyond the tomb. Anguish of a voice which the gaze cannot seize—not as with telecommunications whereby a voice comes from an outside that can be immediately reconstructed—but a voice of a strange "interior." An ironic and treacherous magician—you'd almost say the music of the spheres concentrated in a microcosmic atom. This fantastic is particular, not irrational, but *other*.[16]

The disquieting otherness of the Android's voice, strange sign of presence in an unliving creature (Edison says, "This is not a living being"), reproduces the paradox of recording, of a repetition that doubles yet differs from its original instance. If the Android is able to embody a reproduction of the hated and beloved Alicia that is proof against death, she is also a kind of messenger of death herself, metonymic of its realm, not only an artificial Eve, but an artificial Eurydice as well.

The passage that follows Ewald's shocked hearing of the Android's song underlines the Android's link with death and recording. At the end of Hadaly's song, there is a renewed "infernal" outburst from the bird/crowd, as if to create artificial applause. Villiers employs a similar idea in the story from 1874 and 1877, "La Machine à gloire," imagining an apparatus to create canned applause in a concert hall, and includes mention of a group of "twenty Androids from Edison's workshops" who assist in the mechanical claque.[17] Villiers refers in fact to this ironic piece with the line, "At a gesture from Hadaly, this parody of Glory was instantly cut off." After the tumult following Hadaly's song ceases, the pure "voice" of a nightingale arises, creating a mood of enchantment that seems to contrast its natural sweetness with the preceding recorded voices. A conversation ensues about the bird's "voice," in which Ewald attributes its beauty to its naturalness. Hadaly speaks, advising him not to ask how it is produced; otherwise " 'God would withdraw from the song.' " Edison reveals that it is a recorded song; its freshness has nothing to do with nature. Moreover, the original bird is dead; Edison recorded its last song: " 'Dead, you say? Not altogether, since I've recorded here his song and his spirit. I evoke it by means of electricity; that's spiritualism put in really practical terms, right?' " (*Eve*, 95). Learning he has been deceived, Ewald is disconcerted, chilled to the heart. Hadaly approaches and speaks to him in a sad way that makes him shudder: she is no more living than the nightingale. The enchantment of the recording is proper not to living nature but to the stasis of death, yet the sorrowful tone in her voice suggests living emotion: like a woman from a Poe story, the Android occupies a space compounded of death and a supernatural vitality that transcends it. Beaune writes of the equivocal nature of automata:

Thus the automaton is necessarily a mixture, and as such is deceptive in the same sense as Pascal meant when he said that the imagination was all the more false by not always being so. *The falsity of the automaton does not lie in its inhumanity but in its ambiguity.* The automaton can reach all the way to humanity, can not only imitate life but condense it—*but one is never sure about it.*[18]

The status of Hadaly's sentience shimmers between the poles represented on the one hand by the records on which the Android's speech and thus her nonbeing are inscribed, and on the other by the creation of an enigmatic, new, and synthetic sensibility, invoked through the *deus ex machina* device of Sowana's trance.

In this way the Android anticipates one of the founding questions of artificial intelligence. The attempt to create a machine with human intelligence began in the 1950's with Norbert Wiener's invention of cybernetics. A. M. Turing pursued the question of its possibility in his article "Computing Machinery and Intelligence," and it is a debate that has been continued by Keith Gunderson, Dreyfus, and others. The resonance of the problem of Hadaly's sentience with the scenario of Turing's "Imitation Game"[19] is striking. Gunderson notes that Turing found the question "Can machines think?" ambiguous, if not meaningless, and took the position that a machine that *acted* intelligently, that could fool someone into thinking it thought, could be called so, since sentience or the soul, the "ghost in the machine," was an undemonstrable. Turing describes the game thus:

It is played with three people, a man (A), a woman (B), and an interrogator (C) who may be either sex. The interrogator stays in a room apart from the other two. The object of the game for the interrogator is to determine which of the other two is the man and which is the woman. He knows them by labels X and Y, and at the end of the game he says either "X is A and Y is B" or "X is B and Y is A." The interrogator is allowed to put questions to A and B. . . . It is A's object in the game to try to cause C to make the wrong identification. . . . The answers should be written, or . . . typewritten. . . . The object of the game for the third player (B) is to help the interrogator. The best strategy . . . is probably to give truthful answers. . . . We now ask the question, "What will happen when a machine takes the part of A in this game?" Will the interrogator decide wrongly as often as when the game is played between a man and a woman? These questions replace our original "Can machines think?"[20]

Thus, the classic problem of artificial intelligence sets up the same problem as *L'Eve future*: can you tell the difference between a woman and a "machine"? If she/it can imitate sentience, can create the appearance of it, is there a difference, or is it enough? Turing seems to set up the game as a test of a natural difference: first that between a man and a woman, and then that between a woman and a machine. The logic of his problem, however, breaks down that difference, shows that from where you stand, you just can't know. The woman and the machine are both put in the position of the other, unknowable. The Turing problem shows up in an overdetermined fashion in the figure of Hadaly: both "woman" and machine, she absorbs both sides of the equation into what defines her.

During an extended section of the novel, beginning with a chapter titled "Première Apparition de la machine dans l'Humanité" in which Edison lays open the body of the Android to Ewald's gaze in a crypto-scientific, medically dispassionate disquisition, he explains to him the secret of her voice and implicitly of her being: it lies in twin golden phonographs with the capacity to record and reproduce Alicia's voice. Like the Android's other structures, they are modeled on analogy with those of a real woman's body; thus, Edison calls the phonographs her lungs.

"Here are the two golden phonographs, placed at an angle toward the center of the breast; they are the two lungs of Hadaly. They exchange between one another tapes of those harmonious—or should I say, *celestial*—conversations: the process is rather like that by which printing presses pass from one roller to another the sheets to be printed. A single tape may contain up to seven hours of language. The words are those invented by the greatest poets, the most subtle metaphysicians, the most profound novelists of this century—geniuses to whom I applied, and who granted me, at extravagant cost, these hitherto unpublished marvels of their thought.

"This is why I say that Hadaly replaces *an* intelligence with Intelligence itself." (*Eve*, 131)

The voice of the first Hadaly, the potential Hadaly first presented to Ewald, will become that of Alicia Clary: like the cylinder phonographs of the period, she can record as well as play and will dispose of some 60 hours of recorded conversation. The paradigm of the cylinder serves Villiers as an image to "explain" how the movements and personality of the Android are made to work: the movements, gestures, and expressions of the model are "inscribed" on the Android's central cylinder and can play back some 66 varied movements—many more, assures Edison, than a well-brought-up young woman normally uses. In response to Ewald's question whether her voice will be the same, Edison replies:

"The voice you have heard in Hadaly is her childhood voice, wholly spiritual, like the voice of a sleepwalker, not yet feminine! She will have the voice of Miss Alicia Clary, as she will have all the rest of her properties. The songs and words of the Android will forever be those that your lovely friend will have dictated to her—unknowingly, without ever laying eyes on her. Her accent, her diction, her intonations, down to the last millionth of a vibration, will be inscribed on the discs of two golden phonographs . . . perfected miraculously by me to the point where now they are of a tonal fidelity . . . practically . . . *intellectual*! These are the lungs of Hadaly." (*Eve*, 79)

The multifarious scenes, songs, and intriguing speeches recorded on her cylinders comprise not only the essence of her appeal but also the danger of madness she poses to her captivated lover. It is the enchantment of the Android's voice that fulfills her task of fetishistic seduction:

"An electric spark sets them in motion, as the spark of life sets ours in motion. I should warn you that these fabulous songs, these extraordinary dramatic scenes and unsounded words, spoken first by the living artiste, captured on records, and then given new *seriousness* by her Android phantom, are precisely what constitute the miracle, and also the hidden peril of which I warned you."

Lord Ewald was shaken by these words. He had not dreamed of this explanation of *the Voice*, that virginal voice of the lovely phantom. He had simply wondered. Now the simplicity of the solution erased his smile. The dark possibility—still much disturbed, no doubt, but still a *possibility*—of the total miracle, appeared before him distinctly. (*Eve*, 79)

The possibility begins to dawn on Ewald that his cry of "Who will remove this soul from this body for me?" may be realized through the miraculous recording of Alicia's voice. Instead of her own thoughts, the voice of Alicia will instead act as the vehicle for thoughts more interesting to Ewald: those of men like himself. The perfectly cultivated hetaera, she will mirror his thought for him. Since the Android will repeat new and unknown poetic and philosophic writings by contemporary writers of genius, she will be like a charmingly incarnated book on tape, uttering only the elegant words of great writers, providing the pleasures of an incarnated rare anthology edition of favorite authors. In this metafigurative image one can see the Android's function as the mirror of Ewald's desire, or rather, Echo to his Narcissus: her exquisite lips will pronounce the words men have already spoken. Hadaly is thus a machine for recording presence, for canning Alicia's graceful attributes that obsess Ewald, while leaving out her despised subjectivity. If the public of the time was astonished by the phonograph's seeming capacity to cheat death by preserving the living voice, Villiers's Android is designed to cheat life by providing a simulacrum of its external signs.

The fantasy of the Android points to a certain shift in the representation of women during the late nineteenth century, a moment when women began to be associated more and more with machines, from the girls on bicycles in turn-of-the-century advertisements, to the *bachelor machines* of the Surrealists, to the robot-woman in Fritz Lang's *Metropolis*. The effects of this shift continue to be expressed in contemporary artificial women such as those in Lem's *Solaris* and in *Bladerunner*, and in the feminine voices that urge consumers to buckle their automobile seat belts or to remove their cards from the bank machine.

The phonograph-woman points to a broader shift as well, for the invention of the phonograph marked a turning point in cultural history: the age of new machines that would transform life. In his book *Thomas Alva Edison: An American Myth*, an analysis of the growth and transformations in the popular images of the great inventor, Wyn Wachhorst writes that it was the association of Edison's name with the phonograph in 1877 that impressed him on the public mind as the "Wizard of Menlo Park."

Wachhorst describes the sensation created by the early demonstrations of the phonograph as outstripping by far the response to other inventions. The telephone, first called the "speaking telegraph," was initially viewed as just an extension of that familiar apparatus. Nothing equaled the wild reaction to the phonograph. Scientists at first dismissed it; Edison was accused of ventriloquism; crowds jammed the halls where it was demonstrated (when Edison demonstrated the machine at the National Academy of Sciences in Washington, D.C., the doors had to be taken off their hinges to mitigate the crush). Wachhorst writes that interest in the seemingly inexplicable phenomenon of a machine that talked by itself took on the proportions of a fad, and nothing seemed beyond Edison's powers:

Widespread speculation on the future uses of the invention included the suggestion that a phonograph be placed in the forthcoming Statue of Liberty so that she might give "salutes to the world." The phonograph craze was boosted by the popular press, which depicted typical American families gathered about the machine in their overstuffed parlors. Reporters, discovering that Edison had patented 158 other inventions and that his models filled an entire case at the patent office, hailed him as the nation's greatest inventor. . . . On April 1, 1878, the New York *Daily Graphic* went so far as to print an April Fool's bannerline: "Edison Invents a Machine that will Feed the Human Race—Manufacturing Biscuits, Meat, Vegetables and Wine out of Air, Water, and Common Earth." Other papers around the country picked up the story and ran it straight.[21]

Wachhorst argues that the intense impact of the phonograph on the public mind must be seen in the context of its appearance on the eve of two great transformations in the history of technology: the shift from steam to electric power and the convergence of technology and science. He suggests that both of these shifts can be described by Lewis Mumford's distinction between the "paleotechnic" and "neotechnic" phases of technology: the former was based mainly on the steam engine and was associated with coal and iron. In the steam age, machines were like superbeasts of burden, extensions of the large muscles of the men who were physically degraded in their operation; the latter age emerged with the dynamo and was associated with such things as alloys, synthetics, electronics, and automation. Early in the electrical age, the machine came to appear more benevolent as it increased leisure and physical comfort, and it began to be seen as an extension not only of the finer muscles, but of the ear, eye, and brain.

Wachhorst writes that Edison became associated in the public mind with these new capacities of the machine and seemed, indeed, to be the father of the new electrical age with his light bulb and "Edison effect" (the forerunner of the vacuum tube), and his system of power distribution that brought machines into the homes of ordinary people. Edison was associated not with huge machines like the locomotive but with small, seemingly magical contrivances that could capture the human voice or fill a room with light. The phonograph seems to have been the machine that woke the public imagination to the technological revolution taking place: "In other words, instead of the traditional image of crude power achieved through complicated snarls of tubing, valves, and cogwheels, Edison, to a greater degree than any man before him, suggested to Americans of the 1870's and 1880's a new concept of the machine: the achievement of spectacular ends through inconspicuous means."[22] It is not surprising that Villiers's novel, written during the early 1880's, should reflect this view of Edison and his works.

In fact, the characteristics of Villiers's Android correspond well to those of inventions the public associated with Edison. Wachhorst writes:

Content analysis of the Edison material for adjectives used to describe his inventions reveals that, for the period 1870–1914, "simple" was the most common, followed by "beautiful," "delicate," "sensitive," "curious," and "fragile." Adjectives denoting smallness outnumber those describing bigness in the period 1870–1889 by a ratio of 10 to 1. . . . Although Edison did invent small things, the adjectives disproportionately emphasize such words as "tiny" and "minute"; more important, much of the stress is on delicate parts—especially the lamp filament—rather than on whole devices.[23]

He elaborates this, showing the evolution of Edison's image as the "Wizard of Menlo Park": there was a radical increase in the use of supernatural imagery in popular descriptions of Edison after his introduction of the phonograph and incandescent lamp in 1878 and 1879.

Many of the adjectives, such as sensitive, delicate, fragile, beautiful, curious, found by Wachhorst to be associated with Edison's inventions after the appearance of the phonograph are traditionally associated with women. In fact, they seem to describe the Android quite aptly, particularly considering the extensive vocabulary of fine alloys, precious metals, and rare perfumes that Villiers employs in his descriptions of Hadaly.

In this context, then, Villiers's artificial woman can be seen as emblematic of the innovations that began to transform Europe and America in the late nineteenth century. The phonograph that Edison gives to Ewald in the form of a beautiful woman figures this newly refined, delicate technology that makes a new kind of reproduction possible. The future Eve's status as a copy, a sterile machine, that reproduces in image and recorded sound her original, indicates a shift in the status of art not only produced by mechanical means, as in Benjamin's age of mechanical reproduction, but as reproduction through mechanical recording.

The fascination with machines and the technology of recording appears in other texts of the period, such as Alfred Jarry's *Surmâle*, which presents its superhuman male first defeating a train in a bicycle race, then accomplishing sessions of inhumanly prolonged lovemaking presided over by a trumpeted phonograph. Especially striking in connection with my discussion here, however, is Verne's 1892 novel, *Le Château des Carpathes*, which stages the simulation of a beautiful singer's voice through mechanical "trucs" like those in *L'Eve future*. As in Villiers's novel, the inventor Edison is evoked—here, to rationalize certain mysteries of plot through a delayed introduction and explanation of a telephone. Like the other figures in the texts discussed in this study, La Stilla is evoked as a supremely gifted singer, a specialist in Italian opera. Her voice recalls La Malibran (as does her death). Like Sarrasine and Alicia Clary, she is compared to a Greek statue, a cliché for perfect beauty that yet underlines her relation to artifice. The name "La Stilla," which means "the silent one," is an odd one for a character supposed to be a renowned singer but is emblematic of the general argument I wish to make: feminine subjectivity is silent in these texts that present women singers as figurations of lack, as mirrors to echo male desire.

The machinery of the novel's intrigue works to set up the mystery of La Stilla's reappearance to her fiancé, years after her death during her farewell performance. Having accepted the marriage proposal of young Franz, count of Télek, she agrees to leave the stage—to the rage of her other fanatical admirers, the Baron Rodolphe de Gortz and the peculiar Orfanik. During her last performance as Angélique in *Orlando*, singing "I want to die" (*Voglio morire*), she coughs blood, hesitates, then dies. After five years of mourning, Franz leaves his seclusion to travel to Italy. Chance events and reports of supernatural hauntings at the abandoned castle of the Baron Rodolphe take him near his enemy's stronghold, where Franz sees his dead fiancée on a balustrade, clad as she was the last time he saw her, in white—like an angel, or ghost. He also hears her singing and, believing her to be the Baron's captive, is lured into the castle in search of her. Hearing her voice again singing the last aria she performed before her collapse on stage, he calls to her. Since she fails to respond, he thinks she must be mad.

Finally, he penetrates to a room deep in the castle where he sees her just as she was during her last performance, singing in the voice that he loved, "with an ineffable sweetness." He calls out her name, rejoicing that she is still alive. Rodolphe, also present, curses him and hurls a knife at her, to Franz's horror. Glass shatters, and La Stilla disappears. She is thus revealed to be only an illusion; her portrait was projected against a glass tilted across the little stage like a magic-lantern image. The song, however, continues, only to pause and end, as hers did, with "*Voglio morire*." The repetition Freud identified with death is inscribed in the text as the truth about her: La Stilla is silent. Her voice, like her image, is a simulacrum, recorded by Orfanik during the fatal performance. The deluded fiancé has stumbled into the Baron's private operatic fetish theater. Ignorant of the "trucage" that produced his beloved there, he goes mad, victim to Lord Ewald's own threatened fate.

While the emotive power behind the illusion of La Stilla's presence is based on the phonograph's power to capture the warmth of a human voice, the artifice of her visual apparition derives from the techniques of the phantasmagoria that made their way into the theatrical machinery of the nineteenth century. Eric Barnouw traces the antecedents of film to the magic lantern shows in *The Magician and the Cinema*, where he shows how the tricks and technology of films originated in magic shows and lantern-slide entertainments. The taste for the spectacular, for the sublime as shiver of horror, for the marvelous of the *féerie* came together in a new way in 1797 in

Etienne-Gaspard Robertson's *phantasmagorie*, gothic lantern shows he held in an old monastery: audiences filed through dark, scary corridors to a room decorated with skulls, where they heard gloomy music and tolling bells, and filed past the "Invisible Woman," a piped-in voice. Smoke filled the air, and the lights guttered out:

Then, onto the smoke arising from the braziers, images were projected from concealed magic lanterns. They included human forms and unearthly spectral shapes. The images came from glass slides, but the movements of the smoke gave them a ghoulish kind of life. Among these apparitions were men and women who had died in the French Revolution, such as Danton, Marat, Robespierre. Their faces, with inscrutably changing expressions would suddenly appear. . . . Some spectators sank to their knees, convinced they were in the presence of the supernatural. Robertson climaxed his performance with the projected image of a skeleton, "the fate that awaits us all."[24]

Robertson's shows were fantastically successful, and the history of his imitators becomes that of the nineteenth-century spirit photographers and theater producers putting ghosts on stage by means of projections of figures on glass screens tilted invisibly across the stage, prestidigitators producing floating ladies and their own heads out of nowhere, and eventually, the ex-magician Méliès, with his new bag of old tricks of metonymic concatenation, i.e., montage.

In her article "Phantasmagoria: Spectral Technology and the Metaphorics of Modern Reverie," Terry Castle discusses the symbolic and metaphorical resonances of the phantasmagoria.[25] Over time, the phantasmagoria became a figure for the workings of the mind, what she calls "the inward specter-show" of the romantic and postromantic imagination, associated with the irrational, delirium, and the sublime. The spectacle of the ghostly singer in the baron's Carpathian castle—the neighborhood of vampires and heretics—is subtended not only by certain theatrical conventions, literally by a particular theatrical machinery, but also by a rhetorical tradition that figured the supernatural as outward showing of inner mental spectacle. Hadaly, too, as the answer to Ewald's desire for an Alicia of his dreams, is created as a projection of an interior drama. The disembodied voice that animates her, like the apparition of La Stilla, floats in an odd register compounded of impossible desire and the terror of a sublime threat. It is supported by a mechanical apparatus that ambiguously conjures the supernatural, explains it away, yet whose novel power of re-creation itself leaves a residual sense of the uncanny.

Villiers's Android calls reproduction—in all the senses of the word—into question. She is literally herself a reproduction. In the logic of the text, in fact, the Android is the final term in a relay of reproductions, or copies, with the original repressed, as Marie-Hélène Huet has pointed out in "Living Images: Monstrosity and Representation": "And it could be said that in the line of descent from *Venus Vitrix* to Alicia Clary to Hadaly there is never anything but the representation of a model which is already represented, her origin dissimulated: the cold marble, the immobility of a statue, the soul's vacuity, animated mechanism, disparities."[26] In this piece, Huet considers the Android in terms of the nineteenth-century aesthetic of resemblances and the signature. She analyzes the traditional association of the maternal with the monstrous and the paternal genealogy of the work of art. Huet discusses Hadaly as Edison's artistic creation, a creation imitating a monstrous genetic process in which the maternal function is repressed.

Villiers's Android is, of course, not the first such creation. Here we come back to the history of automata. In his article "The Golem and the Robot," Robert Plank examines the impulse to create artificial human beings as a desire to bypass the woman's role in reproduction. He notes this notion of a male-centered reproduction in the Golem of Judah Loew, Goethe's Sorcerer's Apprentice, Kempelen's Chess Player, Mary Shelley's Frankenstein, and other robots and man-made creatures, and traces their filiation to Paracelsus's homunculus.[27] Paracelsus's writings provide a straightforward version of the fantasy: he boasted that he was able to create a homunculus, prescribing that it be made from sperm and nurtured in a matrix of horse dung. Plank draws a parallel with the legend of the mandrake, which supposedly sprang from the sperm resulting from the death throes of a "pure" young man who had been hanged, and notes the similarity of the homunculus's birth in the dung heap to the golem's formation out of clay.[28] Villiers's imagination of the pure Android's manufacture from gold, iron, and precious jewels thus appears as a refined version of this fantasy of male-centered reproduction in which the woman is replaced or symbolized by a dung heap.

The Android embodies this rejection of the feminine in another sense as well. As artistic artifact, her creation implies the suppression of maternity, while her own sterility suggests the symbolist valuation of virginity, the theme of a refusal of sexuality which one finds in such texts as Mallarmé's *Hérodiade* and Huysmans's *A rebours*. Huet also emphasizes the notion of Mallarmean sterility, quoting Denis Saurat's point that in Mallarmé's *Le Don du poème*, Idumée evokes the sexless kings of Idumea who reproduced without women.[29] The Android is chaste and chastening: not only does she discourage sexual approach with her little electrified dagger, but she cleanses her partner of desire, as Edison explains to Ewald, arguing for the morally salubrious influence of the Android:

"And nobody will be able to raise impudent objections against me, *since it's the normal action of the Android to neutralize within a few hours any low and degrading desires for the original model that may exist in the most inflamed of hearts; and this is accomplished by saturating it with a profound awe hitherto unknown, the irresistible effect of which I do not think anyone can possibly imagine who has not experienced it.*" (*Eve*, 123)

In fact, the Android may be asexual entirely, this being the one point in which she cannot copy her model. In the clinical lesson on the Android's anatomy Edison gives to Ewald, in all other respects minutely detailed, he modestly glosses over any mention of her sexual organs, saying vaguely that her "armor" encloses within itself "the interior organism common to all women" (*Eve*, 79). In another context, he describes her thus: "You see, *she is an angel*! he continued, speaking as solemnly as ever—if indeed it's true, as the theologians teach us, *that angels are simply fire and light*! Wasn't it Baron Swedenbourg who went so far as to add that they are 'hermaphrodite and sterile'?" (*Eve*, 144). Chaste artist, chaste artifact, angel: in this respect Hadaly resembles the chain of sexless singing angels we have seen earlier who so curiously are represented as ideal objects of desire.

Yet the manner in which Hadaly represents the motif of reproduction is not exhausted by the observation that she is sexless and sterile, for her seemingly absent reproductive organs are in a sense not absent at all, but her very essence. The announced project of stealing and re-creating the presence of Alicia that is the raison d'être of the Android may be seen to be accomplished largely through the mechanical apparatus of reproduction that makes up Hadaly. The phonographs which carry Alicia's voice and that central cylinder on which her mannerisms are inscribed are a means of mechanical reproduction. Insofar as the singer Alicia's presence is presented as localized in her voice, Hadaly's golden phonographs are both the instrument of the repression of the feminine in the text and the place where Huet would say "the labor of the maternal imagination is unequivocally present."[30] It is through the emotive power of the voice that repressed, dead mothers customarily reemerge in literature in ways we saw in the texts by Proust and Rousseau. The revalorization of the maternal by the French feminist writers discussed earlier may be seen as a response to a tradition of representation in which the feminine and the maternal have been effaced, and the position from which a woman would speak made over to an artificial Echo.

Inhuman Voices, Sublime Song

Villiers stages the Android in *L'Eve future* as a spectacle. Not only is the female Android's body dissected in such minute fashion as to performatively construct much of the text, but as we saw in the last chapter, she is first presented to her prospective "lover" as if at a recital. Like her model, Alicia Clary, the Android sings: her voice is manifestly a key to her allure. In this way, Villiers's Android resembles the singers in the texts we have considered, which accord a particular privilege to the feminine voice. Although Villiers's novel gives a new turn to the theme in adding the disturbing pleasure of simulation, the doubling of the voice in recording newly made possible by the invention of the phonograph, the singer's voice approaches the register of the inhuman in the earlier texts as well. Moreover, its aesthetic vocabulary, like theirs, is inscribed within the arc described by the trajectory of the development and transformation of romanticism during the nineteenth century.

The voices of the singers in all the fictions we have looked at are characterized as being of an otherworldly purity, inducing a sense of unlimited expansion, uplifting and moving the hearer to a sense of infinite beauty. These voices are compared to larks, bells, aeolian harps, and the voices of angels. In all these texts, the woman's voice becomes assimilated to an inhuman register, promoted in the fictions as able to ravish, elevate, and transport its hearer. These latter terms derive from the original definitions of sublime experience: I propose that one common wellspring of these literary representations of the voice is the idea of the sublime, which played a determining role in the development of romanticism and which persists as an underlying term in these texts.

The sublime has been the focus of discussion during the last ten years or so on both sides of the Atlantic. Readers familiar with French critical debates will recognize in the sublime the subject of work by Philippe Lacoue-Labarthe, Jean-Luc Nancy, and particularly Jean-François Lyotard.[1] Certain arguments in Lyotard's book *L'Inhumain* provide a useful framework for the material under consideration here.

Lyotard argues for the central force of the sublime to the current of artistic modernity, beginning with and including its key role in romanticism. He sees the aesthetic of the sublime persisting in the trace of indeterminacy in art, identifying it with the "inhuman" as a marker of the condition of modernity. In "The Sublime and the Avant-Garde," Lyotard pursues these ideas through a reading of the painter Bernard Baruch Newman's essay "The Sublime Is Now." Newman defines modern art as pure "event" in a "now" colored by the suspense and anguish that attend the state of expectation, the possibility that nothing at all or something extraordinary may happen. Lyotard says this emotion of anguished expectation emerges as the question "*Is it happening?*":

Between the seventeenth and eighteenth centuries in Europe this contradictory feeling—pleasure and pain, joy and anxiety, exaltation and depression—was christened or re-christened by the name of the *sublime*. It is around this name that the destiny of classical poetics was hazarded and lost; it is in this name that aesthetics asserted its critical rights over art, and that romanticism, in other words, modernity, triumphed.[2]

For Lyotard, as for others, the sensibility that lies behind sublime emotion is the aesthetic mode that characterizes modernity;[3] it has been the underpinning of modes of artistic experimentation that have abandoned the beautiful, departing from the classical rule of art as mimetic to turn instead to the shock of surprising or strange combinations. Such a conception rests on the idea of sublime experience as entailing an approach to the limits of the representable and, specifically for Lyotard, on his concept of indeterminacy, what escapes representation, as descriptive of that limit.

Lyotard thus traces the genealogy of the avant-gardes of the twen-

tieth century to a pressure within romanticism toward an abandonment of representativity. Focusing on Kant's analysis of sublime emotion as produced by the "disaster" that the imagination undergoes in
its encounter with what escapes its power of representation—that is,
by the imagination's failure to create forms adequate to represent the
absolute and the pain of the resulting "dislocation of the faculties"—
he correlates the sublime to an experience of the unrepresentable:

> With a view to resolving this paradox of an aesthetics without sensible or
> imaginative forms, Kant's thought looks towards the principle that an Idea
> of Reason is revealed at the same time as the imagination proves to be im-
> potent in *forming* data. In the sublime "situation," something like an Ab-
> solute, either of magnitude or of power, is made quasi-perceptible (the word
> is Kant's) due to the very failing of the faculty of presentation. This Absolute
> is, in Kant's terminology, the object of an Idea of Reason. (Lyotard, 136)

Lyotard's account of the sublime, however, derives not only from
Kant's sublime but from Burke's as well, a filiation of interest here:
in mapping the sublime to what escapes representation, he cites
Burke's use of the image of an angel as an example of a pictorial figure
of the sublime.

In the course of this discussion, we have seen angels also, though
in a different light: the casting of female singers repeatedly in the texts
under consideration as sexless angels. In the reading I am proposing,
these instances of the woman as angel can be seen not simply within
the pattern of the nineteenth-century polarization of woman as demon and angel made familiar to us by critics as widely separated as
Mario Praz and Nina Auerbach. They also suggest that these texts
can be understood in terms of a common recourse to the figures of
angelic singers as a way to stage sublime experience. Lyotard's conception of the indeterminate in the sublime, then, offers one avenue
of approach to disassembling the motor of fascination offered by the
inhuman voice. Another is Thomas Weiskel's account in *The Romantic Sublime* of the psychoanalytic economy that underlies the experience of the sublime. Such an approach is congruent with the readings of texts by Rousseau, Balzac, and Villiers as masochistic and fetishistic I presented earlier.

It is not surprising to find romantic fictional texts offering a vista
of sublime emotion: as is well known, it permeated French romantic

poetry, and Victor Hugo's revolutionary theater owed an explicit debt to the aesthetic of the sublime. At the beginnings of its career it was primarily a literary term, first emerging in the *Peri Hypsous*, the Greek rhetorical text initially attributed to Longinus and long referred to as his work. In *The Sublime: A Study of Critical Theories in Eighteenth Century England*, Samuel Monk shows that it was Nicholas Boileau who first divorced the sublime from its status as a rhetorical term and transferred it to the realm of artistic experience in his distinction between sublime style and the sublime experience, describing the sublime as what is "marvelous" (*merveilleux*) and can "astonish" (*estonner*) and "shake" (*esbransler*): what can ravish, elevate, and transport.[4] As an aesthetic idea, it gave a name to the valuation of emotion in art that characterized the movement away from neoclassicism, and as such it was taken up and extensively discussed in the eighteenth century by a number of English writers first in terms of style, then as an aesthetic mode in and of itself.

Notable among these was Edmund Burke's *Philosophical Inquiry into the Origin of our Ideas of the Sublime and Beautiful*, a discussion of the sublime that emphasized the experience of pain and terror as aesthetic emotions and offered an interpretation of the sublime as the most intense emotion possible. It was finally codified as an adjunct to Kant's philosophical theories in his *Critique of Judgment*, the founding textbook for the sublime. While all approaches go by way of Kant, Monk suggests that it was perhaps less the influence or prestige of Kant's ideas that made them the foundational principles for the art of their time than their predominant role as a synthesis of the current of contemporary aesthetic concepts (see Monk, 6). The progress of interest in the sublime is thus interwoven with elements that become expressed in romanticism: the "drift toward subjectivism, the psychologizing of literature, the concept of 'original genius' . . . and ultimately the rise of romanticism in poetry and the concurrent establishment of aesthetics as a new, separate branch of philosophy."[5]

The topos of the sublime, which enjoyed its most important early dissemination through Boileau, is later reimported to French letters in changed form from English romantic poets such as Byron and the German romantics along pathways that have been well documented:

Madame de Staël in her *De L'Allemagne*; Rousseau in what is often
viewed as the founding text of romanticism in France, *La Nouvelle
Heloïse*; and Diderot, through his writings on genius in his art criticism. Hoffman was read early and enthusiastically in France, and
translations of Kant appeared from the 1830's on.[6]

Kant's discussion of the sublime is to be found in part 1, book 2
of his *Critique of Judgment*. His theory of the sublime takes its definition from the distinction he makes between the sublime and the
beautiful. He locates both kinds of aesthetic experiences not in cog-
nition through conceptualization but in the activity of the imagination; both result from a judgment of reflection and are associated
with the simple presentation of the object of reflection. What results
from this idea is his sense of aesthetic experience as disinterested,
since it is not the result of an attempt to achieve knowledge of the
object.[7] While beauty is a matter of delight in form, contour, in what
is essentially limited, the sublime is to be found in objects that are not
limited by form. It is thus allied with the concept of the infinite. While
the beautiful is associated with quality, the sublime partakes of quantity or magnitude.

Monk's account offers the further distinction that while pleasure
in the beautiful comes from "a feeling of the furtherance of life," the
sense of the sublime arises through "a momentary check to the vital
forces, followed at once by a discharge all the more powerful" for
having been restrained (Monk, 6). As one recent critic, Jean-Luc
Nancy, puts it in his essay "The Sublime Offering," the sublime implies a representation or nonrepresentation not of the infinite but of
the movement of the unlimited at the boundary of representation.[8]
The infinite cannot be thought of as entirely given, states Kant, and
cannot be represented. While the infinite is a numeric concept, the
unlimited is the gesture by which figuration shows the infinite: the
sublime has to do with the movement out of representation traced by
the unlimited.

The sublime for Kant is a matter of *magnitudo*, of absolute grandeur, of quantity as absolute. He distinguishes between the mathematical sublime and the dynamic. The sublime is the name given to
what is absolutely great, what is "beyond all comprehension great"
(Monk, 7). This sense of magnitude of the sublime arises at the limit

of what can be grasped. Natural objects are sublime not in themselves but only as reason responds to them. Thus, while the action of a storm at sea can evoke sublime feelings, it does so because of the ideas the mind conceives in reaction to it. The sublime is thus a product of the mind in response to its inability to represent absolute magnitude. It takes place in a representation of the limitless in which nonetheless the mind seeks to create a sense of a totality.

Kant specifically notes that the sublime may be found in an object without form as well as in a form. What is at stake is the baffling of the mind by its own demand for totality when presented by an object whose magnitude defies this demand. The emotion that then arises is one of reverence or respect, since "reason imposes on us a law (the comprehension of an absolute totality) which as sensuous beings we cannot obey" (Monk, 8). For this reason, the sublime evokes a mingled feeling of pain and pleasure at the perception of a totality beyond what is presentable in a limited form and results from a union of the activities of the imagination and reason. The sublime is thus an experience of (and at) a limit that is rising up out of conceptualization. The mind perceives and is unable to master a totality whose occurrence creates an event at the edge of the limits of the imagination, a totality marking limit and the absence of limit in the same gesture. For Kant, the sublime is associated with a movement of the mind, with a vibration of simultaneous attraction and repulsion. In his discussion of the sublime, Nancy takes up this sense of movement or pulsation as an arrest, like a cardiac arrest or syncope, or as syncopation, a shifting of rhythmic accent within the representational scene:

In the sublime, it is a matter of the syncopated rhythm of the trace of the accord, spasmodic vanishing of the limit all along itself, into unlimitedness, that is into nothing. The sublime schematism of the totality is made up of a syncopation at the heart of the schematism itself: simultaneous reunion and distension of the limit of presentation—or more exactly, and more inexorably: reunion and distension, positing and vanishing *of* simultaneity (and thus of presentation) itself. Instantaneous flight and presence of the instantaneous, grouping and strewn division of a present.[9]

The emotion of the sublime arises at the moment the imagination feels itself reaching its limit: the imagination is moved by the sense of touching the edge of the sensible in a heart-stopping moment of suspension.

Finally, Kant discusses the dynamic sublime as the perception of might in nature on condition that it does not threaten one directly. Examples from nature include volcanoes, lightning, overhanging rocks, waterfalls, the ocean; all must be a source of fear, but not a direct menace, for the emotion of the sublime to occur. Delight arises from the fearful when it does not menace us directly. Instead, it awakens sublime feelings through the mind's ability to stand above nature and be moved, but not crushed, by a sense of enormity. Since the sublime arises not from nature but from the capacities of the mind, the ground of the sublime lies in the mind's capacity to treat moral ideas (see Monk, 8).

These traits explain something of the fascination with the singing voice in the texts we have been considering. The early Sand piece, "L'Histoire d'un rêveur," serves as a very clear example. You will remember that this little story, Sand's first fictional attempt, was written under the spell of Hoffman, whose faith in music as a way to touch the infinite she shared.[10] She named her protagonist Amédée; Ernest Theodore Wilhelm Hoffman had replaced his third Christian name with Amédée in a gesture of admiration for Mozart. In this story, a quintessentially sublime scene provides the backdrop for its hero's emotional audition of an ambiguously beautiful voice, at once haunting and overwhelming.

The scene takes place in a specifically sublime spot: the exploding crest of a volcano, a textbook location for sublimity. The voice Amédée hears, compared to the aerial harmonies of the aeolian harp, fills the air, "so strong and so dazzling that space does not seem vast enough to contain it." Its strange register and ambiguity thwart gender identification: it seems to include the qualities of all voices, at once contralto, tenor, and bass. Amédée and the singer agree to leap into the volcano together, and once this is decided, "violent quakes shook the mountain; bursts of red flames and smoke poured forth from the volcano's mouth while dreadful percussive crashes rang out." All the while, the cryptic words "temporale, temporale" fall from the air. The mysterious youth (ultimately revealed to be a woman) mingles a wrenching song filled with madness and pain with the noise, while "walls of flame criss-crossed about them and a hail of smoking rocks rained down without touching them." Amédée is "intoxicated by this horrible and sublime spectacle."[11]

In this first effort, Sand lays it on pretty thick, and her intent is quite unmistakable: markers of sublimity frame the text throughout: the presence of the protagonists on an exploding volcano that does not threaten them physically but instead evokes terror and wonder; a totality that escapes the understanding (evoked by the ambiguous multiple gender of the singer, the volcano, the voice filling the air); and the sense of magnitude evoked by the whole, including the seemingly infinite vastness of the singer's voice. What is interesting about the story in the context of this discussion is its placement of a voice of seemingly inhuman nature and power among the elements of natural sublimity.

Crude as it is, this story makes a gesture characteristic of the other texts we have been looking at: in them, the voice renders sublimity. Although the sublime is often associated with the visual, it can be elicited by other kinds of experience. Kant's statement that the sublime may reside in objects that have no form opens a place for auditory experiences, while Burke's discussion of the sublime specifically identifies certain sounds (section 17) as a source of the emotion of the sublime (as well as other sensations such as those from bitter tastes and stenches, certain colors such as fustian and black, and mercurial changes in light):

The eye is not the only organ of sensation by which a sublime passion may be produced. Sounds have a great power in these as in most other passions. I do not mean words, because words do not affect simply by their sounds, but by means altogether different. Excessive loudness alone is sufficient to overpower the soul, to suspend its action and to fill it with terror. The noise of vast cataracts, raging storms, thunder, or artillery awakes a great and aweful sensation in the mind, though we can observe no nicety or artifice in those sorts of music.[12]

In this passage, Burke offers an explanation of the sublime effects of sounds in terms of the impressions produced by loudness, but in a later passage titled "The Artificial Infinite," he associates the sublime in sound with the sense of infinity produced by the tension that results from a sustained repetition of sounds: "We have observed, that a species of greatness arises from the artificial infinite; and that this infinite consists in a uniform succession of great parts: we observed too, that the same uniform succession had a like power in sounds" (Burke, 264). He goes on to give an illustration of the state of suspense created by the sound of something being struck repeatedly with the resulting vibration produced in the ear and the hearer's resulting state of suspension awaiting the next tone. Although Burke does not discuss music, the step from this definition of the artificial infinite to the effects produced by music is a short one: again, one finds a kind of key in the idea of rhythmical beating. It is within the space opened by this pulse that one may perhaps place the value of indeterminacy in music and painting as it emerges from Lyotard's account of the sublime.

A sense of the voice as vehicle of the sublime may be drawn directly, however, from the definitions of the sublime in Kant. We have seen that sublime emotion is evoked by an object that seems unlimited, that invokes a sense of infinite expansion, a spilling over of a feeling of great magnitude moving the subject to a state in which he feels brought to the edge of what may be presented in form. The qualities inherent in a powerfully moving singing voice may be the source of such an emotion: the amplitude of a voice filling a space; the liquid sense it can create at once of pure presence and continual movement, and of an expansion beyond the body of the singer and beyond the song form that structures it; the exquisite sense of pain and pleasure experienced by the listener. What better than an accomplished singing voice can evoke in its hearer the sense of a flooding over from the limits of form, of being taken to the edge of the representable, the sense of "instantaneous flight and presence of the instantaneous, grouping and strewn division of a present" in Nancy's account? Nancy's formulation is suggestive here: not only does the liquidity of the voice convey such a paradoxical sense of "spasmodic vanishing of the limit all along itself," but as music it also bears the pulse of rhythm—Nancy's "syncopation" in the heartbeat. In this connection, too, one cannot help but think of the value of rhythm in both Lacoue-Labarthe's and Kristeva's accounts of subjectivity in its formation within a vocal/acoustic mode.

Further, in Boileau, as in the eighteenth-century English theorists of the sublime such as John Baillie and Joseph Priestley, the sublime in art is linked with artistic genius: the superlatives are matched, and supernal experience becomes associated with superlative talent, the common denominator being intensity of emotion. Romantic ideology fused the concept of the sublime with the governing idea of the power of original genius as it evolved through the writings of Archibald Alison and others in the eighteenth century (see Monk, 233–36). Sand's "L'Histoire d'un rêveur" provides an explicit mise-en-scène of the fusion of these ideas, emphasizing the mysterious singer's extraordinary artistry against a conventionally sublime backdrop.

In *La Comtesse de Rudolstadt* Sand again employs some trappings of sublime landscape to furnish the decor of the novel, while the singing of the genially talented Consuelo exalts her audience. Consuelo's singing excites the passionate admiration of the composer Marcello in a scene set in a cathedral; Consuelo's features are illuminated by a "divine flame" as she fills the huge vault with her "grand" voice. Marcello weeps with ecstasy; he cries out, comparing her to Saint Theresa and Saint Cecilia, calling her poetry, music, faith personified. Elsewhere she is said to be, as a woman of genius, priestess, sibyl, and initiatrix of the sacred, formed for the contemplation of the "sublime ideal."

Sand is far from alone in employing this vocabulary. Balzac also draws from the lexicon of the sublime in *Sarrasine* in staging the moment Sarrasine hears La Zambinella sing: "The effect was delirium. The artist felt cold." Sarrasine's sensation recalls the heart-stopping action of sublime emotion. This sense of the subliming voice informs Stendhal's language in *La Vie de Rossini*, where he speaks of the capacity of the great Giuditta Pasta to imbue the same note with different nuances of feeling on different occasions (one might say anticipating Lyotard's conception of indeterminacy in the artistic sublime): "Madame Pasta may indeed sing the same *note* on two different occasions; but, if the spiritual context is different, it will not be the same *sound*. These are the sublimest heights to which the art of singing can attain."[13]

I have earlier quoted what Stendhal writes of the singer Catalani's power to transport her audience: her "prodigiously beautiful" voice fills its listeners with awe, as if before some great "miracle"; our hearts are "confused."[14] The words "astonished wonder," "miracle," "confusion of [the] heart" inscribe his discussion of Catalani within the table of superlatives indexed to sublimity.

If we look again at descriptions of the quality of singing in the castrato voice, we find the same terms: the purity and agility of this voice is compared to a flute or a lark; it suggests the infinite. Enrico Panzacchi had observed that "when it seems that the voice has reached the loftiest peaks of altitude, it starts off again . . . a voice that gives the immediate idea of sentiment transmuted into sound, and of the ascension of a soul into the infinite on the wings of that sentiment. . . . [It] captivated me with the power of a most gracious sensation never before experienced."[15] Du Maurier taps into this same tradition, calling Trilby's hypnotized voice "infinite." Trilby's recital under the spell of Svengali elicits this description:

> But her voice was so immense in its softness, richness, freshness, that it seemed to be pouring itself out from all round; its intonation absolutely, mathematically pure; one felt it to be not only faultless but infallible; and the seduction of it, the novelty of it, the strangely sympathetic quality! How can one describe the quality of a peach or a nectarine to those who have only known apples? Until La Svengali appeared, the world had only known apples—Catalanis, Jenny Linds, Grisis, Albonis, Pattis! The best apples . . . for sure, but still only apples![16]

The immensity of Trilby's voice and its absolute quality assimilate it to the register of what is unrepresentable: the world's greatest singers are only "apples"; she is something else. Her voice is of a different order, belonging to a register until then unknown, its quality seemingly impossible to convey in words. The narrator compares her singing to that of an "archangel"; it seems to Little Billee to be a "revelation of some impossible golden age"; the audience is reduced to tears; her singing is the "apotheosis of voice and virtuosity" and gives a "heavenly glimpse beyond the veil"; du Maurier even helpfully invents a review by Gautier titled "Madame La Svengali—Ange ou Femme?"[17] The rhetoric du Maurier employs to suggest the magic of Trilby's voice (when Trilby is Svengali's creation, his doll) draws from the same well as Stendhal, Balzac, and Sand.

The singing Android in *L'Eve future*, Edison's talking doll, is not just cast in the same mold but typifies it in a heavily overdetermined way. When Ewald first sees Hadaly, the scene takes place in Edison's gothic subterranean vault, a place of which Burke might approve. Again, the context is a "recital," here attended by an audience of two: Hadaly sings in tones of a "supernatural femininity"; hearing this unexpected song, Ewald is "overwhelmed by a kind of fearful amazement." Her song, moreover, is attended by the song of a nightingale: "This voice, coming straight from Nature and recalling the forests, the skies, and the immensity of space, seemed strange indeed in this place."[18] The voice of the nightingale, sign of the soul, turns out to be "dead," implying the Android's to be the same. The supernatural song of the Android heard in the macabre depths of the underground chamber invokes the aesthetic assumptions that underlie these nineteenth-century texts associating the affective power of song with sublimity.

Like Consuelo, Trilby, and La Zambinella, Hadaly is described as an angel. In a passage quoted earlier, Edison discourses to Ewald on the workings of the Android over her opened body as he argues for the superiority of the artificial woman to the human one. He takes her hand and says, "You see, *she is an angel*! . . . if indeed it's true, as the theologians teach us, *that angels are simply fire and light*! Wasn't it Baron Swedenbourg who went so far as to add that they are 'hermaphrodite and sterile'?" (*Eve*, 144). The "supernatural" voice of the artificial angel is not the only term that links the Android with the sublime: the scene of her encounter with Ewald after her "incarnation" as Alicia Clary is very explicitly set up to represent a sublime event. Called during this passage a "stupefying machine for manufacturing the Ideal" (*Eve*, 194), she is a machine for sublime production.

Ewald goes to meet Alicia one evening in Edison's garden in order to break with her, before accepting her substitute. During the course of their conversation, he is struck by her solicitude and sensitivity, the first such signs he has seen. Ewald is moved to surprise and passion: "At this emotion, this expression, the young man felt himself transported by a veritable access of amazement. He was in ecstasy. He no longer gave thought to *the other*, the terrible new creation. A single human word had been enough to touch his heart, and to rouse in it indescribable hopes" (*Eve*, 191–92). It is, however, not a human word that touches his soul: it is the voice of the inhuman Hadaly. Declaring his renewed love for Alicia, after anathematizing the "ridiculous, senseless doll" to himself, he kisses her and finds on her breath the telltale scent of roses and amber that is the sign of the Android:

As his kiss melted on her lips, he caught a vague scent of amber and roses. A deep shudder shook him from head to foot, even before his understanding was able to grasp the thought which had just struck his mind like a thunderbolt.

At the same time, Miss Alicia Clary rose from the bench and, placing on the young man's shoulders her hands *glittering with their many rings*, she said to him in a melancholy voice—in that melodious, supernatural voice that he had heard before: "Dear friend, don't you recognize me? I am Hadaly." (*Eve*, 192)

Trembling, shocked by an event that dazzles his understanding in a terrible way, Ewald feels the blood flood back into his heart, sees his life pass before his eyes, and fixes his eyes, "dilated by the complex horror of the facts," on the Android. This moment of horrified recognition, which parallels Nathanael's *unheimlich* horror at the revelation of Olympia as a wooden doll, is marked by the attributes of the sublime: he is shocked by a hair-raising event that terrifies him and baffles his reason, stops his heart and lifts him out of himself; his heart is "confounded, humiliated, thunderstruck." Villiers insists on the word sublime itself as the passage continues. Ewald examines her features, dress, and manner, and sees Alicia. The only difference is that her look is "sublime," and on reflection, he is struck to an even more profound astonishment by a sudden idea: "It was simply this: that the woman represented by this mysterious doll at his side *had never found within herself the power to make him experience the sweet and overpowering instant of passion that had just shaken his soul*" (*Eve*, 192).

Agitated by "extraordinary feelings," Ewald listens to his mechanical hetaera address him in terms of a mystical idealism, speaking to him of a supernatural reality that transcends the world of forms, and whose beings send him signs of their presence. In dreams, she tells him, he sees figures or a face which he cannot distinguish and which trouble him profoundly. She informs him that the reality governed by reason is only one enclosed within the infinite, that the "most certain of all realities—you know perfectly well, it is that in which we are lost and which exists within us in purely ideal form (I speak, of course, of the Infinite)—that reality is simply not accessible to reason." In visions that bring a "further election" one receives intimations of "a new and inexpressible dimension of space all around him of which the apparent and accepted space in which we are trapped, is *merely the metaphor*. This living ether is a region without limits or restrictions" (*Eve*, 195). The beings that visit him from that region, the Android tells Ewald, seek to communicate with him through the wind, reflections of light on metal, folds of fabric. The soul responds to them. "And the first *natural instinct* of the Soul is to *recognize* them, in and through that same holy terror which bears witness to them" (*Eve*, 196). This terror is of course the terror she has provoked in him.

Hadaly thus offers herself to Ewald's imagination, grounding her being in a supernal realm in a discourse couched in transcendentalist rhetoric and emphatically evocative of the vocabulary of sublimity. It is divided into several short sections. In the central one, which is entitled "Struggles with the angel" and prefaced by a pseudo-quote attributed to "Someone" to the effect that positivism lies in the forgetting of the infinite, she reminds him that the comforts of logic and common sense are illusory and make him forget his destiny to embrace the higher world: "And so, not without a skeptical laugh or two, you conclude by hailing this Reason of yours. . . . You propose to see it as the unquestioned 'Legislator' of the *incomprehensible, shapeless, inescapable* INFINITE" (*Eve*, 197). In the scene of Ewald's struggle with his artificial angel, Villiers's own struggle is to invoke her as a figure of a suprasensory world, in a scene manifestly framed as sublime.

At this juncture, let us recall Michel Poizat's idea about women as the last avatar of the angel in nineteenth-century opera and place it beside Nina Auerbach's homologous observation, made in the context of her discussion of the polarity between angel and demon that structured Victorian thinking about women, that it was only in the nineteenth century that angels became feminized. Since the sublime is not normally associated with femininity—quite the opposite, in fact—these arguments help account for the assimilation of singing women to the angelic and the angelic to the sublime in the fictions we have considered here.

In section 4 of his treatise on the sublime, Burke postulates a feeling of profound uncertainty as the source of intense emotion, hence of the sublime, proposing the idea of infinity as the most affecting of all among those which provoke this emotion, since "hardly anything can strike the mind with its greatness, which does not make some sort of approach towards infinity" (Burke, 105). He follows this argument with an example from the book of Job, which he calls "amazingly sublime," attributing its effectiveness to the "terrible uncertainty of the thing described." The passage he quotes is the text of Job's visitation by a messenger from God:

In thoughts from the visions of the night, when deep sleep felleth upon men, fear came upon me and trembling, which made all my bones to shake. Then a spirit passed before my face. The hair of my flesh stood up. It stood still, but I could not discern the form thereof: an image was before mine eyes; there was silence; and I heard a voice,—Shall mortal man be more just than God? (Burke, 108)

The angel here is presented as an ideal figure for the infinite and so a quintessentially sublime one: its form cannot be discerned, and the ideas to which it gives rise escape representation, instilling the terror that was a hallmark of sublimity for Burke.

Burke returns to the angel as image of sublimity toward the end of his treatise, when advocating the superior evocative force of poetry over painting as a medium for the sublime. Saying that a picture cannot evoke the same effect as words, he writes, "To represent an angel in a picture, you can only draw a beautiful young man winged; but what painting can furnish out any thing so grand as the addition of one word, 'the angel of the *Lord*'?" (Burke, 336). He gives as a "further instance" the passage from Milton in which he "describes the fallen angels through their dismal habitations," finding the line "Rocks, caves, lakes, dens, bogs, fens and shades" to be quite sublime, but says that the last words, "and Death," raise a higher degree of sublimity with the addition of a "universe of Death" (Burke, 337–

38). Undoubtedly, Burke would find Edgar Allan Poe's poetry to be extremely sublime, and clearly Poe's aesthetic inherits much of its quality from the gothic taste for darkness and horror Burke's text expresses. As an aside, it is tempting to think of Poe's *Fall of the House of Usher* as making reference to the eighteenth-century theorist of the sublime, James Usher, who published in 1769 a book that Monk calls "what comes very near being a mystical interpretation of sublimity" (Monk, 142).

Thus, Burke accords the angel particular prestige as an effective figure for the sublime: the angel stands for an experience of what is supernal, hence unrepresentable. Evoked repeatedly in the nineteenth-century fictional representations of extraordinary female singers, it serves as a shorthand figure in received romantic vocabulary for their function as liminal figurations of an idealized aesthetic experience understood to be taking place at the edge of, and indeed as escaping, representation. The fictional descriptions of the singing voices that move their hearers to painful wonder through their magnitude, through their seemingly infinite expansion, through the sense of the beauty of a soul in flight they are said to convey, repeatedly typify the singer as angel, a term implicitly coded as sublime.

The voices of these fictional singers are much like the sexless voice that Poizat argues is key to the position of the female voice in nineteenth-century opera. He emphasizes the importance of the female voice for opera at this time, arguing that the soprano voice in particular becomes the primary object of musical *jouissance* for the opera lover. As we have seen, Poizat grounds his thesis of the object-voice in Lacanian theory, tracing the appeal of the feminine voice to the primordial lost object of psychoanalysis, as well as to the related question of sexual difference, an argument whose critical context and various formulations we reviewed earlier. One reading, then, of the voice as aesthetic object finds its grounding in a line of psychoanalytic argumentation that presents it within the framework of nostalgia for the maternal voice.

Such a reading is enriched by the argument Thomas Weiskel has made in *The Romantic Sublime* about the role of sublimation in the economy of the psychology of the sublime. He suggests that the "semiology of the sublime requires for its working principle the category of 'sublimation' which suggests in turn the psychological concept of 'identification.'"[19] His analysis of the role of sublimation as determinative of the "I" of the romantic poem is useful for an understanding of the dynamics at work in the pleasure in the feminine voice insofar as they reveal certain masochistic and fetishistic grounds.[20]

In "The Logic of Terror," Weiskel suggests that the motor of transcendence in the sublime is fueled by an intense anxiety: this anxiety is particularly visible in Burke's emphasis on terror as a catalyst of sublime emotion. Weiskel argues that Burke's sense of terror derives from what suggests the idea of danger, from a perception of power, in particular as it gives rise to an indirect threat of danger. Sublime experience in this reading arises, then, from a "fantasy of injury": castration anxiety. The perception of defeat (which emerges strongly in Kant's account) is joined to a realization that the threat is not a real one. The initial anxiety is subsumed by a "positive resolution of the anxiety in the delight of the third phase, which is psychologically an identification with the superior power" (Weiskel, 93). Thus, in the parallel Weiskel draws between the sublime experience and the structure of castration anxiety, a way out becomes possible through an act of identification that establishes the superego. The subject neutralizes the danger by internalizing it, then identifying with an ideal. Weiskel signals that the ambiguity of this identification with an ideal both internal and external to the psyche is to be met throughout Kant's account of the sublime. He notes that the importance of the sublime lies in its functioning as the very moment in which the mind turns within and performs its identification with reason. The sublime moment recapitulates and thereby reestablishes the Oedipus complex, whose positive resolution is the basis of culture itself (see Weiskel, 93–94).

In this connection, Weiskel cites Freud's own assessment in "The Economic Problem of Masochism" that "the categorical imperative of Kant is thus a direct inheritance of the Oedipus-complex" (Weiskel, 93). Weiskel buttresses this suggestion of a masochistic component in sublime delight by pointing out the theological forms Burke takes in his meditation on God as authority; this emerges more clearly still in Kant's stress on the necessity to identify with a disposition consonant with the will of God. Thus "the best defense against fear is a strong superego, which the sublime both requires and nourishes. The identification is so strong that the mind voluntarily submits to punishment. . . . Sublimity enjoins a divided self sitting in judgment on its own impulses" (Weiskel, 94). Weiskel goes on to trace out how melancholy and guilt issue from the aggressive impulse released by this process of identification that defuses the threat. This impulse in turn must be neutralized by an increased identification with the "dictatorial harshness" activated in the superego.

This masochism and the melancholy associated with it are hallmarks of romantic feeling, as Weiskel points out, and call to mind the type of masochistic pleasure that Praz isolates in his reading of the late romantic femme fatale figure. It is also homologous with Lacoue-Labarthe's characterization of musical pleasure as essentially theatrical and masochistic. We have seen something of this at work in the parallel developed earlier between those icy sirens, Hadaly and Wanda: in both cases, desire becomes imbricated with an idealizing impulse that reifies the woman as statue. Since the linchpin of fetishistic preoccupation is, of course, oedipal anxiety over sexual difference, it is resolved through a denial of female difference. The ghost of the denial of the feminine haunts Weiskel's account as well: like Lacoue-Labarthe, who alludes to nostalgic reminiscence of the lost maternal voice at the end of "The Echo of the Subject," Weiskel appends a short discussion of the role of the mother in the structure of sublimation, noting that the "other side of superego anxiety presents itself as having been ignored. The superego is a precipitate of the mother as well as the father, and its displeasure may thus be manifested not only in the fantasy of castration but also in the sense of loss" (Weiskel, 102).

This anxiety of loss, which Weiskel associates with romantic melancholy, is for Lacoue-Labarthe the sense of originary loss at the source of musical pleasure. Poizat's theory that the pleasure offered by the object-voice in nineteenth-century opera is keyed to longing for the maternal lost object bears affinities with Weiskel's analysis of the economy of sublimation in which oedipal fear of injury is resolved through a masochistic identification with a powerful ideal.

Weiskel, Lacoue-Labarthe, and Poizat all point to a similar conclusion: superego identification is interwoven with anxiety over originary loss, paradoxically creating the conditions for aesthetic delight.

Such a reading of the role of sublimation in the fascination with the voice as aesthetic object parallels the suggestion that the sublime aesthetic lends energy to the romantic singer texts. Taken together, these readings provide a framework for the demonstrations I have given that the literary representations of singing voices assimilate them to an inhuman register of inhuman entities: bird song, bells, struck crystal, violins, and so on. Angels, too, are inhuman. This thesis is further supported by an argument both Poizat and Lyotard make separately in the contexts of their discussions for a progressive focus on the materiality of the artistic object during this period.

Poizat's thesis, that the feminine voice in opera as it became the focus of operatic pleasure was constructed as angelic and sexless, must be taken in the context of the historical frame of his argument. Poizat traces opera's evolution away from its early emphasis on the intelligibility of sung speech toward a progressive focus on song detached from intelligibility in favor of what he calls the "angel's voice," the voice from "on high"—the very high, soaring voice—and ultimately, pure cry. The evolution of operatic form in the nineteenth century thus resolves, as it were, the long debate that dogged the history of opera over the respective importance of aria and recitative, of "music" versus "drama" or speech. In his writings on music Rousseau recounts the famous dispute between Piccinists and Gluckists that divided the court on this issue between the "Queen's Corner" and the "King's Corner"—that is, between Italian and French music. The antinomy was ultimately broken down, as intelligible song became absorbed by music, culminating in the Wagnerian continuity of aria and orchestral music. Thus, the character of the diva's voice in the singing of bel canto and after renders the text not only insignificant beside the pleasure obtained from the pure quality of the singing itself but essentially unintelligible. The audience's pleasure becomes intensively focused on the aria, with its essentially nonlinguistic emotive power. Poizat's thesis that the angelic voice, the soprano voice, becomes the pure object of musical pleasure assumes added coherence in light of Lyotard's association of the sublime, the indeterminate, and the inhuman.

Lyotard cites Burke's use of the angel as exemplar of the sublime as part of his argument. He asserts that he derives his formulation of the sublime moment as the question *Is it happening?* not directly from Kant, but rather from Burke's association of the sublime with the fear that "nothing" will happen: "What is terrifying is that the *It happens that* does not happen, that it stops happening" (Lyotard, 99). He argues that Burke's conception of the sublime is based on terror, in turn based on various sorts of privations, on suspense, and the delight that arises as the threat of danger subsides. He bases his definition of the sublime on that of Burke:

Here then is an account of the sublime feeling: a very big, very powerful object threatens to deprive the soul of any "it happens," strikes with "astonishment." . . . The soul is thus dumb, immobilized, as good as dead. Art, by distancing this menace, procures a pleasure of relief, of delight. Thanks to art, the soul is returned to the agitated zone between life and death, and this agitation is its health and its life. For Burke, the sublime was no longer a matter of elevation (the category by which Aristotle defined tragedy), but a matter of intensification. (Lyotard, 98)

He then cites Burke's use of Milton's angel to suggest the capacity of poetry to move its public, freed from the "verisimilitudes of figuration." Drawing on Burke's celebration of literature's power to employ powerful *combinations* of ideas to influence the passions, Lyotard enrolls this idea of the sublime in support of his contention that with romanticism art became freed to abandon the imitation of beautiful models, to try combinations of effects that would be "surprising, strange, shocking"; he thus identifies the *it happens* of the sublime as the shock "par excellence." In this way, the aesthetic ground is prepared for a new world of artistic experimentation that becomes modern art, and the avant-gardes in particular. Lyotard does not claim that the artist of the late nineteenth and twentieth centuries reads Burke:

It is more a matter of an irreversible deviation in the destination of art, a deviation affecting all the valencies of the artistic condition. The artist attempts combinations allowing the event. The art-lover does not experience a simple pleasure, or derive some ethical benefit from his contact with art, but expects an intensification of his conceptual and emotional capacity, an ambivalent enjoyment. Intensity is associated with an ontological dislocation. The art-object no longer bends itself to models, but tries to present the fact that there is an unpresentable; it no longer imitates nature, but is, in Burke, the actualization of a figure potentially there in language. (Lyotard, 101)

Lyotard, here calling the art object in the French text a "simulacrum," is arguing for the decline of the Aristotelian unity of form and content or "matter" in art, along with its attendant assumption of a natural correspondence, an organic harmony, between form and matter (stemming naturally, as it were, as *phusis*, from *phuein*, to grow). This decline for Lyotard is implicit in the Kantian analysis of the sublime and is both revealed and hidden by romantic aesthetics. With the gradual abandonment of the idea of art as nature and nature as art, a new set of stakes emerges: the need to approach matter, the material itself, "which means approaching presence without recourse to the means of presentation" (Lyotard, 139). In music and painting, then, a new place is made for progressive exploration of nuance and timbre, elements that militate against positive determination. In this context, Lyotard presents his notion of the indeterminate in art, an idea he elsewhere identifies with the incursion of an "other inhuman" into the modern condition and which emerges as an aesthetic term within the register of the sublime.

This notion of the indeterminate in music and painting offers a suggestive avenue to approach the inhuman voice as vehicle for sublime feeling. Nuance and timbre are differences that are subtly perceptible between sounds or colors otherwise identical in their physical parameters. They are what emerge as the distinctions one hears between the same note played by a flute, violin, or piano, in his example, or in the same color rendered in pastels, watercolor, or oils. Lyotard speaks of this quality of shading in tone and color indeterminacy as opening up a space of experience outside any identifiable formal quality:

Within the tiny space occupied by a note or a colour in the sound- or colour-continuum, which corresponds to the identity-card for the note or the colour, timbre or nuance introduces a sort of infinity, the indeterminacy of the harmonics within the frame determined by this identity. Nuance or timbre is the distress and despair of the exact division and thus the clear composition of sounds and colours according to graded scales and harmonic temperaments. From this aspect of matter, one must say that it must be immaterial. (Lyotard, 140)

The perception of this immateriality of musical or painterly artistic material thus described by Lyotard entails a kind of suspension of the critical faculty in a state of aesthetic receptivity, a state of mind in which it is subject to "presence," not in the sense of a here and now, but of an aesthetic event in which the material is simply perceived as "there," as something that touches and moves the sensibility. Terms like timbre or nuance are interchangeable and designate the event of a passion, a possibility for which the mind will not have been prepared, which will have unsettled it, and of which it conserves only the feeling—anguish and jubilation—of an obscure debt (see Lyotard, 141). This "debt" is the one owed to the tradition of aesthetic suspension opened up by the sublime, which pries apart the congruence of beauty and form, creating a place for an aesthetic of nuance and timbre.

These qualities that escape formal description correspond to those qualities of the voice that make it available as a pure object of aesthetic experience—paradoxically, since nuance and timbre are essentially tiny impurities in color and sound: they derive from the very materiality of the media. Like Roland Barthes's "grain of the voice," they communicate feeling in a mode that lies outside signification as it can be systematized by language or theoretical constructs, the realm of pure *jouissance*. The grain of the voice, like Lyotard's indeterminate in art, provokes aesthetic pleasure within a register that presents it in its essential materiality. In this context, Stendhal's praise of Pasta's capacity to exploit just such an indeterminacy in musical notation takes on added resonance: "For Mme. Pasta, the same note in two different situations of the soul is not, so to speak, the same sound. Here, quite simply is the sublimity of the art of singing."[21]

The aesthetic space of the indeterminate occupies the place of Lyotard's inhuman, the element in art that escapes representativity, where the material of art offers itself to the senses outside its conceptual frame of presentation. Implicit in Lyotard's thesis is the notion that this indeterminacy is the trace of a sense of infinity as what eludes the formal, as what escapes the totalizing activity of the mind in its apprehension of an aesthetic object. What in the earlier formulations of the sublime is seen in terms of sheer magnitude in Kant, or very intense sensory experiences in Burke, elements that provoke a suspension of the critical faculties, persists in representation through romanticism as a gesture toward the supernal and the absolute. It is allied with an exploration of the material properties of the aesthetic object that lead to the object's divorce from mimesis or representativity, to the progression from "art as nature and nature as art" to the aesthetic that dominates the late romantic era of "art for art's sake," which emphasizes the artistic object as artifact, as "simulacrum," to use Lyotard's term.

This argument for a process of "dehumanization" in art is congruent with my discussion of Baudelaire and the artificial woman. In examining Baudelaire's preference for the "painted woman" in terms of the dandyist posture of hostility to nature and taste for the artificial, we have seen how Baudelaire's "Eloge du maquillage" criticizes the eighteenth-century moral conception of nature as the source and type of artistic beauty, to relocate art in the realm of artifice. We have seen the association in Baudelairean aesthetics of art and modernity with the artificial, itself assimilated to the supernatural and to the strange or unexpected, *l'insolite*. Baudelaire's antinaturalism is shared by the socialist utopian movements of the period, specifically the Saint-Simonians, and by a certain current of Marx's thought.[22] Likewise, I have presented the filiation of the Baudelairean preference for the inorganic (things cold, mineral, and metallic) as elements of modernity and the aesthetic of artificiality that emerges in Villiers's *L'Eve future* and such symbolist works as Huysmans's *A rebours*, as well as in the antinaturalist gestures of Jarry's works and in Maurice Maeterlinck's waxwork theater. The prestige of Baudelaire's aesthetic gives expression to what may be thought of as an antinaturalistic thread that emerges in romanticism and becomes progressively pronounced in later aesthetic ideas.

In this context, I have argued for the association of this antinaturalistic impulse with the figure of the statuelike, remote femme fatale, which Praz shows to be an obsessive image in the latter half of the century, and with the figure of the dancer with the dead face which Kermode argues to be a central aesthetic motif of late romantic and symbolist poetry. According to Kermode's argument, dance for these artists meant not classical ballet but the unconventional, free-form dance of Loïe Fuller (since her performances eliminated the extraneous element of scenery). Still, his argument that the stylized gesture of the dancer figures forth the romantic image allows for the suggestion that the aesthetic of the artificial can be seen to emerge from within the matrix of romanticism not only in literary art but in ballet as well, which saw at this time the cultivation of a progressive stylization of the human body—the female body in particular—in poses and movements that are unnatural and severely taxing to achieve. In this sense, ballet becomes during this period one staging—again through the woman—of the triumph of artifice over nature. In this connection, one may think of Balinese dance, also characterized by an extreme artificiality of movement: these dancers combine stiff, abrupt motions alternately with a gliding stride, as they extend their fingers in a trembling motion and tilt their heads. It is often said that this form of dance takes its character from its imitation of the shadow puppet theater which plays such an important role in Balinese society. While ballet dancers cannot be said to be imitating marionettes (except in Stravinsky's *Petrouchka*), their impassivity as they dance, the distinctive costumes they wear, and the conventionalized forms of ballet, which exploit to an extraordinary degree a rigidification of the body, suggest the scene of ballet as a special world of artifice in which, as in the marionette theater, the stakes are to make artificial figures look almost—but not quite—natural.

Within this framework of the identification of art with the artificial arises the fascination with the representations of the female voice as dehumanized object in the texts we have considered here. The constructed, inhuman voices in these texts present an aspect of the persistence of the aesthetic of the sublime: within the matrix of the antinaturalist tendency, with its valuation of the artificial—the paradoxical offspring of the urge to represent the suprasensory that emerges in romanticism—the inhuman voice occupies the space of inhuman otherness opened by the aesthetic of the sublime, which persists from the eighteenth century through romanticism and after. The shiver of pleasure offered by the inhuman voice thus reveals itself as a constituent impulse of modernity at work within romanticism and as a trace of the idea of infinity codified in the sublime. The transcendental siren song of Villiers's late-nineteenth-century artificial angel recalls this nostalgia already evident at the outset of romanticism. Writing of the concept of infinity in Baudelaire's *Correspondences* and Kleist's "On the Marionette Theater," Paul de Man calls the idea of innocence recovered through experience, "of paradise consciously regained after the fall into consciousness, . . . one of the most seductive, powerful and deluded *topoi* of the idealist and romantic period"[23] and refers the reader to the passage from Kleist's piece with which I will conclude:

Just as two intersecting lines, converging on one side of a point reappear on the other after their passage through infinity, and just as our image, as we approach a concave mirror, vanishes to infinity only to reappear before our very eyes, so will grace, having likewise traversed the infinite, return to us once more, and so appear most purely in that bodily form that has either no consciousness at all or an infinite one, which is to say, either in the puppet or the god.[24]

Reference Matter

Notes

Chapter 1

1. Doane, "The Voice in the Cinema," 45.
2. Irigaray, *L'Ethique*, 14. Translations, when not otherwise noted, are my own.
3. Ibid., 17.
4. Goux, *Symbolic Economies*, 215–16.
5. See Plaza, "Pouvoir 'phallomorphique' et psychologie de 'la femme.'"
6. Fraser, "Introduction," 3.
7. Goux, *Symbolic Economies*, 236.
8. Proust, *Remembrance of Things Past*, 2: 134.
9. Rousseau, *Confessions*, 6–7.
10. Marin, "Un Filet de voix fort douce," 12.
11. Grosrichard, "L'Air de Venise," 134.
12. Quoted in Grosrichard, "L'Air de Venise."
13. I will return to this point later in my discussion. See Berenson, *The Trial of Madame Caillaux*.
14. See Poovey, *Uneven Developments*.
15. See Kittler, *Discourse Networks: 1800/1900*, 25–69.
16. Vasse, *La Voix et l'ombilique*, 14.
17. Anzieu, *The Skin-Ego*, 40.
18. See, for example, the special issue of *Yale French Studies* in which Doane's essay appears. Rick Altman's essay on film as ventriloquism ("Moving Lips: Cinema as Ventriloquism") offers the suggestion that sound plays a much more important role than is generally understood, and provocatively offers as a model for film the metaphor of the ventriloquist (the sound track), who uses the dummy (the image track) to his own ends.

19. See Chion, *La Voix au cinéma*.
20. See Chodorow, *The Reproduction of Mothering*.
21. Khomsi, "Langue maternelle, langue adressé à l'enfant," 93.

Chapter 2

1. Silverman's book appeared after I had worked out the argument developed in my study. Since it bears so closely on the topics at hand, I felt it necessary to provide some comment.
2. Stanton, "Difference on Trial," 158.
3. See Fraser, "Introduction."
4. Kahane, "Questioning the Maternal," 82.
5. Gallop, *The Daughter's Seduction*, 124–25.
6. Moi, *Sexual/Textual Politics*, 165–66.
7. For further discussion of the *chora* as site of splitting and abjection, see Fletcher and Benjamin, eds., *Abjection, Melancholy, Love: The Work of Julia Kristeva*.
8. Moi, *Sexual/Textual Politics*, 168.
9. Kristeva, "The Novel as Polylogue," 191.
10. See, for example, Smith's discussion, "Julia Kristeva Et Al.; Or, Take Three or More" in *Feminism and Psychoanalysis*.
11. See Butler, "The Body Politics of Julia Kristeva."
12. Silverman, *The Acoustic Mirror*, 109.
13. The importance of rhythm in language and subjectivity cannot be overestimated for Meschonnic. In his *Critique du rhythme* he generates a complex analysis of rhythm not only in poetry but in the evolution and determination of meaning in discourse in general. Rhythm comes from the body and informs the subject and his perceptions; Meschonnic argues that language is rhythm. Like Foucault and Derrida, he believes that discourse structures the subject, but he also thinks that "a theory of discourse is no longer effective without a theory of rhythm, which transforms the prevailing discontinuity of the units of the sign into the primacy of continuity, with rhythm defined as the continuous movement of *signifiance*, such a movement being the historical activity of a subject, the very possibility of the passing on of significance from subject to subject—the *energeia* spoken about by Humboldt" ("Interview," 95). Although Meschonnic shares with Kristeva this sense of the centrality of rhythm to language and the subject, like Derrida he is a critic of structuralism, semiotics, and their immediate heirs in the conception of the sign. Thus he attacks those, like Anthony Wilden and Kristeva, whom he sees as subscribing to a conception of the sign as duality, product of a binary rationalism. Meschonnic criticizes Kristeva for feminist, hence dualistic, thinking: "The problem shared by women and poets is to change

the relation, not just to reverse the terms. But in France, at least a few years ago, feminist theory figured theory as male, and the relation to the body as feminine. Thus Kristeva tied rhythm to the impulse. That is precisely nineteenth-century dualist anthropology: reason versus emotion, male versus female, mathematics versus embroidery. The more that 'feminist theory' rebelled against the male, the more it reinforced the model" ("Interview," 96).

14. Lacoue-Labarthe, "The Echo of the Subject," 159.

Chapter 3

1. Sand, *Lettres inédites de George Sand et Pauline Viardot, 1839–1849*, 159.

2. Christiansen, *Prima Donna: A History*, 78.

3. Gautier, *Histoire de l'art dramatique en France*, 1: 304.

4. Marix-Spire, *Les Romantiques et la musique*, 24.

5. See Christiansen, 76–77.

6. Ibid., 77.

7. Decades later, Saint-Saëns would liken her voice to " 'not velvet or crystal . . . but bitter-sweet oranges' " (ibid., 83).

8. Musset, *Mélanges de littérature et de critique*, 108–9.

9. Ibid., 118–19.

10. Stendhal, *The Life of Rossini*, 367.

11. Gautier, 305–6. Gautier gives a detailed description of Viardot's voice in this passage, some of which I include here:

During the pause in the *andante* of the cavatina (taken from Rossini's *Elisabetta* and intercalated here), she executed two and a fifth octaves, from the tenor's bottom "F" to the soprano's high "C." But the timbre of the "F" and the facility with which she attacked the "C," which she displayed frequently in the course of the piece, clearly show that she will eventually produce at the theater the three full octaves, at least, of which she is capable at home. In the contralto roles, like those of Tancredi, Arsace, and Malcolm, which she will learn, they say, she will give us the exact measure of her lower register, which will undoubtedly acquire one day more force, if not more reach. As for the high notes, it would behoove her never to force them nor to overdo them before reaching her full physical development. . . . Her sensitive and practiced ear attends accurately to the details of accompaniment, as numerous recommendations and remarks at rehearsals have proved to us.

See also my discussion of Gautier's "Contralto" on pages 105–10.

12. Christiansen, 82.

13. See Marix-Spire, 57–58. Marix-Spire includes here a copy of a letter Viardot published in *Le Siècle* to explain that a bad review of Pauline in the

Revue des Deux Mondes had him as its real target: "There are some noble-hearted people who strike a woman in order to wound a man."

14. Quoted in *Lettres inédites*, 41. The rest of the quote is as follows:

The debut of Mlle. García will be a brilliant moment in the history of art practiced by women. The genius of this musician at once consummate and inspired testifies to a progess in intelligence that has not yet been manifested by the feminine sex in such a conclusive manner. . . . [Passage quoted in my text follows.] Her talent as an actress is analogous: all the desirable faculties and innate qualities inspire her almost spontaneously; but this talent has not been submitted, as has her singing, to rigorous study. . . . One has noticed in the young actress a certain awkwardness, yet full of grace and modesty, and one has willingly let her be governed by her impressions . . . without seeking too much before her mirror what the boards will give her soon enough. One has also noticed that her figure was admirably lovely. . . . The painters admire the instinctive poetry that presides over her manner. She is always in the midst of movement full of elegance and truth.

15. Guichard writes in *La Musique et les lettres au temps du Romantisme*, "Rousseau, who sings the praises of these *scuole*, never missed vespers at the school of the *Mendicanti* . . . where all the music lovers met—amateurs, that is, of music and of little girls." Regarding Rousseau and his revelations about the voice in Venice, see Grosrichard, "L'Air de Venise." Regarding Rousseau and the mother's voice, see Marin, "Un filet de voix fort douce." See also my previous chapter.

16. Sand fictionalizes a number of historical figures in this ambitious, extensively researched novel, including Frederick the Great of Prussia, Empress Maria Theresa, Haydn, Cagliostro, Metastasio, and others, some of whom were authors of memoirs she used to render an approximation of historical accuracy. One example is the sister of Frederick, Frederica Sophie Wilhelmina of Prussia, Margrave of Bareith, whose unhappy attachment to the Baron of Trenck provides Sand with much romantic material.

17. Guichard, *La Musique et les lettres au temps du Romantisme*, 355.

18. Marix-Spire, 215.

19. Bailbé, "Musique et personnalité dans *Consuelo*," 119.

20. Ibid., 127.

21. One thinks of the "flexible timbre" of Amélie's voice, the sign of her light character (1: 225), of the "vulgar accent" of Anzoleto's tenor voice (1: 30), of Zdenko's voice, "shrill and broken but penetratingly true and sweet" (1: 270), of the sonority of Albert's voice that "flatters Consuelo's musical ear" (1: 222), of the sweet and harmonious sound of Haydn's voice (2: 105). Even the good canon "in raising a bit his tone" condemns the voice of dame Brigide as "harsh as a rattle" (2: 239). Finally the "clear and full timbre" of Consuelo's voice touches Albert, who tells her: "The words you pronounce in your songs are nothing but an abbreviated theme, a partial in-

dication. . . . What I hear, what penetrates to the depth of my heart, is your voice, your accent, your inspiration," and he adds: "I am not a musician except while I listen to you" (1: 378). All page references are to Sand, *La Comtesse de Rudolstadt*.

22. Sand, *Consuelo*, vol. 1 of *La Comtesse de Rudolstadt*, 23.

23. See Christiansen, 96–99, 108–9.

24. Marix-Spire notes that Sand might have had the opportunity to see both Malibran and Pasta perform in the opera *Tancredi* in the same year, 1831.

25. See Marix-Spire, 241–42.

26. See Boney, "The Influence of E. T. A. Hoffman on George Sand."

27. Hoffman, *Tales of E. T. A. Hoffman*, 114.

28. See Freud, "The Uncanny," 152–53.

Chapter 4

1. Stendhal, *Life of Rossini*, 357.

2. See chapter 35, "Madame Pasta," in ibid., 361–76.

3. Quoted in Marix-Spire, *Les Romantiques et la musique*, 246–47.

4. Lindenberger, *Opera: The Extravagant Art*, 236–37.

5. Fulcher, *The Nation's Image*, 8.

6. Anderson, *Imagined Communities*, 145.

7. Stendhal, *Life of Rossini*, 113.

8. Heriot, *The Castrati in Opera*, 13.

9. Poizat, *The Angel's Cry*, 68–69.

10. Christiansen, *Prima Donna*, 126.

11. See Clément, *Opera, or the Undoing of Women*.

12. Lindenberger, *Opera: The Extravagant Art*, 267–68.

13. Musset, *Mélanges de littérature et de critique*, 125.

14. See the discussion in the next chapter on Baudelaire and the painted woman.

15. Sand, *Consuelo*, vol. 1 of *La Comtesse de Rudolstadt*, 146–47.

16. Simone Vierne, "Le Mythe de la femme dans *Consuelo*," 44.

17. See ibid., 45.

18. Nerval, *Les Filles du feu*, 131.

19. Professor Chambers kindly sent me this monograph after hearing about my study. Its corroboration of my own ideas has been very encouraging.

20. Chambers, *L'Ange et l'automate*, 19.

21. Balzac, "Sarrasine," reprinted in Roland Barthes, *S/Z*, 253.

22. Gautier, "Contralto," in *Emaux et camées*, 51–52.

23. Hugo's lines are:

> Le carillon, c'est l'heure inattendue et folle
> Que l'oeil croit voir vêtue en danseuse espagnole
> Elle vient, secouant sur les toits léthargiques
> Son tablier d'argent plein de notes magiques
> Par un frêle escalier de cristal invisible,
> Effaré et dansante, elle descend des cieux;
> Et l'esprit, ce veilleur fait d'oreilles et d'yeux,
> Tandis qu'elle va, vient, monte et descend encore,
> Entend de marche en marche errer son pied sonore!

[The pealing of bells, the unexpected and mad hour / That the eyes thinks it sees dressed as a Spanish dancer. / She comes, shaking over the lethargic roofs / Her silver pinafore full of magic notes. / Alarmed and dancing, she descends from the sky; / And the spirit, that watchman made of eyes and ears / While she comes, goes, rises and descends again / Hears her pass step to step, her foot ringing on the stair.]

Quoted in *Emaux et camées*, notes to "Contralto," 238, note 3.

24. Ibid.

25. See chapter 3, n. 11.

26. Vierne, "Le Mythe de la femme dans *Consuelo*," 47.

27. See Butler, "Gender Trouble, Feminist Theory, and Psychoanalytic Discourse," 338.

28. I learned of the topos of the hypnotized woman under the spell of the mesmerizer while attending Raymond Bellour's course on "Hypnose et Cinéma" at the Centre Odéon in Paris, 1981. It can be found in a number of nineteenth-century novels like *Trilby* and the Cagliostro novels of Dumas, and in certain films, such as Fritz Lang's Mabuse series.

29. Du Maurier, *Trilby*, 14, 16.

Chapter 5

1. Kittler, *Discourse Networks, 1800/1900*, 348.

2. While it is true that social change and the feminist movements of the late nineteenth century may have rendered it easier for women to be more active, "1900" with its futurists and surrealists continued to eroticize and objectify women.

3. Kittler, *Discourse Networks*, 229.

4. See ibid., 238.

5. See Praz, *The Romantic Agony*.

6. See Kermode, *The Romantic Image*.

7. See Benjamin, *Illuminations*, 155–200.

8. See Djikstra, *Idols of Perversity*.

9. Baudelaire, *The Painter of Modern Life*, 30.

10. Baudelaire, *Oeuvres complètes*, 2: 1426, n. 2.

11. Ibid., 2: 1427.

12. Ibid., 2: 766–67.

13. Jean de la Bruyère, *The Characters of Jean de La Bruyère*, trans. Henry Van Laun (London, 1929), 59–60, quoted in Lichtenstein, "Making Up Representations: The Risks of Femininity," 77.

14. Lemaitre, "Modernité et surnaturalisme," xxxi.

15. Sartre, *Baudelaire*, 100.

16. Villiers de l'Isle-Adam, *Tomorrow's Eve*, 92.

17. See Beaune, *L'Automate et ses mobiles*, 54–60.

18. I am indebted for this reference to Rosi Braidotti, who discussed it during the course she co-taught with Marie-Jo Dhavernas on technology at the College International de Philosophie, Paris, spring 1986.

19. Again, I first heard this reference from Rosi Braidotti during her talk on *L'Eve future*.

20. See Mayr, *Authority, Liberty, and Automatic Machinery in Early Modern Europe*.

21. Descartes, *Selected Philosophical Writings*, 44.

22. See Gunderson, *Mentality and Machines*.

23. See Loraux, "Le Fantôme de la sexualité."

24. Theweleit notes that Jean Paul disliked Kempelen's "plan to construct playing and talking machines, for this promised to take bread from the mouths of sportsmen, on the one hand, and women on the other" (*Male Fantasies*, 356–57).

25. Quoted in Ziolkowski, review of *Marionetten, Maschinen, Automaten*, 302.

Chapter 6

1. She moves from a consideration of Hadaly as *emblazoned woman* through a comparison of her with the eighteenth-century Waxen Venus of Clemente Susini, a complex and elegant anatomical doll, to an evocation of Condillac's statue as model for Villiers's ambiguously quickened Android. See Michelson, "On the Eve of the Future."

2. Bellour has developed a theory of hypnosis as a model for the cinema that posits the cinema as a hypnotized, speaking woman. In this argument, which follows the development of a series of narratives in nineteenth-century fiction by Dumas, Villiers, du Maurier, and Verne through to the Mabuse films of Fritz Lang, Bellour traces the theme of the hypnotized woman who proffers vision for her master. A key term of Bellour's analysis of *The Future Eve* is the novel's anticipation of the invention of cinema, evoking the ref-

erence to Alicia's "horrible *camera obscura*," to be replaced with the sublime illusion of Hadaly. He also emphasizes the way the Android stages the nineteenth-century Promethean dream of a rivalry with God: Hadaly both allows man to occupy the place of the creator, and as ideal machine does so herself; he notes also the parallel between the Android and Mallarmé's "Livre." See Bellour, "Ideal Hadaly."

3. Villiers, *Tomorrow's Eve*, 7.

4. Perriault, *Mémoires de l'ombre et du son*, 203.

5. This sketch appeared in *La Semaine parisienne*, 21 mai, 1874.

6. Villiers, *Oeuvres complètes*, 672.

7. Charbon, *La Machine parlante*, 20.

8. Nadar, "Daguerréotype acoustique," *Le Musée franco-anglais*, 1856, quoted in Perriault, *Mémoires de l'ombre et du son*, 133.

9. Nadar, *Les Mémoires du géant*, quoted ibid., 133–34.

10. Kittler, "Gramophone, Film, Typewriter," 111.

11. Ibid., 104.

12. Deleuze, *Présentation de Sacher-Masoch*, 17–18.

13. For rich discussions of the discourse on sexuality, fetishism, and prostitution in French literature of the nineteenth century, see Bernheimer, *Figures of Ill Repute*, and Apter, *Feminizing the Fetish*.

14. Lacoue-Labarthe, "The Echo of the Subject," 188.

15. See Raitt, "Villiers de l'Isle-Adam et Edgar Allan Poe," in *Villiers de l'Isle-Adam et le mouvement symboliste*.

16. Beaune, *L'Automate et ses mobiles*, 167.

17. Villiers, *Contes Cruels, Oeuvres complètes*, 2: 593.

18. Beaune, *L'Automate et ses mobiles*, 11.

19. My thanks to Malcolm Brodwick for bringing the Turing article to my attention.

20. Quoted in Gunderson, "The Imitation Game," in *Mentality and Machines*, 39–40.

21. Wachhorst, *Thomas Alva Edison*, 212.

22. Ibid., 23.

23. Ibid., 22.

24. Barnouw, *The Magician and the Cinema*, 11.

25. See Castle, "Phantasmagoria."

26. Huet, "Living Images," 81.

27. See Plank, "The Golem and the Robot."

28. Robert Alter has pointed out that this clay comes from *Genesis* 2, where a male God fashions men out of it.

29. Huet, "Living Images," 87.

30. Ibid.

Chapter 7

1. A collection of some of their writings on the subject has recently been translated in *Of the Sublime: Presence in Question. Essays by Jean-François Lyotard, et al.*, ed. Philippe Lacoue-Labarthe, trans. Jeffrey Librett (Albany: State University of New York Press, 1993).

2. Lyotard, *The Inhuman*, 92.

3. Lyotard is not alone in arguing for the sublime as a key to the rise of modernism in France. Suzanne Guerlac has recently published a reading of romantic and modernist writers through the perspective of the sublime that emphasizes the importance of this aesthetic to modernism and shows how its structures map modernity's crises of metaphysics and mimesis. See *The Impersonal Sublime*.

4. Monk, *The Sublime*, 32.

5. "The Sublime," in *The Princeton Encyclopedia of Poetry and Poetics*, 819.

6. See Furst, *Counterparts*, 112.

7. Quoted and paraphrased from *Critique of Aesthetic Judgment*, trans. J. C. Meredith (Oxford, 1911), and Victor Basch, *Essai critique sur l'esthétique de Kant* (Paris, 1927), in Monk, *The Sublime*, 6.

8. See Nancy, "The Sublime Offering."

9. Ibid., 42–43.

10. See Chapter 3, 76–77, 82.

11. Summarized in Marix-Spire, *Les Romantiques et la Musique*, 201.

12. Burke, *A Philosophical Inquiry into the Origin of our Ideas of the Beautiful and Sublime*, 150–51.

13. Stendhal, *The Life of Rossini*, 370 (translation modified).

14. Ibid., 167; see Chapter 4, 84–85.

15. Heriot, *The Castrati in Opera*, 36–37.

16. Du Maurier, *Trilby*, 318.

17. See ibid., 319–33.

18. Villiers, *Tomorrow's Eve*, 94.

19. Weiskel, *The Romantic Sublime*, 41.

20. See my discussions of Rousseau in Chapter 1, of the artificial woman in Chapter 4, and of the parallels between Villiers's Android and Sacher-Masoch's Wanda in Chapter 6, 154–56.

21. Stendhal, *Life of Rossini*, 184.

22. See Chapter 5, 129–30.

23. De Man, "Aesthetic Formalization," 267.

24. Kleist, *An Abyss Deep Enough*, 216.

Bibliography

Altman, Rick. "Moving Lips: Cinema as Ventriloquism." *Yale French Studies* 60 (1980): 67–79.

Anderson, Benedict. *Imagined Communities*. London: Verso, 1983.

Anzieu, Didier. *Le Moi-Peau*. Paris: Dunod, 1985.

———. *The Skin-Ego*. Trans. Chris Turner. New Haven, Conn.: Yale University Press, 1989.

Apter, Emily. *Feminizing the Fetish: Psychoanalysis and Narrative Obsession in Turn-of-the-Century France*. Ithaca, N.Y.: Cornell University Press, 1991.

Auerbach, Nina. *Woman and the Demon: The Life of a Victorian Myth*. Cambridge, Mass.: Harvard University Press, 1982.

Bailbé, Joseph Marc. "Musique et personnalité dans *Consuelo*." In Léon Cellier, ed., *La Porporina, Entretiens sur Consuelo*. Grenoble, Presses Universitaires de Grenoble, 1976.

Balakian, Anna. *The Symbolist Movement, A Critical Appraisal*. New York: New York University Press, 1977.

Balzac, Honoré de. *Sarrasine*. In Roland Barthes, *S/Z*. Trans. Richard Miller. New York: Hill and Wang, 1974.

Barnouw, Eric. *The Magician and the Cinema*. New York: Oxford University Press, 1981.

Barthes, Roland. *Image-Music-Text*. Trans. Stephen Heath. New York: Hill and Wang, 1977.

———. *S/Z*. Paris: Editions du Seuil, 1970.

———. *S/Z*. Trans. Richard Miller. New York: Hill and Wang, 1974.

Barzun, Jacques. *Berlioz and the Romantic Century*. New York: Columbia University Press, 1969.

Baudelaire, Charles. *Petits poèmes en prose (Le Spleen de Paris).* Ed. Henri Lemaitre. Paris: Editions Garnier Frères, 1962.

———. *Oeuvres complètes.* Vol. 2. Paris: Gallimard, 1975.

———. *The Painter of Modern Life and Other Essays.* Ed. and trans. Jonathan Mayne. New York: Phaidon, 1965.

Baudrillard, Jean, ed. *Traverses: la voix, l'écoute* 20 (1981). Paris: Editions de minuit. Centre national d'art et de culture Georges Pompidou.

———, ed. *Traverses: le simulacre* 10 (1978). Paris: Editions de minuit. Centre national d'art et de culture Georges Pompidou.

———, ed. *Traverses: les rhétoriques de la technologie* 26 (1982). Paris: Editions de minuit. Centre national d'art et de culture Georges Pompidou.

Beaune, Jean-Claude. *L'Automate et ses mobiles.* Paris: Flammarion, 1980.

Bedetti, Gabriella. "Henri Meschonnic: Rhythm as Pure Historicity." *New Literary History* 23 (spring 1990): 431–50.

Bellour, Raymond. "Ideal Hadaly." *Camera Obscura* 15 (fall 1986): 111–34.

Benjamin, Walter. *Illuminations.* Ed. and intro. Hannah Arendt. Trans. Harry Zohn. New York: Schocken, 1968.

Berenson, Edward. *The Trial of Madame Caillaux.* Berkeley: University of California Press, 1991.

Bernheimer, Charles. *Figures of Ill Repute: Representing Prostitution in Nineteenth-Century France.* Cambridge, Mass.: Harvard University Press, 1989.

Boney, Elaine. "The Influence of E. T. A. Hoffman on George Sand." In Janet Glasgow, ed., *George Sand: Collected Essays.* New York: Whitston Publishing Company, 1985.

Burke, Edmund. *A Philosophical Inquiry into the Origin of our Ideas of the Sublime and Beautiful.* London: R. and J. Dodsley, 1764.

Butler, Judith. "The Body Politics of Julia Kristeva." *Hypatia* 3, no. 3 (winter 1989): 104–17.

———. "Gender Trouble, Feminist Theory, and Psychoanalytic Discourse." In Linda J. Nicholson, ed., *Feminism/Postmodernism.* New York: Routledge, 1990.

Carrera, Roland, and David Fryer. "Androids." *FMR* 6 (November 1984): 65–92.

Carrouges, Michel. *Les Machines célibataires.* Paris: Chêne, 1976.

Castle, Terry. "Phantasmagoria: Spectral Technology and the Metaphorics of Modern Reverie." *Critical Inquiry* 15 (autumn 1988): 26–61.

Chambers, Ross. *L'Ange et l'automate: Variations sur le mythe de l'actrice de Nerval à Proust.* Paris: Lettres Modernes, vol. 5, #128, 1971.

Charbon, Paul. *La Machine parlante.* Rosheim: Editions Jean-Pierre Gyss, 1981.

Chion, Michel. *La Voix au cinéma.* Paris: Editions de l'Etoile, 1982.

Chodorow, Nancy. *The Reproduction of Mothering: Psychoanalysis and the Sociology of Gender.* Berkeley: University of California Press, 1978.

Christiansen, Rupert. *Prima Donna, a History.* New York: Viking, 1984.

Clair, Jean, and Harold Szeeman. *Les Machines célibataires.* Paris: Alfieri, 1975. Musée des Arts Décoratifs.

Clément, Catherine. *L'Opéra ou la défaite des femmes.* Paris: Grasset, 1979.

————. *Opera, or the Undoing of Women.* Trans. Betsy Wing. Minneapolis: University of Minnesota Press, 1988.

Deleuze, Gilles. *Présentation de Sacher-Masoch avec le texte intégral de* La Vénus à la fourrure. Trans. Aude Willm. Paris: Editions de minuit, 1967.

Delevoy, Robert. *Symbolists and Symbolism.* New York: Rizzoli, 1978.

de Man, Paul. "Aesthetic Formalization: Kleist's *Über das Marionettentheater.*" In *The Rhetoric of Romanticism.* New York: Columbia University Press, 1984.

Descartes, René. *Selected Philosophical Writings.* Trans. John Cottingham et al. Cambridge: Cambridge University Press, 1988.

Djikstra, Bram. *Idols of Perversity: Fantasies of Feminine Evil in Fin-de-Siècle Culture.* New York: Oxford University Press, 1986.

Doane, Mary Ann. "Voice in the Cinema: The Articulation of Body and Space." *Yale French Studies* 60 (1980): 33–50.

du Maurier, George. *Trilby.* New York: Harper & Brothers, 1894.

Else, Gerald F. "Sublime." In Alex Preminger, ed., *The Princeton Encyclopedia of Poetry and Poetics.* Princeton: Princeton University Press, 1965.

Feldstein, Richard, and Judith Roof, eds. *Feminism and Psychoanalysis.* Ithaca, N.Y.: Cornell University Press, 1989.

Figuier, Louis. *Les Grands Inventions modernes dans les sciences, l'industrie et les arts.* Paris: Hachette, 1912.

Fletcher, John, and Andrew Benjamin, eds. *Abjection, Melancholy, Love.* Warwick Studies in Philosophy and Literature. London: Routledge, 1990.

Franklin, H. Bruce. *Future Perfect: American Science Fiction of the Nineteenth Century.* New York: Oxford University Press, 1978.

Fraser, Nancy. "Introduction." *Hypatia* 3, no. 3 (1989): 1–9.

Freud, Sigmund. "The Uncanny." In James Strachey, ed. and trans., *New Introductory Lectures.* New York: Norton, 1965.

Fulcher, Jane. *The Nation's Image: French Grand Opera as Politics and as Politicized Art.* Cambridge: Cambridge University Press, 1987.

Furst, Lillian. *Counterparts.* Detroit: Wayne State University Press, 1977.

Gallop, Jane. *The Daughter's Seduction: Feminism and Psychoanalysis.* Ithaca, N.Y.: Cornell University Press, 1982.

Gautier, Théophile. *Emaux et camées.* Ed. Claudine Gothot-Mersch. Vol. 1. Paris: Gallimard, 1981.

————. *Histoire de l'art dramatique en France depuis vingt-cinq ans.* Vol. 1. Paris: Editions Hetzel, 1858.

Geduld, Harry M. *The Birth of the Talkies.* Bloomington: Indiana University Press, 1975.

Gelatt, Roland. *The Fabulous Phonograph.* 2nd edition. New York: Macmillan, 1977.

Goux, J. J. *Les Iconoclastes.* Paris: Editions du Seuil, 1978.

————. *Symbolic Economies: After Marx and Freud.* Trans. Jennifer Curtis Gage. Ithaca, N.Y.: Cornell University Press, 1990.

Grosrichard, Alain. "L'Air de Venise." *Ornicar?* 25 (1982): 109–40.

Guerlac, Suzanne. *The Impersonal Sublime.* Stanford, Calif.: Stanford University Press, 1990.

Guichard, Léon. *La Musique et les lettres au temps du Romantisme.* Paris: Presses Universitaires de France, 1955.

Gunderson, Keith. *Mentality and Machines.* 2d edition. Minneapolis: University of Minnesota Press, 1985.

Heriot, Angus. *The Castrati in Opera.* New York: Da Capo Press, 1974.

Hoffman, E. T. A. *Tales of E. T. A. Hoffman.* Ed. and trans. Leonard Kent and Elizabeth Knight. Chicago: University of Chicago Press, 1969.

Huet, Marie-Hélène. "Living Images: Monstrosity and Representation." *Representations* 4 (fall 1983): 73–87.

Irigaray, Luce. *Ethique de la différence sexuelle.* Paris: Editions de minuit, 1984.

————. *Speculum de l'autre femme.* Paris: Editions de minuit, 1974.

————. *Speculum of the Other Woman.* Trans. Gillian C. Gill. Ithaca, N.Y.: Cornell University Press, 1985.

Jardine, Alice. *Gynesis: Configurations of Woman and Modernity.* Ithaca, N.Y.: Cornell University Press, 1985.

Kahane, Claire. "Rethinking the Maternal Voice." *Genders* 3 (fall 1988): 82–91.

Kermode, Frank. *Romantic Image.* London: Routledge and Kegan Paul, 1957.

Khomsi, A. "Langue Maternelle, langue addressé à l'enfant." *Langue française: langue maternelle et communauté linguistique* 54 (May 1982): 93–113.

Kilmartin, Terence. *A Reader's Guide to Remembrance of Things Past.* New York: Vintage Books, 1984.

Kittler, Friedrich. *Discourse Networks: 1800/1900.* Trans. Michael Metteer, with Chris Cullens. Stanford, Calif.: Stanford University Press, 1990.

————. "Gramophone, Film, Typewriter." *October* 41 (summer 1987): 101–18.

Kleist, Heinrich von. "On the Puppet Theater." In Philip B. Miller, ed. and trans., *An Abyss Deep Enough: Letters of Heinrich von Kleist, with a Selection of Essays and Anecdotes.* New York: E. P. Dutton, 1982.

Kristeva, Julia. *Desire in Language.* Ed. Leon S. Roudiez. New York: Columbia University Press, 1980.

———. *The Kristeva Reader.* Ed. Toril Moi. New York: Columbia University Press, 1986.

Lacoue-Labarthe, Philippe. "L'Echo du sujet." In *Le Sujet de la Philosophie (Typographies I).* Paris: Aubier-Flammarion, 1979.

———. *Typography: Mimesis, Philosophy, Politics.* Ed. Christopher Fynsk. Cambridge, Mass.: Harvard University Press, 1989.

Lake, Carolyn Dawn. "Virgins and Dynamos: The Myth of the Machine in French Literature at the Turn of the Century." Ph.D. diss., University of California, Berkeley, 1978.

La Mettrie, Julien-Offray de. *L'Homme-Machine.* Holland: Jean-Jacques Pauvert, 1966.

Lemaitre, Henri. "Modernité et surnaturalisme." In *Petits poèmes en prose,* by Charles Baudelaire. Paris: Editions Garnier Frères, 1962.

Lichtenstein, Jacqueline. "Making Up Representations: The Risks of Femininity." *Representations* 20 (fall 1987): 77–87.

Lindenberger, Herbert. *Opera, the Extravagant Art.* Ithaca, N.Y.: Cornell University Press, 1984.

Litman, Theodore. *Le Sublime en France (1660–1714).* Paris: A. G. Nizet, 1971.

Loraux, Nicole. "Le Fantôme de la sexualité." *Nouvelle Revue de la Psychanalyse: La Chose Sexuelle* 29 (spring 1984): 11–31.

Lyotard, Jean-François. *L'Inhumain: causeries sur le temps.* Paris: Galilée, 1988.

———. *The Inhuman. Reflections on Time.* Trans. Geoffrey Bennington and Rachel Bowlby. Stanford, Calif.: Stanford University Press, 1991.

Marin, Louis. "Un Filet de voix fort douce." In Jean Baudrillard, ed., *Traverses: La voix, l'écoute.* Paris: Editions de minuit, 1981.

Marix-Spire, Thérèse. *Les Romantiques et la musique: le cas George Sand.* Paris: Nouvelles éditions latines, 1954.

Mayr, Otto. *Authority, Liberty and Automatic Machines in Early Modern Europe.* Baltimore: Johns Hopkins University Press, 1986.

Meschonnic, Henri. *Critique du rhythme: anthropologie historique du langage.* Paris: Verdier, 1982.

———. "Interview with Gabriella Bedetti." *Diacritics* 18 (fall 1988): 93–109.

Michelson, Annette. "On the Eve of the Future: The Reasonable Facsimile and the Philosophical Toy." *October* 29 (summer 1984): 3–21.

Moi, Toril. *Sexual/Textual Politics*. London: Methuen & Co., 1985.

Monk, Samuel. *The Sublime: A Study of Critical Theories in Eighteenth Century England*. Ann Arbor: University of Michigan Press, 1960.

Musset, Alfred de. *Mélanges de littérature et de critique*. Paris: Charpentier, 1867.

Nancy, Jean-Luc. "L'Offrande sublime." *Po&sie* 30 (1984): 76–103.

——. "The Sublime Offering." In Jeffrey Librett, trans., *Of the Sublime: Presence in Question*. Albany: State University of New York Press, 1993.

Nerval, Gérard de. *Les Filles du feu*. Paris: Gallimard, 1972.

Perriault, Jacques. *Mémoires de l'ombre et du son*. Paris: Flammarion, 1981.

Plank, Robert. "The Golem and the Robot." *Literature and Psychology* 15 (winter 1965): 12–27.

Plaza, Monique. "Pouvoir Phallomorphique et la psychologie de 'la femme.'" *Questions féministes* 1, no. 1 (1978): 91–119.

Poizat, Michel. *L'Opéra ou le cri de l'ange*. Paris: A. M. Métailié, 1986.

——. *The Angel's Cry*. Trans. Arthur Denner. Ithaca, N.Y.: Cornell University Press, 1992.

Pool, Ithiel de Sola. *The Social Impact of the Telephone*. Cambridge, Mass.: Massachusetts Institute of Technology Press, 1977.

Poovey, Mary. *Uneven Developments: The Ideological Work of Gender in Mid-Victorian England*. Chicago: University of Chicago Press, 1988.

Praz, Mario. *The Romantic Agony*. Trans. Angus Davidson. New York: Oxford University Press, 1970.

Proust, Marcel. *A la Recherche du temps perdu*. Vol. 2, *Le Coté de Guermantes*. Paris: Gallimard, 1954.

——. *Remembrance of Things Past*. Trans. C. K. Scott Moncrief and Terence Kilmartin. Vol. 1, *The Guermantes Way*. New York: Random House, 1981.

Raitt, A. W. *The Life of Villiers de l'Isle-Adam*. Oxford: Clarendon Press, 1981.

——. *Villiers de l'Isle-Adam et le mouvement symboliste*. Paris: Libraire José Corti, 1965.

Rosolato, Guy. *Essais sur le symbolique*. Paris: Gallimard, 1969.

Rousseau, Jean-Jacques. *Les Confessions*. Paris: Editions Garnier-Frères, 1926.

——. *Confessions*. Ed. and trans. P. N. Furbank. New York: Alfred A. Knopf, 1931.

Sand, George. *La Comtesse de Rudolstadt*. 3 vols. Ed. Léon Cellier and Léon Guichard. Paris: Editions Garniers-Frères, 1959.

——. *Lettres inédites de George Sand et Pauline Viardot, 1839–1849*. Ed. Thérèse Marix-Spire. Paris: Nouvelles editions latines, 1959.

Sartre, Jean-Paul. *Baudelaire*. Trans. Martin Turnell. London: Horizon, 1949.

Silverman, Kaja. *The Acoustic Mirror: The Female Voice in Psychoanalysis and Cinema*. Bloomington: Indiana University Press, 1988.

Smith, Paul. "Julia Kristeva Et Al.; Or, Take Three or More." In Richard Feldstein and Judith Roof, eds., *Feminism and Psychoanalysis*. Ithaca, N.Y.: Cornell University Press, 1989.

Stanton, Domna. "Difference on Trial: A Critique of the Maternal Metaphor in Cixous, Irigaray and Kristeva." In Nancy K. Miller, ed., *The Poetics of Gender*. New York: Columbia University Press, 1986.

Stendhal. *The Life of Rossini*. Trans. Richard N. Coe. London: John Calder, 1956.

———. *La Vie de Rossini*. Paris: Le Divan, 1929.

Theweleit, Klaus. *Male Fantasies*. Minneapolis: University of Minnesota Press, 1987.

Thiher, Alan. *Words in Reflection: Modern Language Theory and Postmodern Fiction*. Chicago: University of Chicago Press, 1984.

Vasse, Denis. *Le Poids du réel, la souffrance*. Paris: Editions du Seuil, 1983.

———. *La Voix et l'ombilique*. Paris: Editions du Seuil, 1974.

Verne, Jules. *The Carpathian Castle*. Trans. I. O. Evans. London: Arco Publications, 1963.

Vierne, Simone. "Le Mythe de la femme dans *Consuelo*." In Léon Cellier, ed., *La Porporina: Entretiens sur Consuelo*. Grenoble: Presses Universitaires de Grenoble, 1976.

Villiers de l'Isle-Adam. *Oeuvres complètes*. Ed. Alan Raitt and Pierre-Georges Castex. Paris: Gallimard, 1986.

———. *Tomorrow's Eve*. Trans. Robert Martin Adams. Urbana: University of Illinois Press, 1982.

Wachhorst, Wyn. *Thomas Alva Edison*. Cambridge: Massachusetts Institute of Technology Press, 1981.

Weiskel, Thomas. *The Romantic Sublime: Studies in the Structure and Psychology of Transcendence*. Baltimore: Johns Hopkins University Press, 1976.

Ziolkowski, Theodore. Review of *Marionetten, Maschinen, Automaten: Der Künstliche Mensch in Der Deutschen Und Englishchen Romantik*, by Liselotte Sauer. *Comparative Literature* 38, no. 3 (summer 1986): 302–4.

Index

In this index an "f" after a number indicates a separate reference on the next page, and an "ff" indicates separate references on the next two pages. A continuous discussion over two or more pages is indicated by a span of page numbers, e.g., "57–59." *Passim* is used for a cluster of references in close but not consecutive sequence.

Library of Congress Cataloging-in-Publication Data

Miller Frank, Felicia.
  The mechanical song : women, voice, and the artificial in
nineteenth-century French narrative / Felicia Miller Frank.
      p.   cm.
  Includes bibliographical references and index.
  ISBN 0-8047-2381-8
    1. French literature—19th century—History and criticism.
2. Literature and technology—France—History—19th century.
3. Women and literature—France—History—19th century.   4. Women
singers in literature.   5. Technology in literature.   6. Singing in
literature.   7. Voice in literature.   8. Narration (Rhetoric).
1. Title.
PQ283.M53   1995
843'.709352042—dc20   94-34279
                                                            CIP

♾ This book is printed on acid-free, recycled paper.

WITHDRAWN